NEW YORK
ENCOUNTER

GINGER ADAMS OTIS

New York Encounter

Published by Lonely Planet Publications Pty Ltd
ABN 36 005 607 983

Australia	Head Office, Locked Bag 1, Footscray, Vic 3011
	☎ 03 8379 8000 fax 03 8379 8111
	talk2us@lonelyplanet.com.au
USA	150 Linden St, Oakland, CA 94607
	☎ 510 250 6400
	toll free 800 275 8555
	fax 510 893 8572
	info@lonelyplanet.com
UK	2nd fl, 186 City Rd
	London EC1V 2NT
	☎ 020 7106 2100 fax 020 7106 2101
	go@lonelyplanet.co.uk

This title was commissioned in Lonely Planet's Oakland office and produced by: **Commissioning Editors** Jay Cooke, Jennye Garibaldi **Coordinating Editors** Carolyn Boicos, Simon Williamson **Coordinating Cartographers** Barbara Benson, Julie Dodkins **Assisting Cartographer** Brendan Streager **Layout Designers** Katherine Marsh, Carol Jackson **Senior Editors** Helen Christinis, Katie Lynch **Managing Cartographer** Shahara Ahmed **Cover Designer** Pepi Bluck **Project Manager** Chris Love **Managing Layout Designers** Laura Jane, Celia Wood **Thanks to** Lucy Birchley, Sally Darmody, Heather Dickson, Alison Lyall, Wayne Murphy, Raphael Richards, Jacqui Saunders

ISBN 978 1 74104 995 4

Printed by Hang Tai Printing Company.
Printed in China.

Acknowledgements New York City Subway Map © 2008 Metropolitan Transportation Authority. Used with permission. New York City Bus Map © 2008 Metropolitan Transportation Authority. Used with permission.

HOW TO USE THIS BOOK
Colour-Coding & Maps

Colour-coding is used for symbols on maps and in the text that they relate to (eg all eating venues on the maps and in the text are given a green knife and fork symbol). Each neighborhood also gets its own colour, and this is used down the edge of the page and throughout that neighborhood section.

Shaded yellow areas on the maps denote 'areas of interest' – for their historical significance, their attractive architecture or their great bars and restaurants. We encourage you to head to these areas and just start exploring!

Send us your feedback We love to hear from readers – your comments help make our books better. We read every word you send us, and we always guarantee that your feedback goes straight to the appropriate authors. The most useful submissions are rewarded with a free book. To send us your updates and find out about Lonely Planet events, newsletters and travel news visit our award-winning website: **lonelyplanet.com/contact**.

Note: We may edit, reproduce and incorporate your comments in Lonely Planet products such as guidebooks, websites and digital products, so let us know if you don't want your comments reproduced or your name acknowledged. For a copy of our privacy policy visit **lonelyplanet.com/privacy**.

GINGER ADAMS OTIS

As a working reporter in New York City, Ginger is intimately acquainted with all the nooks and crannies of the five boroughs, and often winds up riding the subway or walking the streets alongside visitors who are using her books. Thanks to the vagaries of being a print and radio reporter, Ginger gets to experience the city anew each day, getting pushed into off-the-beaten-track locales and brought into contact with new groups of people through her assignments. When she's not busy working for Lonely Planet, Ginger likes to travel in Latin America, where she has also done extensive reporting.

GINGER'S THANKS

Muchas gracias to Jay Cooke, my stalwart editor of many years. His humor, patience and appreciation for NYC made every project a pleasure to tackle. Thanks to Jennye Garibaldi, an equally talented member of the Encounter team, who juggles multiple professional responsibilities and yet is always available with encouragement and information. Thanks to Lonely Planet Oakland, Brice and, of course, mapping genius Alison Lyall and the Oz carto team, without whom I'd be lost in a pile of POIs.

THE PHOTOGRAPHER

Dan Herrick has been based in New York City for the past six years after having lived and studied in Latin America and Europe. He enjoys documenting the city's changes and its frenetic way of life. On occasion he is able to pull himself away from it all to travel abroad, or more often to travel to one of the many different worlds that exist within the city's boundaries.

Our readers Many thanks to the travelers who wrote to us with helpful hints, useful advice and interesting anecdotes: Mark Broadhead, Simon Dillon, Juan Edwards, Michael Gardner, Seena Gosrani, Robert Goundry, Keith Houghton, Suzanne Lee, Ciaran Lennon, Amy Millott, Shanna Van Der Laarse.

Central Park (p174) – sun worshippers, not livestock, congregate on Sheep Meadow

CONTENTS

Why is our travel information the best in the world? It's simple: our authors are passionate, dedicated travelers. They don't take freebies in exchange for positive coverage so you can be sure the advice you're given is impartial. They travel widely to all the popular spots, and off the beaten track. They don't research using just the internet or phone. They discover new places not included in any other guidebook. They personally visit thousands of hotels, restaurants, palaces, trails, galleries, temples and more. They speak with dozens of locals every day to make sure you get the kind of insider knowledge only a local could tell you. They take pride in getting all the details right, and in telling it how it is. Think you can do it? Find out how at **lonelyplanet.com**.

THIS IS NEW YORK CITY

It's a mad, mad world in Manhattan, where taxis, pedicabs, commuters, pedestrians – even horse-drawn carriages – careen around looking for space. The city is heady, frustrating, shocking, almost overwhelming in its intensity and, ultimately, incredibly exhilarating.

And yet it's not all chaos and grit. Inside New York's pocket-sized parks, like Riverside (p195) and Tompkins Sq (p95), bluesy buskers blow their horns, delighted toddlers run through sprinklers, chess players frown in fierce concentration, and dogs nip and bark inside their runs.

The bigger green spaces, such as Central Park (p174) and Prospect Park (p219), whisk you away from the grimy streets and set you down alongside flowing rivers, dark, primal ponds and gently tangoing couples, who gather on Saturday nights in summer to flirt with their feet in the shadows of birch trees.

Romance and ruin weave together in New York City, a group of five boroughs offering endless contrasts and captivating diversity. Anchored by back-to-back buildings and more than nine million people, the city is a series of interlocking enclaves, each with its own flavor and appeal. Brooklyn is the domain of writers, artists, young couples and families seeking to live in creative peace without the yoke of Manhattan's sky-high rents. Vibrant Queens is a maelstrom of ethnicities and nationalities that live together – for the most part – in quiet harmony. This sprawling borough, studded with housing projects, alternative museums and galleries, and countless neat, single-family homes, contains some of the tastiest Indian, Korean, Greek and Albanian food anywhere. The boogie-down Bronx is still New York City's least appreciated borough, but even Manhattanites know there's no better place than Arthur Ave for an authentic Italian dinner – not even Staten Island, full of third-generation Napolitanos, can compare.

In the middle of it all is glorious Manhattan, that scintillating sliver of land where anything – absolutely *anything* – can happen.

Top left Different races, same song – New York subway (p257) **Top right** Brooklyn Bridge and Lower Manhattan (p42) as night moves in and lights flicker on **Bottom** Mural on the pulsing heart of Harlem: 125th St (p202)

>HIGHLIGHTS

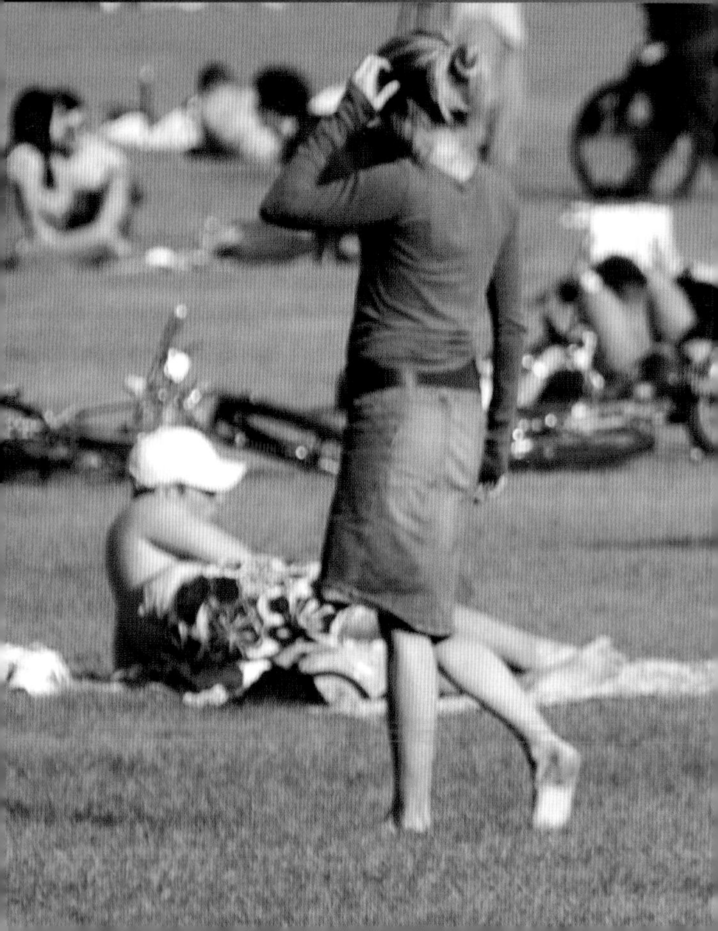

Get horizontal in Central Park (p12), a relaxing swath of green in a hectic, vertical city

>1 NEW YORK HARBOR

RIDE THE WAVES TO THE STATUE OF LIBERTY

Half tourist attraction, half busy industrial byway, the wide, watery mouth of Lower Manhattan is full of things to see and do. Hugging the island's southernmost tip, New York's harbor offers stellar views of Brooklyn's creaky old waterfront to the west, Staten Island to the south, and a nice chunk of the Jersey coast to the east.

But the best views of all, of course, are of Lady Liberty (p46) herself: tall, lean and green, and rising up proudly out of the waters. Whether you admire her from afar or take one of the ferries constantly circling the harbor out to her rocky toehold, she is magnificent. Guarding the entrance to Lower Manhattan since 1886, Lady Liberty is positioned to gaze sternly across the waters at 'unenlightened Europe.' Known as the 'Mother of Exiles,' the statue serves as an admonishment to the rigid social structures of the old world. 'Keep your ancient lands, your storied pomp!' says Lady Liberty's famous

poem. 'Give me your tired, your poor, your huddled masses yearning to breathe free.'

When those masses came – which they did in droves – they most likely ended up behind the statue at Ellis Island, a must-see New York experience. Its moving exhibits include early photos of gaunt, hollow-eyed émigrés clutching papers and their worldly goods.

Ferries to and from the islands depart from Battery Park (p44), which is worth a stroll in its own right. The park's thick green grass leads to an esplanade along the Hudson River, and it's studded with outdoor installations and other works of art.

For a less personal but still stellar look at the Old Green Lady, skip the official tour and jump on the Staten Island Ferry (p46), which departs from Whitehall Terminal, also in Battery Park. This free half-hour ride swings you right past the Statue of Liberty. Another ferry ride that gives you spectacular Manhattan-skyline views takes you to Governor's Island (p47), a small strip of land in New York Harbor that used to be an old coast guard base. Soon it will be completely transformed into public parkland.

>2 CENTRAL PARK

GET LOST IN THE MIDDLE OF MANHATTAN

Hard to believe that verdant grasses, dappled forests, rioting wild-flowers and cool, meandering streams exist in such a cacophonous, car-heavy city, but – praise be – they do. 'The People's Park' was designed in the 1860s and '70s by Frederick Law Olmsted and Calvert Vaux, and it serves as the city's collective backyard.

Stretching from Midtown at 59th St to the beautifully restored Harlem Meer at 110th St, these rolling hills are thronged every morning with roller-bladers, cyclists, walkers, joggers and yoga enthusiasts. Couples, friends and sometimes even strangers meet at the center, Bethesda Tce, recognizable by the famous *Angel of the Waters* statue (p178) in its middle.

Walkers and joggers gravitate to the Jacqueline Kennedy Onassis Reservoir (p176), while the park's west side, near the 79th St Transverse Rd, is home to an ever-evolving, changing memorial to John Lennon, who liked to hang out in the ethereal stretch of park now known as Strawberry Fields (p178) and who was shot by a deranged fan while entering his apartment across the street in 1980. The list of must-sees and dos goes on and on in Central Park; for more information, visit the **Dairy Visitor Center** (☎ 212-794-6564; www.centralpark.org).

>3 EMPIRE STATE BUILDING

FALL IN LOVE WITH A SKYLINE

It's famous for its sky-high observatory deck that allows visitors a bird's-eye view of Manhattan, but New Yorkers love this art deco delight for its quirky facade. No matter where you are in the city, its jutting silhouette – sometimes bathed in red, sometimes green, other times both – is the perfect landmark. Its legendary observation decks, although encased in safety wire, are not for the faint of heart. On a windy day, the top floors of this sturdy structure bend and sway like Fred Astaire (it can feel that way, at least).

Conceived during the prosperous 1920s, the Empire State Building (p152) didn't actually go up until after the stock market crash of 1929. Thrown together in 410 days for $41 million, the 102-story landmark opened in 1931 and immediately became the most exclusive business address in the city. But who could afford the equally exclusive rent? It sat empty for years, earning it the nickname 'Empty State Building.' The top level was meant to serve as a zeppelin mooring mast, but the Hindenburg disaster in 1937 put a stop to that.

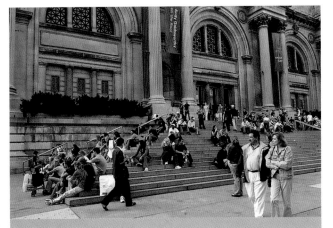

>4 METROPOLITAN MUSEUM OF ART

MEET AN EGYPTIAN MUMMY AT THE TEMPLE OF DENDUR

One of the first things that will greet you as you walk into this Fifth Ave behemoth is the Sackler Wing, home to an ancient Egyptian temple from 15 BC. This 82ft sandstone wonder, saved in 1967 from submersion in the Aswan Dam, doesn't even come close to dwarfing the room – that's how big the Met is.

Its permanent collection holds three million pieces, and an average of five million art-lovers tramp through every year.

You'll want plenty of time to explore. The European galleries above the marble staircase at the Fifth Ave entrance could easily consume a day, as could the larger-than-ever Greek and Roman galleries, and the newly expanded Egyptian gallery, with its perfectly preserved mummies. Don't miss the dark and lovely medieval galleries, full of glinting Byzantine enamels, or the Lehman Wing, full of glowing Renaissance works by Rembrandt, El Greco and others.

For more information, see p185.

>5 MUSEUM OF MODERN ART

DINE AMID PICASSOS AT THE MOMA

Tucked into a Midtown sidestreet, the Museum of Modern Art (p164) is a gleaming gem. It's easy to spend a day here, starting at the top of its spiraled multilevel floors and strolling ever downward, stopping at any of its excellent coffee shops or restaurants for a break, before winding up the day with a contemplative exploration of its 1st-floor sculpture garden.

If you follow the museum's contours, you'll move downward from floor to floor, and chronologically through the major art movements of the 20th century. Floors five and four are MoMA's intro to modern art – Picassos, Matisses, Dalis, Mondrians, Pollocks, de Koonings and a few Marcel Duchamp originals.

The museum's world-class restaurant, the Modern, overlooks the first-floor sculpture garden with its crooked trees and eclectic installations. On the 2nd floor there's a rustic Italian eatery with an airy espresso bar.

>6 BROADWAY & TIMES SQUARE

TAKE IN THE DAZZLING LIGHTS OF THE GREAT WHITE WAY

There's a reason it's known as the 'Crossroads of the World' –
because everybody who comes to town has to take a peek at the
crazy, zany intersection of 42nd St and Broadway.

All traces of its early 1900s incarnation as a tranquil horse-trading
plaza are long gone, as are its days as a seedy sex-shop hangout.
Now there are a thousand blinking lights and flashing neon adver-
tisements, and Times Sq is defined by its blazing kilowatt power.

But it's not all big-name chain stores, novelty restaurants and
gaudy billboards. Many of the marquee lights belong to the theaters
running along Broadway. When electric signs first came into vogue
back in the day (1906, to be precise), the colored bulbs burned out
too quickly, so only white lights were used. The sprawling length of
Broadway held so many new-fangled theaters it soon got the nick-
name 'The Great White Way.' Many are the legends who've pulled
into town nameless, faceless and penniless, only to find fame and
fortune amid the worn out floorboards of historic old theaters like
the Ambassador (p171), the Biltmore (p171) and Longacre.

For more information on the area, see p162.

>7 FIFTH AVENUE & ROCKEFELLER CENTER

ZIP TO THE TOP OF THE ROCK

A ritzy, upscale enclave full of big media companies and fine wine bars, Rockefeller Center (p154) also doubles as a public art plaza. It's most famous mural, done by the Socialist-leaning Mexican painter Diego Rivera, is long gone (Rivera included Lenin in his commissioned mural, which didn't please his capitalist boss) but other works abound.

Prometheus overlooks the famous skating rink, there's an Atlas Carrying the World on Fifth Ave, and the aptly named News, an installation by Isamu Noguchi, sits not far from NBC studios. On the Sixth Ave side, red-velvet-seated Radio City Music Hall (p153) houses the high-kicking Rockettes.

Inside Rockefeller Center, you can zip up to its vertigo-inducing observation deck (pictured above; see p154) in a stomach-dropping elevator with blue neon lights for unobstructed views into Central Park. From Rockefeller Center, a stroll north on Fifth Ave will bring you past the soaring St Patrick's Cathedral (p154) into a glitzy shopping district: Fendi, Prada, Saks Fifth Avenue, Bergdorf's, Bulgari, Ferragamo, Tiffany's and more.

>8 SOHO, NOHO & NOLITA

SHOP TILL YOU DROP DOWNTOWN

These three neighborhoods (p76), all on the cusp of Lower Manhattan, function as an urban Bermuda Triangle for celebrities: they get sucked in and – given the shopping, restaurants and nightlife – they simply never leave.

Noho is the northernmost section, a tiny crossroads of shops and trendy eateries that stretches across Bond St and Great Jones St and then flows into the East Village. Nolita, an even smaller warren of crooked streets just south of Houston St and east of Broadway, is – if it's possible – even more hip than Noho. The name means North of Little Italy, and its four quaint main streets (Elizabeth, Mott, Mulberry and Prince) retain an enticing aura of Old Italy. Film director Martin Scorsese grew up on Elizabeth St and was an altar boy at the original St Patrick's Old Cathedral (p80) on the corner of Mott and Prince Sts. For an afternoon of shopping, café-hopping and then fine dining, Nolita can't be beat.

On the west side of Broadway, below Houston St (but north of Canal St) is Soho, the original hipster haven. It's slightly more corporatized than a decade ago, but is still infused with that unique New York glamour, courtesy of its big old loft buildings, quirky cobblestone streets and endless shops and galleries.

>9 CHELSEA & THE MEATPACKING DISTRICT

COMBINE YOUR GALLERY TOUR WITH A PUB CRAWL

Who says high art and a good beer don't mix? Certainly not the residents of Chelsea (p126). Their free-spirited neighborhood has now supplanted Greenwich Village as the locus of gay life, even as it continues to nurture the art world and most of the city's clubbing activities.

Much of Chelsea's extreme west side contains huge galleries and art studios. Its wide, industrial streets are sometimes lonesome and windswept, but it suits the neighborhood's avant-garde mood. White Box (p132), an artist collective, and White Columns (p117) – no connection, despite the names – are bringing new life to the scene.

Chelsea's not particularly up-to-the-moment when it comes to fab new eateries – although it's got more than its share of arty standouts like Klee Brasserie (p136). Where Chelsea does shine is in its nightlife: big, brash clubs that line up along 27th and 28th Sts, and upscale gay/straight bars clustered in the lower 20s.

Whatever Chelsea lacks in trendy restaurants can be found in its neighbor, the always-packed Meatpacking District (p116). This abattoir-turned-hipster-hangout was once a working butchery – and nobody wanted to live among the fecund, fetid smells. Now people can't stay away, and this popular pocket has stellar eateries, insane shopping and is even catching up with Chelsea in nightclubs.

>10 WEST VILLAGE

LAZE AWAY THE AFTERNOON ON OLD, CROOKED STREETS

It's hard to find traces of the former political and social fervor that at one time had this quaint, serene residential neighborhood buzzing with radical activities. Only a few old bars and relics of the seminal gay rights fight of the 1960s and '70s remain: Stonewall, the Duplex (p115) and a string of S&M shops on Christopher St. But otherwise its pioneering spirit is mostly gone. Where it once attracted literary lights like ee cummings, Edna St Vincent Millay, Williams S Burroughs, James Baldwin and more, it now has A-list celebrities raising families, wealthy bankers, investors and a few grown-up rock stars. Nonetheless, the West Village's (p104) striking visual charm is intact – winding streets built on old cow paths, and hidden courtyards behind narrow, tree-lined alleys. It's still worth visiting, as much for its history as its quirky cafés and specialty shops and its people-watching.

>11 EAST VILLAGE & LOWER EAST SIDE

PARTY IN THE MIDST OF ROCK 'N' ROLL HISTORY

Separated by busy Houston St, these two closely intertwined neighborhoods are but a stone's throw apart: the East Village (p90) begins on Houston's north side, while its close cousin the Lower East Side (p62) sits on the southeast side. The resemblance is striking. Both of the formerly grungy and gritty enclaves are still full of crumbling tenements and graffiti-scarred buildings – but not for long.

Waves of gentrification continue to knock down the old squatter lofts and turn community-run cooperatives into luxury condos, particularly in the East Village. Tompkins Sq Park (p95) and St Marks Pl, two bastions of punk-rocker energy and counter-culture upheaval, are now attractive areas to hang out in and get a beer (or a tattoo).

Still, both neighborhoods retain a singular, electric energy, fueled mostly by the burgeoning nightlife along Second Ave in the East Village and Rivington St in the Lower East Side. There's a continuous influx of new bars, restaurants and nightclubs to draw you in. The constant change lends both areas the kind of creative buzz that lured in jazz great Charlie Parker, the Ramones, the Rolling Stones and a young Madonna.

>12 BROOKLYN

GO OFF THE BEATEN PATH IN BROOKLYN

Welcome to 'Breukelen,' a former Dutch settlement of neatly divided little towns. Those outlines can still be traced in the many small neighborhoods that today make up Brooklyn (p214), New York's most populous borough (2.5 million residents) outside of Manhattan.

For most people, Brooklyn is Coney Island (p219), that strange stretch of sea and sand on the coast that's also a famous outdoor amusement park and freak show (now slated for a major face-lift). But there's so much more: the gentle slopes of laid-back Prospect Park (p219), the often overlooked Brooklyn Museum of Art (p215) and its five floors of Egyptian, African and European art, including one whole wing of Rodin sculptures. Brooklyn Botanical Gardens, next door, is a 52-acre flowery oasis. In spring its Japanese Hill and Pond garden comes alive with cherry blossoms, and its Rose Garden blooms seem to scent the whole nabe.

Northwest Brooklyn includes some of the borough's most breath-taking brownstones, mostly in the fairly affluent enclaves of Brooklyn Heights, Carroll Gardens, Park Slope and Vinegar Hill. Up-and-coming Red Hook and Fort Greene are now attracting the creative, 20-somethings priced out of the artistic haven of Williamsburg.

Borough Park is home to a large ultra-Orthodox Jewish community, and Besonhurst is still largely Italian, while Sunset Park contains a flourishing community of Mexican and Chinese-American families.

Brighton Beach, right behind Coney Island, is where you go to practice your Russian. 'Little Odessa,' as the area is known, has become the haven of immigrants from former Soviet Union nations, and it's where you can get a good cup of hot tea, caviar and sturgeon, and pick up a souvenir samovar.

For those who wish to experience Brooklyn without straying too far from Manhattan, a trip to Dumbo (Down under Manhattan Bridge Overpass) fits the bill. An easy and panoramic walk across the slender span of steel known as the Brooklyn Bridge (onlookers on Brooklyn Bridge, pictured opposite) will bring you to this waterfront neighborhood, full of old warehouses and factories. The abandoned

and decaying loft buildings were gradually reclaimed in the 1980s by artists priced out of fast-gentrifying Tribeca. Now Dumbo is the driving force for Brooklyn's artistic community; even those creative types who don't live here benefit from its residents' willingness to share gallery space and put on cutting-edge shows.

>13 LOWER MANHATTAN

WANDER NEW YORK'S COLONIAL BYWAYS

An eye-catching combination of old and new, Lower Manhattan (p42) contains some of the island's most grandiose skyscrapers, crammed on to tiny colonial streets. If you've always wanted to eat lunch in one of George Washington's old watering holes, this is the place for you.

Lower Manhattan overflows with both Revolutionary and modern landmarks. Not only did Washington eat at Fraunces Tavern (p44), he was sworn in at Federal Hall (pictured opposite; p44), he worshipped at St Paul's Chapel (p46) and Trinity Church (p47), and he buried many of his contemporaries in its cemetery. Another Lower Manhattan fixture, the New York Stock Exchange (p46), got its start on Wall St, named after the original Dutch fortifying wall, and remains headquartered there.

On the east side of Lower Manhattan you'll find South Street Seaport (p46), an old working port reached by cobblestone streets. Amid these colonial byways you'll find an influx of trendy eateries and bars, with a strong international feel. Japanese sushi, New Zealand seafood, traditional Irish pub fare and Aussie eats are all available in these few small blocks.

Busy Fulton St is a great place to shop for souvenirs, T-shirts and trinkets, and if you want a glimpse of New York City's bureaucratic heartbeat, City Hall is right across the street from legendary electronics/music/computer store, J&R (p48).

GROUND ZERO

Lower Manhattan has largely rebounded from the terrible events of September 11, 2001, though a gaping hole still marks the spot where the Twin Towers fell. Despite every effort from city leaders, money issues, insurance red tape and a plague of other problems have blocked progress on a planned memorial park and tower. There are ways to pay homage, however, from the surrounding observation decks, or in a tour of the site led by a volunteer from the WTC Tribute visitors center (p45).

> 14 HARLEM

DISCOVER THE HIDDEN DELIGHTS OF HARLEM

Everything is changing in New York City, and Harlem (p202), the mecca of urban African American life for over a century, is no exception. Or is it?

All the signs of gentrification are here – high-rise condos, an influx of banks and new business, sky-rocketing rents and home prices. But, the traditional base of Harlem, working-class and middle-income earners, mostly African American but with a hefty mix of other ethnicities and nationalities, hasn't crumbled in the face of developers. The result is a neighborhood on the upswing, with pockets of former blight right next to sleek, $2-million glass skyscrapers, and a diverse but solid offering of restaurants, clubs and entertainment.

For many decades Harlem was overlooked as a tourist destination, and its many neighborhood treasures went unnoticed by the world below 96th St. Thankfully, that's all changed now, and long-standing cultural icons are being restored and revitalized, such as the Apollo Theater (p204), the Lenox Lounge (p212), the Studio Museum (p208) and the Schomburg Center for Research in Black Culture (p206). Famous soul food restaurants like Sylvia's (p210), Amy Ruth's (p210) and Miss Mamie's Spoonbread (pictured above) flourish next to newcomers like Melba's (p210) and Mobay Uptown (p212) and a growing crop of African eateries where the waiters speak colonial French.

>A YEAR IN NEW YORK CITY

Celebration is a way of life in busy New York City, where the population's diversity means plenty of reasons for fun. The biggest annual events include New Year, Chinese New Year, the Puerto Rican Day Parade, Gay Pride Month, Fourth of July, the West Indian American Day Carnival, Halloween and the Thanksgiving Day Parade. In December, when Hanukkah, Christmas and Kwanzaa usually collide, the city is truly a movable feast.

Stilt-walkers at West Indian American Day Carnival in Brooklyn

JANUARY

Three Kings Parade
www.eastharlempreservation.org
On January 5, Spanish Harlem, up Fifth Ave to 116th St, is full of parading schoolchildren, donkeys and sheep.

Winter Restaurant Week
www.nycvisit.com
High-profile restaurants offer three-course lunches or dinners from $20 to $30.

Martin Luther King Jr Parade
Civil rights leader Martin Luther King is commemorated annually with a birthday gala parade down Fifth Ave from 86th to 61st Sts.

FEBRUARY

Olympus Fashion Week
www.olympusfashionweek.com
The couture world descends upon Manhattan in the second week of February to flounce, and gawk at the new looks. A second fashion week is held in the second week of September.

Westminster Kennel Show
www.westminsterkennelclub.org
Catch the much-mocked parade of show dogs at this dead-serious annual showcase for purebreds.

The city turns green for the St Patrick's Day Parade down Fifth Ave

Moments before take-off – LGBT Pride parade (p30)

APRIL

Easter Parade
www.ny.com
From 10am to 4pm on Easter Sunday, cars are blocked off of Fifth Ave from 57th to 49th Sts. People show off their Easter costumes and fine, fluffy Easter hats.

Orchid Show
www.rockefellercenter.com
This massive display of orchids, well into its second decade, includes competitions in both the orchid-art and fragrance categories.

MAY

Bike New York
www.bikemonthnyc.org
May is Bike Month, with weekly bike-oriented tours, parties and other events for pedal-pushing New Yorkers.

Fleet Week
www.intrepidmuseum.com
Ships arrive from around the world for this annual end-of-the-month celebration.

JUNE

Puerto Rican Day Parade
www.nationalpuertoricandayparade.org
Thousands of revelers show up in the second week of June for this massive march along Fifth Ave from 44th to 86th Sts.

MARCH

New York Underground Film Festival
www.nyuff.com
Edgy, sexy and just plain weird documentaries and narratives at the Anthology Film Archives.

St Patrick's Day Parade
www.saintpatricksdayparade.com/nyc/newyorkcity.htm
On March 17 everything goes green along Fifth Ave, from 44th to 86th Sts, when the world-famous parade starts at 11am.

Ctrl-Alt-Del...computer virus on Halloween (p32)

JULY

July Fourth Fireworks
www1.macys.com
Independence Day fireworks start at 9pm.
For good viewing spots, try the Lower
East Side waterfront park, Williamsburg,
Brooklyn or high rooftops.

Nathan's Hot Dog Eating Contest
www.nathansfamous.com
A celebration of gluttony brings food inhalers to Coney Island each Fourth of July.

Philharmonic in the Park
www.newyorkphilharmonic.org
Enjoy free concerts in Central Park, Prospect
Park, Queens, the Bronx or Staten Island.

AUGUST

Fringe Festival
www.fringenyc.org
This annual festival features the edgiest,
most creative stage talent in New York.

Howl! Festival
www.howlfestival.com
A week-long celebration of arts in the East
Village, including the Charlie Parker Jazz Festival and other readings and performances.

US Open Tennis Tournament
www.usopen.org
One of the four Grand Slam tournaments for
professional tennis players; held in Queens.

Lesbian, Gay, Bisexual & Transgender Pride
www.heritageofpride.org
Gay Pride Month lasts throughout June and
culminates in a major march down Fifth Ave
on the last Sunday of the month.

Restaurant Week
www.nycvisit.com
Big-time discounts at top-notch eateries
during the last week of June; three-course
lunches and dinners for $20 to $35.

Mermaid Parade
www.coneyisland.com
Elaborately costumed folk display their
mermaid finery along the Coney Island
boardwalk on the last Saturday of the month.

Harlem Week
www.harlemweek.com
Throughout the month of August there are ongoing street celebrations – including music, theater performances and food fairs – all over Harlem.

SEPTEMBER

West Indian American Day Carnival
www.wiadca.com
Two million Caribbean Americans head to Eastern Parkway in Brooklyn for the annual Carnival Parade.

Olympus Fashion Week
www.olympusfashionweek.com
Round two for designers and fashionistas strutting their stuff on the catwalk.

OCTOBER

Dumbo Art under the Bridge Festival
www.dumboartscenter.org
Celebrates local artists; you can enjoy open studios, performances and street displays.

Blessing of the Animals
www.stjohndivine.org
In honor of the Feast Day of St Francis, pet owners flock to the grand Cathedral of St John the Divine with their creatures.

Open House New York
www.ohny.org
For one weekend a year, the doors to New York's secret places are thrown open.

Each year a primeval battle between human and hot dog takes place at Nathan's

ANNUAL FESTIVALS

Chinese Lunar New Year Festival (www.explorechinatown.com) An awesome display of fireworks and dancing dragon parades, usually in either late January or February depending on the lunar calendar.

Cherry Blossom Festival (www.bbg.org) Held during the first weekend in May, this festival celebrates the annual flowering of cherry trees in Brooklyn's Botanic Gardens.

Tribeca Film Festival (www.tribecafilmfestival.com) This film fest invigorates Lower Manhattan in the first week of May.

JVC Jazz Festival (www.festivalproductions.net/jvcjazz.htm) Forty jazz shows take place around the city during this mid-June fest.

River to River Festival (www.rivertorivernyc.org) Performers bring theater, music, dance and film to downtown parks all summer long (June to August).

San Gennaro Festival (www.sangennaro.org) Rowdy crowds descend on Little Italy for carnival games, sausage-and-pepper sandwiches, deep-fried calamari and more during the Feast of San Gennaro, usually mid-to-late September.

Halloween Parade

www.halloween-nyc.com

Freaks and geeks gather in the streets for a wild night of prancing about in costume.

NOVEMBER

New York City Marathon

www.ingnycmarathon.org

This annual 26-mile run through the five boroughs draws thousands of athletes from around the world.

Thanksgiving Day Parade

www.macys.com

Famous floats waft down Broadway, from 72nd St to Herald Sq. Balloons are inflated at the southwest corner of Central Park the night before.

DECEMBER

Rockefeller Center Christmas Tree Lighting

Join the hundreds encircling Rockefeller Center in Midtown and watch the world's tallest Christmas tree lit up to a chorus of 'ooohs' and 'aaahs.'

New Year's Eve

www.nycvisit.com

In addition to the world-famous countdown to midnight in Times Sq, the city has plenty of other celebratory events, namely the **Midnight Run in Central Park** (☎ 212-860-4455) and midnight fireworks in Central Park, Prospect Park and the South Street Seaport.

Fresh food heaven, Chelsea Market (p133)

ITINERARIES

Public transportation is your best friend in New York City. Sure, the subway system is a bit old, smells funny and sometimes goes a bit fitfully. But, overall, it zips up and down Manhattan with dependable regularity. For the scenic route, take the aboveground buses that trundle along Manhattan's famous avenues.

You'll need a MetroCard (p261) to get around, and you can buy them at newsstands or from vending machines inside subway stations.

Taxis are a good option if you're trekking to the far edges of the city, but during rush hour (anywhere from 7am to 9am and 4pm to 7pm), traffic is brutal. Fast-moving pedicabs will also compete for your business; there's nothing wrong with these rickshaws, but keep in mind that few of the operators are insured.

ONE DAY

Head to Lower Manhattan and walk around Battery Park (p44), Ground Zero (p45) and the South Street Seaport (p46). If you're really dying to see the Statue of Liberty, skip the lengthy lines on the official visit and grab the Staten Island Ferry (p46) for the drive-by-view instead. Head to Chinatown for lunch, and spend the afternoon exploring Soho, Noho and Nolita. Dine amid the neon of Times Sq, and then try to catch a show. If you're out of the theater before 11pm, rush to the Empire State Building (p152) to catch the last elevator (at 11:15pm) to the observation deck.

TWO DAYS

Spend a leisurely morning on the Upper West Side, with a breakfast bagel at Barney Greengrass (p197), a stop to pick up some snacks at Zabar's (p197), and then a stroll around the mom-and-pop shops clustered near 79th St and Broadway. Make your way to the American Museum of Natural History (p194), but before you go in, step into Central Park (p174) and picnic on your snacks. Hit the museum for the afternoon, and then meander south, ending your day with dinner in either Chelsea or the Meatpacking District. Spend your next morning exploring Lower Manhattan, and aim to have lunch in Greenwich Village. Walk through

---

Top Immerse yourself in a classic New York read (p241) **Bottom** The Guggenheim (p186) – Interior view of The Solomon R. Guggenheim Museum New York © The Solomon R. Guggenheim Foundation, New York.

Washington Sq Park (p105) and head into East Village to shop, sightsee and have some drinks in the late afternoon. Head south across Houston St to have dinner on the Lower East Side.

THREE DAYS

You've got the time to tackle the Metropolitan Museum of Art (p185), so make that your first project. Grab a hearty breakfast and then head inside. Later in the afternoon, exit on Fifth Ave and stroll south, parallel to Central Park. At 59th St, consider a hansom-cab ride, or continue south along the fabled Fifth Ave shopping district. Refresh yourself with some tea at Takashimaya department store (p156). Explore the UN (p155) to the east, and splurge on a romantic, Upper East Side dinner at La Goulue (p189). Day two starts off with a walk through Central Park (p174) and then a visit to the Museum of Modern Art (p164). From there it's an easy transition to Rockefeller Center (p154), where you can tour NBC studios and zip to the Top of the Rock (p154). You can swing by Macy's (p166), then choose from Little Brazil or Little Korea for dinner. Day three, head to Lower Manhattan and hit the Statue of Liberty and Ellis Island (p46). Have dinner in Greenwich Village.

RAINY DAY

The Guggenheim (p186) is perfect for any inclement weather because the out-of-this-world atmosphere creates its own little reality bubble anyway. Spend the day enjoying the museum, then check out the Schomburg Center (p206) in Harlem. It's not far from the Cathedral of St John the Divine (p205), where you can admire the still-unfinished spires before topping off the day with some soul food at Amy Ruth's or Sylvia's (p210).

FORWARD PLANNING

Three weeks before you go Pick a Broadway show and book tickets, and pick a back up as well in case you need to try your luck at the TKTS booth (www.tdf.org/tkts).

Two weeks before you go Visit www.opentable.com and make a reservation for Babbo (p110) or another restaurant you'd like to try.

Three days before you go Start checking out what will be going on while you're in town at www.freeinnyc.net and www.clubfreetime.com.

The day before you go Start testing your online reflexes and see if you can snag a seat at Momofuku (p98). Check out what sample sales will be on while you're in town.

NYC ON A SHOESTRING

The greatest things in life are free, as the saying goes, and that's true in New York, where it costs you nothing to enter Central Park or check out the city's iconic architecture. Catch the splendors of Grand Central Terminal (p152) and admire the jutting lines of Le Corbusier's UN building (p155) without spending a dime. Head to Midtown and lunch at the Hallo Berlin food cart at Fifth Ave and 54th St. Bargain hunters do well in Chinatown, and while it'll cost you a mint to eat in Little Italy, strolling there is free. Head uptown to Morningside Heights to check out the Cathedral of St John the Divine (p205), then dine with the students at Community Food and Juice (p209).

OPEN ALL DAY

Many museums are closed on Monday, making that the perfect day to really explore Central Park (p174). Start at the northern tip and head south, through the Ramble and the Mall, taking a peek at the Central Park Wildlife Center and Strawberry Fields. If you emerge on the park's west side, take the subway to Chelsea. Not all the galleries will be open – but the stores will be. Do a little window-shopping and inhale the fresh-cookie smell of the Chelsea Market (p133).

Explore the Lower East Side, stopping for some gourmet bar food at Schiller's Liquor Bar (p72). Then hit the bargain shops along Orchard St before heading north into the East Village. End the night with a pub crawl along Second Ave.

>NEIGHBORHOODS

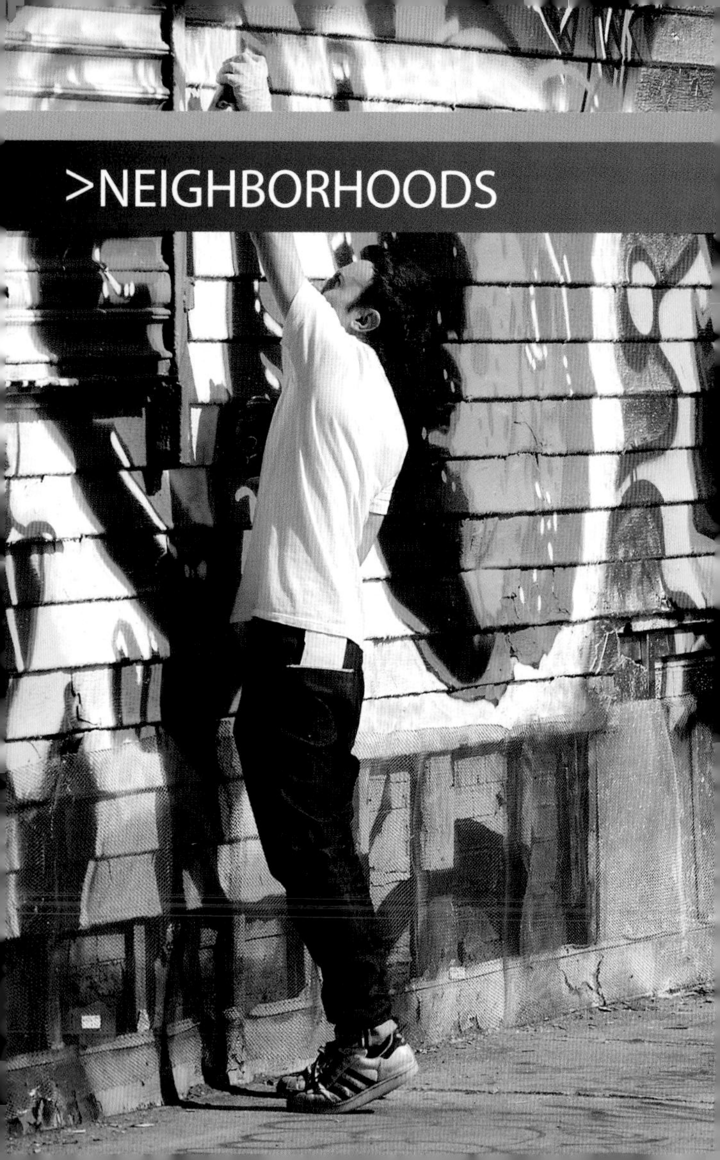

Art comes in all shapes, forms and locations in New York City

NEIGHBORHOODS

Manhattan rolls south from Harlem in a wave of arbitrarily drawn but identifiable neighborhoods, each with its own sense of community and pace. Real estate agents like to coin trendy monikers for on-the-cusp enclaves (SoHa for South Harlem, for example), but don't believe the hype. New York has always been defined by its traditional neighborhoods.

Harlem's wide boulevards, lined with brownstones and beaux-arts buildings, stretches from 100th St into Washington Heights. On the west side, from 110th St to about 116th St, is Morningside Heights, full of students, young professionals and old-timers from when the area was called Spanish Harlem. To the east, from 125th St south, is El Barrio, a working-class enclave with a diverse population.

In the city's center sits that glorious green no-man's land, Central Park. From 96th St south, the neighborhood on the west of Central Park is the Upper West Side, to the east is the Upper East Side. It's as simple as that.

Busy Midtown takes over at 59th St, stretching down to 42nd St. The same rule applies, this time divided by Fifth Avenue: everything to the west is Midtown West, everything to the east is Midtown East. Below 42nd St is a mish-mash of Manhattan's best-known nabes, starting with arty Chelsea, full of gay-friendly nightclubs, which overlaps with the trendy Meatpacking District, which in turn blends into bohemian Greenwich Village, all on the west side of Fifth Ave. On the east side is Union Sq, the center of activist life in New York, and a dizzying array of bars, gastropubs and bistros that make up the East Village, Lower East Side and Nolita.

The city converges in Lower Manhattan, where the 'concrete canyons' of Wall St are filled with hulking skyscrapers. Lower Manhattan's Brooklyn Bridge crosses the Hudson River into artistic Dumbo and tony Brooklyn Heights. Behind them, the rest of the borough stretches southeast, all the way to Coney Island and the Atlantic Coast.

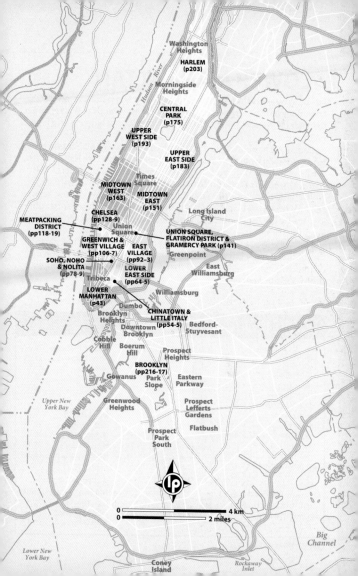

WASHINGTON
HEIGHTS
**HARLEM
(p203)**

Morningside
Heights

**CENTRAL
PARK
(p175)**

**UPPER
WEST SIDE
(p193)**

**UPPER
EAST SIDE
(p183)**

Times
Square

**MIDTOWN
WEST
(p163)**

**MIDTOWN
EAST
(p151)**

Long Island
City

**CHELSEA
(pp128-9)**

Union
Square

**MEATPACKING
DISTRICT
(pp118-19)**

**UNION SQUARE,
FLATIRON DISTRICT &
GRAMERCY PARK (p141)**

**GREENWICH &
WEST VILLAGE
(pp106-7)**

**EAST
VILLAGE
(pp92-3)**

Greenpoint

**SOHO, NOHO
& NOLITA
(pp78-9)**

Tribeca

**LOWER
EAST SIDE
(pp64-5)**

East
Williamsburg

**LOWER
MANHATTAN
(p43)**

Williamsburg

Dumbo

**CHINATOWN &
LITTLE ITALY
(pp54-5)**

Brooklyn
Heights

Downtown
Brooklyn

Bedford-
Stuyvesant

Cobble
Hill

Boerum
Hill

Prospect
Heights

**BROOKLYN
(pp216-17)**

Gowanus

Park
Slope

Eastern
Parkway

Greenwood
Heights

Prospect
Lefferts
Gardens

Flatbush

Upper New
York Bay

Prospect
Park
South

Big
Channel

Lower New
York Bay

Coney
Island

Rockaway
Inlet

Hudson River

0   4 km
0   2 miles

>LOWER MANHATTAN

Full of byways and sky-high structures, Lower Manhattan comes splendidly to life every weekday morning as thousands of workers pour through the narrow streets, hurrying to their jobs in banking and high finance.

Coming to a rounded tip at its southern end, Lower Manhattan is surrounded by water: the East River to the east, New York Harbor at its center and the mighty Hudson to the west. Boats to Lady Liberty, Ellis Island, Governor's Island and Staten Island depart from Battery Park, which is full of memorials and public art and great views of New Jersey. Colonial New York is south of Wall Street – named after the barrier put in place by the Dutch over 200 years ago – and around South Street Seaport, a briny and somewhat touristy old docking area.

The World Trade Center site is still a barren hole, marred by construction efforts that try but never quite seem able to make progress on a planned memorial park. North of that is trendy Tribeca, full of gorgeous shops and gourmet eateries.

LOWER MANHATTAN

👁 SEE

Battery Park	1	B6
Bowling Green	2	B5
Federal Hall	3	C4
Ferry to Statue of Liberty & Ellis Island	4	B6
Fraunces Tavern Museum	5	C5
Ground Zero	6	B3
Museum of Jewish Heritage	7	A5
National Museum of the American Indian	8	B5
New York Stock Exchange	9	B4
Skyscraper Museum	10	A5
South Street Seaport	11	D4
South Street Seaport Museum	12	D4
St Paul's Chapel	13	B3
Staten Island Ferry Terminal	14	C6
Trinity Church	15	B4
WTC Tribute Visitors Center	16	B4

🛍 SHOP

A Uno	17	B2
Century 21	18	B4
Issey Miyake	19	A1
J&R	20	B3
Urban Archaeology	21	A1

🍴 EAT

Financier Patisserie	22	C5
Financier Patisserie	23	A4
Financier Patisserie	24	C4
Nelson Blue	25	D3
Soda Shop	26	B2
Stella Maris	27	D3
Zaitzeff	28	C4

🍸 DRINK

Another Room	29	B1
Brandy Library	30	A1
Rise	31	B5
Ulysses	32	C5

⭐ PLAY

TKTS Booth	33	D4
Tribeca Film Center	34	A1
Tribeca Performing Arts Center	35	A2

◉ SEE
◉ BATTERY PARK
☎ 311; www.nycgovparks.org;
Broadway at Battery Pl; ☽ sunrise–1am;
◉ 4, 5 to Bowling Green, 1 to South
Ferry; ♿
With its 13 works of public art,
the Holocaust Memorial, the NYC
Police Memorial, the Irish Hunger
Memorial, the rose-filled Hope
Garden and sweeping views of
Lady Liberty, this delightful bit
of green is practically an outdoor
museum. Check out the **Museum of
Jewish Heritage** (☎ 646-437-4200; www
.mjhnyc.org; 36 Battery Pl; adult/child/student/
senior $10/free/5/7, admission free 4-8pm Wed;
☽ 10am-5:45pm Sun-Tue & Thu, to 8pm Wed,
to 5pm Fri; ◉ 4, 5 to Bowling Green) and
the **Skyscraper Museum** (☎ 212-968-
1961; www.skyscraper.org; 39 Battery Pl; adult
$5, senior & student $2.50; ☽ noon-6pm
Wed-Sun; ◉ 4, 5 to Bowling Green), an ode
to the art of vertical building.

◉ BOWLING GREEN
cnr Broadway & State St; ◉ 4, 5 to
Bowling Green
A handkerchief-sized piece of
grass with an important past,
Bowling Green is believed to be
the spot where Dutch settler Peter
Minuit paid $24 to the Lenape for
the island of Manhattan. Now it's
home to *Charging Bull*, Arturo di
Modica's famous bronze statue
that symbolizes America's economic vitality.

◉ FEDERAL HALL
☎ 212-825-6888; www.nps.gov/feha;
26 Wall St; admission free; ☽ 10am-4pm
Mon-Fri; ◉ 2, 3, 4, 5 to Wall St, N, R to
Rector St
The big daddy of all founding fathers – George Washington – was
inaugurated at this Greek Revival–style building, and the museum
inside is dedicated to postcolonial
New York and its struggle to define
freedom of the press, as well as
many other 'inalienable' rights.

◉ FRAUNCES TAVERN
MUSEUM
☎ 212-425-1778; www.frauncestavern
museum.org; 54 Pearl St; adult $4,
senior, student & child $3; ☽ noon-5pm
Mon-Sat; ◉ 4, 5 to Bowling Green, 2, 3,
4, 5 to Wall St, R, W to Whitehall St, J, M,
Z to Broad St
This unique museum-restaurant
combo, a complex of four early-
18th-century structures, is an
homage to the nation-shaping
events of 1783 – when the British
left New York and General George
Washington gave a farewell
speech to his officers. It was the
most popular watering hole
of its day, and is still a working
pub/restaurant that serves up
hearty farmer fare like shepherd's
pie and roast-beef platters. The
museum section hosts rotating
exhibits, walking tours and lunchtime lectures.

GROUND ZERO

Church St btwn Vesey & Liberty Sts;
E, 2, 3 to World Trade Center, N, R to Rector St

The site is as blighted as ever, but signs of progress are finally showing up around the perimeter of Ground Zero. The **WTC Tribute visitors center** (☎ 866-737-1184; www.tributewtc .org; 120 Liberty St; admission $10; 10am-6pm Mon & Wed-Sat, noon-6pm Tue, noon-5pm Sun; E, 2, 3 to World Trade Center, N, R to Rector St), a nonprofit run by the WTC Families' Association, features a gallery of moving images and artifacts, and leads tours of the site. All the tours are led by New Yorkers who experienced the Twin Towers' destruction on September 11, or lost a loved one to the disaster.

Around the corner, on the west side of the Engine 10 Ladder 10 Firehouse is a massive bronze plaque that tells the story of what happened on September 11 from the firefighters' point of view. It's dedicated to all the lost firefighters, and Glenn Winuk, a partner in a nearby law firm and a volunteer medic who dashed into the burning buildings to help fleeing victims and perished himself.

NATIONAL MUSEUM OF THE AMERICAN INDIAN

☎ 212-514-3700; www.nmai.si.edu;
1 Bowling Green; admission free;
10am-5pm Fri-Wed, to 8pm Thu;
4, 5 to Bowling Green

Housed in an ornate building right behind Bowling Green, this Smithsonian-run museum has crafts, art and everyday objects from American Indian tribes, augmented

Onlookers contemplating the somber sight of Ground Zero

by interactive displays offering insights into Indian beliefs and culture. The building was once the US Customs House where Herman Melville wrote parts of *Moby Dick*.

◉ NEW YORK STOCK EXCHANGE
☎ 212-656-5168; www.nyse.com; 8 Broad St; ◉ 2, 3, 4, 5 to Wall St, N, R to Rector St

There's no getting inside the adrenaline-filled NYSE, but you can enjoy the gorgeous Roman-esque facade and the hordes of blue-jacketed traders who step outside to puff furiously on cigarettes and gobble a hotdog during their two-minute lunch break. During the holiday season Exchange Place gets seriously decked out – it rivals Rockefeller Center with the size of its tree.

◉ SOUTH STREET SEAPORT
☎ 212-732-7678; www.southstseaport .org; Pier 17 btwn Fulton & South Sts; ◷ 10am-9pm Mon-Sat, 11am-8pm Sun; ◉ J, Z, 3, 4, 5 to Fulton St; &

Slated for an overhaul that will turn this kitschy tourist trap into a sleek, waterfront hangout, South St is for now still an old collec-tion of waterlogged boats, naval memorabilia, and the **South Street Seaport Museum** (☎ 212-748-8600; 12 Fulton St; adult $10, student & senior $8, child under 12 $5; ◷ 10am-5pm Fri-Sun Nov-Mar, 10am-6pm daily Apr-Oct) for history

buffs who like to know everything about historic ships.

◉ ST PAUL'S CHAPEL
☎ 212-233-4164; www.stpaulschapel .org; Broadway at Vesey St; ◉ 2, 3 to Park Pl

St Paul's Chapel was built as a companion to the larger, more elaborate Trinity Church. Its homey style wasn't too humble for George Washington, who had – and still has – a pew inside. St Paul's was the center of rescue and recovery operations post–September 11 and has a permanent exhibit about that effort.

◉ STATEN ISLAND FERRY
☎ 718-815-2628; www.nyc.gov/html /dot/html/masstran/ferries/statfery.html; Whitehall Terminal at Whitehall & South Sts; admission free; ◷ 24hr; ◉ 1 to South Ferry; &

This is the life – a nice breeze, plenty of room, and a good long look at Lower Manhattan, the Statue of Liberty and Ellis Island – and it costs nothing. The Staten Island Ferry has got to be the best deal in town.

◉ STATUE OF LIBERTY & ELLIS ISLAND
☎ ferry info 212-363-3200, Time Passes 212-269-5755, toll-free reservation number 866-782-8834; www.nps.gov/stli, www.statuereservations.com; ferry adult/ child $12/5; ◷ Liberty Island 9am-5pm

GOVERNOR'S ISLAND

For decades, New Yorkers knew the 172-acre swath of **Governor's Island** (☎ 212-514-8285; www.nps.gov/gois; admission free; ◷ 10am-5pm Fri, to 7pm Sat & Sun May 31-Oct 12; ◉ 4, 5 to Bowling Green) only as an untouchable, mysterious patch of green out in the harbor. Now that the island has become part of the National Park Service, it's transforming into an elaborate public parkland. A ferry service (a 5-minute ride from Manhattan) brings you to the green gem, with three-tiered, sandstone Castle Williams and unsurpassed city views. Under future plans, there will also be a botanic forest, amphitheaters, bike trails and a waterfront promenade.

Sep-May, to 6:30pm Jun-Aug; ◉ 4, 5 to Bowling Green, 1 to South Ferry; ♿

She's great, grand, and somewhat of a challenge to visit. Lady Liberty, that beacon of freedom, ironically keeps her visitors under tight scrutiny. At research time her upper reaches were still closed off, but there was some discussion of opening them back up. If you want to get inside, you have to have a pass that says 'Monument Access.' The best way to be sure you'll get in is to order your tickets online in advance (www.nps.gov/stli has all the details). Ferries load at Battery Park City, and it's wise to disembark right away and enter the Statue of Liberty; stroll the grounds after. The Circle Line ferry departs Battery Park every 15 to 30 minutes from 9:30am to the late afternoon.

Nearby Ellis Island, where the ferries go before returning to Manhattan, is even more fascinating, with detailed accounts of the harrowing journeys made by immigrants to the US.

☑ TRINITY CHURCH
☎ 212-602-0800; Broadway at Wall St; ◷ 8am-6pm Mon-Fri, 8am-4pm Sat, 7am-4pm Sun; ◉ 2, 3, 4, 5 to Wall St, N, R to Rector St

A hugely influential church in the annals of New York history, Trinity was built in 1697 by King William III. Its clergy were required to be Loyalists, even though many of its members were dedicated to American independence by the mid-1700s. Its serene and tiny cemetery has headstones bearing some last names that would be very familiar to any student of the American Revolution.

☐ SHOP

☐ A UNO *Fashion*
☎ 212-227-6233; 123 W Broadway near Duane St; ◷ 11am-7pm; ◉ 1,2,3 to Chambers St

Sleek European brands for the 30-plus crowd who like to look sophisticated and fashionable without sacrificing comfort.

☐ CENTURY 21 *Fashion*
☎ 212-227-9092; www.c21stores.com;
22 Cortlandt St at Church St; 🕙 7:45am-
8pm Mon-Wed & Fri, to 8:30pm Thu,
10am-8pm Sat, 11am-7pm Sun; ⊕ A, C,
4, 5 to Fulton St/Broadway-Nassau St
Designer duds at gasp-inducing
prices keep the crowds pouring
into Century 21. It gets crowded
and competitive, so keep your elbows out, and if you see something
you like, get hold of it fast. Not everything is a knockout or a bargain,
but persistence pays off.

☐ ISSEY MIYAKE *Fashion*
☎ 212-226-0100; 119 Hudson St;
🕙 11am-7pm Mon-Sat, noon-6pm Sun;
⊕ 1 to Franklin St

The downtown crowd goes wild
for Miyake's pretty and delicate
dresses, blouses, skirts and slen-
derizing slacks.

☐ J&R Music *Electronics*
☎ 800-221-8180; www.jr.com; 15 Park
Row; 🕙 9am-7:30pm Mon-Sat, 10:30am-
6:30pm Sun; ⊕ 4, 5, 6 to Brooklyn
Bridge-City Hall
Three multistory stores line up
between Ann and Beekman Sts
and basically sell anything and
everything that's related to computers, phones, stereos, radios,
iPods, recording equipment and
other electronic goods. There's
also a store packed with CDs and
video games.

Run the bargain-shopper gauntlet at Century 21

📷 URBAN ARCHAEOLOGY
Homewares

☎ 212-571-8880; www.urbanarchaeology
.com; 143 Franklin St; ⏱ 9am-6pm Mon-
Fri; 🚇 1 to Franklin St

A pioneer in recycled design, owner Gil Shapiro continues his tradition of remixing, reconstructing and re-claiming old parts from abandoned buildings and construction sites. What he salvages and restores (or repurposes) is now sought after in the hippest Manhattan apartments; check out his Tribeca showroom/studio for his latest designs.

🍴 EAT
🍴 FINANCIER PATISSERIE
Bakery & Sandwiches, Desserts $

☎ 212-334-5600; 62 Stone St at Mill
Lane; ⏱ 7am-8:30pm Mon-Fri, to 7pm
Sat; 🚇 2, 3, 4, 5 to Wall St, J, M, Z to
Broad St;

There are now three Patisserie out-posts in Lower Manhattan (the sec-ond is in the World Financial Center and the third is at 35 Cedar St) because nobody can get enough of the flaky, buttery croissants, almond, apricot and pear tarts, aromatic coffee, homemade soups, creamy quiches and fresh salads on the regular menu. Dig in.

🍴 NELSON BLUE
New Zealand Cuisine $$

☎ 212-346-9090; www.nelsonblue
.com; 233-235 Front St; ⏱ lunch &
dinner; 🚇 A, C, J, M, Z, 2, 3, 4, 5 to Fulton
St/Broadway-Nassau St; 🚫 🚹

Good for a drink as well as a lamb curry pie, Nelson Blue claims to be the only Kiwi pub in town. It's certainly the only one in Lower Manhattan. The beer and wine list is heavy on New Zealand brews, which are perfect accompaniment for the pie, or New Zealand crab cakes or mussels, all sorts of skew-ers, burgers and grilled fish platters.

🍴 SODA SHOP
American Comfort $

☎ 212-571-1100; 125 Chambers St;
⏱ 8am-9pm; 🚇 A, C, 2, 3 to Chambers
St; 🚫 Ⓥ 🚹

Lunch and dinner are great – full of American classics like hearty mac 'n' cheese, and spaghetti with rich, flavorful meatballs – but locals love the breakfasts. Soda Shop's homey interior is the perfect place to grab a short stack or a fluffy omelette on the way to work.

🍴 STELLA MARIS
Irish Pub, Seafood $$

☎ 212-233-2417; 213 Front St;
⏱ breakfast, lunch & dinner; 🚇 J, M, Z,
1, 2, 4, 5 to Fulton St/Broadway-Nassau St

An Irish-owned spot with a polished and modern vibe on a cobblestoned, old-world corner of the city. Tuck into warm asparagus salad topped with a poached egg, done-right steak *frites*, charcuterie plates, grilled Scottish salmon or

NEIGHBORHOODS

LOWER MANHATTAN

an array of fresh shellfish from the black-onyx raw bar.

ZAITZEFF *Organic Diner* $
☎ 212-571-7272; www.zaitzeffnyc.com; 72 Nassau St; 🕑 8am-10pm Mon-Fri, 10am-6pm Sat & Sun; 🚇 A, C, J, M, Z, 2, 3, 4, 5 to Fulton St/Broadway-Nassau St; ♿ Ⓥ ♨

Classic New York diner food served with everything but the grease. The burgers, sandwiches and hot dogs are organic, as are the buns, and there are plenty of veggie dishes too.

🍸 DRINK
🍸 ANOTHER ROOM *Bar*
☎ 212-226-1418; 249 W Broadway; 🕑 5pm-3am; 🚇 1, 2 to Franklin St

Mellow and artsy and filled with long-time Tribeca residents, Another Room manages to be welcoming despite its narrow space and industrial decor. Wine and beer only; no mixed drinks.

🍸 BRANDY LIBRARY *Bar*
☎ 212-226-5545; www.brandylibrary .com; 25 N Moore St at Varick St; 🕑 5pm-2am Sun-Wed, 4pm-4am Thu-Sat; 🚇 1 to Franklin St

When sipping means serious business, it's easy to settle into this library, with soothing reading lamps and club chairs facing backlit, floor-to-ceiling, bottle-filled shelves. Go for top-shelf cognac, malt scotch or 90-year-old brandies (prices range from $9 to $280). Call ahead about tastings and other events.

Alfresco dining in Lower Manhattan

🍸 RISE *Bar*

☎ 917-790-2626; www.ritzcarlton.com; Ritz Carlton, 2 West St at Battery Pl; 🕐 noon-1am; 🚇 N, R, W to Rector St, 4, 5 to Bowling Green

What better place to sip a drink than 14 stories above the Hudson River? Rise is a sleek, sexy, comfortable bar that's great anytime of year, but absolutely phenomenal in the summer months when it opens up the outdoor patio. The dress code calls for 'casual chic,' meaning smart but not fussy.

🍸 ULYSSES *Pub*

☎ 212-482-0400; 95 Pearl St; 🕐 11am-4am Mon-Fri, to 3:30am Sat & Sun; 🚇 2, 3 to Wall St

An Irish bar with big easy chairs and comfy couches, Ulysses is part laid-back lounge and part neighborhood watering hole. The crowd's diverse and fun, the choice of drinks immense, and the owners run a shuttle between this and their two other bars, Puck Fair and Swift.

PLAY

⭐ RIVER TO RIVER FESTIVAL
Festival

www.rivertorivernyc.com; various locations around Lower Manhattan; admission free; 🚇 any train to Lower Manhattan; ♿

All summer long this nonprofit organization puts on film screenings, live music performances, dance nights, children's events and many other culturally enriching activities all across Lower Manhattan. Each summer's schedule is posted on the website. Favorite local choices include Latin nights at South Street Seaport.

⭐ TRIBECA FILM CENTER
Cinema

☎ 212-941-2000; www.tribecafilm.com; 375 Greenwich St btwn N Moore & Franklin Sts; 🕐 hours vary; 🚇 1 to Franklin St

It's not a working movie theater, but this labor of love from movie legend Robert DeNiro encourages the public to attend special screenings held throughout the year. It's also the de facto headquarters of the Tribeca Film Festival, another DeNiro production.

⭐ TRIBECA PERFORMING ARTS CENTER *Theater*

☎ 212-220-1460; www.tribecapac.org; 199 Chambers St; 🕐 hours vary; 🚇 A, C, 1, 2, 3 to Chambers St

A grassroots artists' collective, Tribeca PAC likes to put on performances from local residents on diverse topics related to city life. Works are multidisciplinary and unexpected, like *Lost Jazz Shrines*, which celebrates New York jazz clubs no longer in existence.

>CHINATOWN & LITTLE ITALY

One of Manhattan's busiest, most chaotic sections, vibrant Chinatown has all but eclipsed tiny Little Italy, which spiritually is still the soul of New York's Italian heritage but physically has been reduced to just a few quaint, picturesque blocks along Mott and Mulberry Sts.

The 15,000 Chinese immigrants who call this enclave home have turned it into a vibrant shopping market – all manner of snakes, snails, frogs and fish slither and flop in the open-air markets, and glistening, golden-skinned roast ducks hang in restaurant windows. Knock-off designer bags and watches – faux versions of Louis Vuitton, Chanel and Rolex – are hawked up and down Canal St.

With a growing Vietnamese presence and waves of Chinese immigrants from Fuzhou, Guangdong and Toisan, there's a constant overlapping of festivals, holidays and traditions. Get oriented at the official **Explore Chinatown information kiosk** (☎ 212-484-1216; www.explorechinatown .com; Canal St btwn Baxter & Walker Sts; ☷ 10am-6pm Mon-Fri & Sun, to 7pm Sat), where helpful, multilingual folk can guide you to specific eateries, shops, sights and events.

CHINATOWN & LITTLE ITALY

◉ SEE
Chatham Square............ 1 D6
Church of the
    Transfiguration 2 D6
Columbus Park 3 C6
Eastern States Buddhist
    Temple.....................4 D5
Edward Mooney House ..5 E5
Mahayana Buddhist
    Temple.....................6 E4
Mulberry Street.............7 C3
Museum of Chinese
    in America 8 B4

◻ SHOP
Canal Street....................9 G4
Pearl Paint Company....10 A4
Pearl River Mart 11 A3
Wing Fat Shopping.......12 E6

◍ EAT
Big Wong.....................13 D5
Bo Ky Restaurant.........14 C5
Canton........................15 E5
Focolare......................16 C4
Original Chinatown
    Ice Cream Factory......17 D5
Peking Duck House.......18 D6
Tai Pan Bakery.............19 C5

▼ DRINK
Gold Bar......................20 C2

★ PLAY
Explore Chinatown
    Information Kiosk 21 C4
Santos Party House......22 B4

Please see over for map

◉ SEE
◉ BUDDHIST TEMPLES
There are Buddhist temples all over Chinatown. The **Eastern States Buddhist Temple** (64 Mott St btwn Bayard & Canal Sts; ☯ 9am-6pm; ◉ J, M, Z, 6 to Canal St) holds hundreds of statues in all different sizes. It's a landmarked site, as is the **Mahayana Buddhist Temple** (133 Canal St & Manhattan Bridge Plaza; ☯ 8am-6pm; ◉ B, D to Grand St, J, M, Z, 6 to Canal St), which holds one large 16ft Buddha. You'll know you've arrived when you see two golden lions guarding a door.

◉ CHATHAM SQUARE
btwn Doyers & Catherine Sts; ◉ J, M, Z, 6 to Canal St
You've hit Chatham Sq when you see a large arch on two columns, with fresh flowers on each one. That's the Kim Lau Memorial Arch, built in 1962 to commemorate fighter pilot Benjamin Ralph Kim Lau and other Chinese Americans who were killed in WWII. The other statue in Chatham Sq is an homage to Lin Ze Xu, a 19th-century Ching-dynasty anti-drugs crusader who fought against the opium trade. Looking to the east, to Division St, you'll see a statue of Confucius; he's standing next to what's believed to be the tallest building in Chinatown. At St James Pl, just behind Chatham Sq, is the First

Shearith Israel Cemetery, which dates to 1683 and is believed to be the oldest Jewish cemetery in the city.

◉ CHURCH OF THE TRANSFIGURATION
☎ 212-962-5157; 29 Mott St; admission $2; ☯ noon-6pm Tue-Sun; ◉ J, M, N, Q, R, W, Z, 6 to Canal St
It's been serving New York's immigrant communities since 1801, and the Church of the Transfiguration doesn't stop adapting. First it was the Irish, then Italians, and now Chinese. The same priest delivers sermons in Cantonese, English and sometimes even Latin. This small landmark is not far from Pell St and Doyers Sts, two winding paths worth exploring.

◉ COLUMBUS PARK
Mulberry & Park Sts; ◉ J, M, Z, 6 to Canal St
You'd never guess from the gentle sounds of neighborhood residents playing mah-jongg and dominoes, but this park was once part of the notorious Five Points neighborhood that was the inspiration for Martin Scorsese's *Gangs of New York*. Although the tiny triangle is now a peaceful playground, the surrounding tenements are the same ones that were built in 1890.

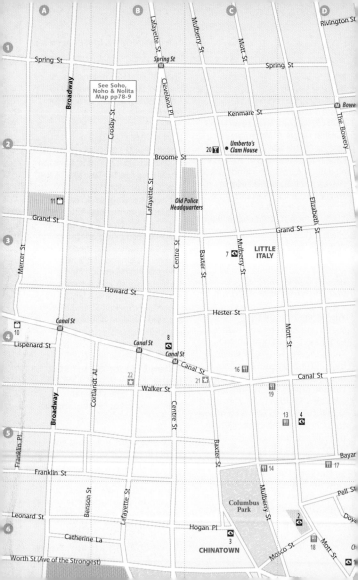

⊙ EDWARD MOONEY HOUSE
cnr 18 Bowery & Pell St; 🕙 **9am-5pm Mon-Fri, to 3pm Sat;** 🚇 **J, M, Z, 6 to Canal St**

The oldest townhouse in Manhattan stands at the corner of Bowery and Pell St, courtesy of a Mr Edward Mooney, who in 1785 took the wealth he made as a butcher and invested it in real estate. His post–Revolutionary War townhouse became a tavern in the 1800s, then a store, hotel, pool hall, restaurant, private club and now a bank. The architecture is a combination of Georgian and Federalist styles.

⊙ MULBERRY STREET
🚇 **C, E to Spring St**

Even though the original Italian essence is long gone, Mulberry St still bursts with true ethnic pride. Mobster Joey Gallo was shot to death at the former location of Umberto's Clam House (now found at 386 Broome St) in the '70s, John Gotti was wiretapped by the Feds in the long-gone Ravenite Social Club, and Ol' Blue Eyes himself, Frank Sinatra, caroused his way up and down this street back in the day. It's worth a walk just to take in the festive sights, sounds and fragrant smells. Most weekend days during summer, cars are blocked, leaving more room for the gelato carts.

⊙ MUSEUM OF CHINESE IN AMERICA
☎ **212-619-4785; www.moca-nyc.org; 211-215 Centre St near Grand St; suggested admission $3;** 🕙 **noon-6pm Tue-Sun;** 🚇 **J, M, N, Q, R, W, Z, 6 to Canal St**

This newly relocated museum – now housed in a 12,350-sq-ft space designed by architect Maya Lin (who did the famed Vietnam Memorial in Washington DC) – is chock-full of facts about Chinese American life . Browse through interactive multimedia exhibits, maps, timelines, photos, letters, films and artifacts, and catch rotating exhibits. Its anchor exhibit is the Chinese-American Experience, which touches on subjects such as immigration, activism and globalization.

🛍 SHOP
🛍 CANAL STREET *Bric-a-Brac*
🚇 **M, N, Q, R, W, Z, 6 to Canal St**

Bustling, busy and perpetually congested, Canal St is packed with everything from treasure to junk; sifting through takes a keen eye and loads of patience. Or, you can simply walk around, taking in the strange creatures flopping in the food markets, the homeopathic drugstores with Chinese remedies, and the sound of a thousand tongues speaking at once.

Countless shoppers, numerous vendors, many goods – but only one Canal St

PEARL PAINT COMPANY
Arts & Crafts

☎ 212-431-7932; 308 Canal St; ⏰ 10am-7pm Mon-Fri, to 6:30pm Sat, to 6pm Sun; ⊕ J, M, N, Q, R, W, Z, 6 to Canal St

An institution in art circles, Pearl Paint sticks out a mile on Canal St. Taking up four floors of a sprawling warehouse, it's got an obscene amount of space and it's all filled with anything and everything to do with painting, drawing, arts and crafts, gold leaf, glitter, glue – the list is endless.

PEARL RIVER MART
Bric-a-Brac

☎ 212-431-4770; 477 Broadway; ⏰ 10am-7pm; ⊕ J, M, N, Q, R, W, Z, 6 to Canal St

An Asian emporium that stocks all sorts of knick-knacks, Pearl River Mart's swanky storefront showcases bright kimonos, bejeweled slippers, Japanese teapots, paper lanterns, jars of mysterious spices, herbs, teas (and a Zen-like tea room) and more.

WING FAT SHOPPING *Mall*

8-9 Bowery btwn Pell & Doyers Sts; ⏰ 10am-6pm; ⊕ J, M, N, Q, R, W, Z, 6 to Canal St

One of the most unique malls you'll ever see, it lies underground and has businesses offering reflexology, collectible stamps and feng-shui services. The most fascinating aspect is its history, as the tunnel is said to have served

Bo Ky Restaurant – all those happy customers can't be wrong

as a stop on the Underground Railroad, as well as an escape route in the early 20th century for members of rival Tong gangs. They'd wage battle up on the street and then disappear down into the darkness before police could even begin to search.

🍴 EAT
🍴 BIG WONG Asian $
☎ 212-964-0540; 67 Mott St btwn Walker & Bayard Sts; ☷ breakfast, lunch & dinner; Ⓣ J, M, N, Q, R, W, Z, 6 to Canal St; ♿ Ⓥ ♨

A fast-moving favorite that's famous for its roast pork and BBQ-style chicken, duck and ribs, Big Wong also does a mean rice crepe for breakfast. You'll likely have to share a table, and the food

(and your check) comes lightning quick, but it's a fun, communal (and affordable) experience.

🍴 BO KY RESTAURANT
Pan Asian $
☎ 212-406-2292; 80 Bayard St btwn Mott & Mulberry Sts; ☷ breakfast, lunch & dinner; Ⓣ J, M, N, Q, R, W, Z, 6 to Canal St; Ⓥ

Cheap, quick and delicious, Bo Ky's meat-studded soups, fish-infused flat noodles and curried rice dishes keep customers rotating in and out the door, usually in twos and threes. Join the crowds and dig in.

🍴 CANTON *Cantonese* $$$
☎ 212-226-4441; 45 Division St btwn Bowery & Market St; ☷ lunch & dinner; Ⓣ F to East Broadway; ♨

It's been around for 50 years, so Canton must be doing something right – no, make that everything right. Underneath the Manhattan Bridge, it churns out delectable dishes such as ginger scallion noodles, sautéed tofu with pork, mixed vegetables and garlicky chicken.

FOCOLARE *Italian* $$$
☎ 212-993-5858; 115 Mulberry St btwn Canal & Hester Sts; ☼ lunch & dinner; Ⓔ J, M, Q, R, W, Z to Canal St

If you're determined to experience a Little Italy dinner while in the city, this friendly newcomer is a fine choice. With a cozy interior warmed by a fireplace in winter and adorned with photos of Frank Sinatra and company, the kitchen turns out classics in fine style: homemade pasta, cooked al dente, is an excellent base for various red and cream-based sauces; crisp rice balls ooze with cheese; fried calamari zings with flavor.

ORIGINAL CHINATOWN ICE CREAM FACTORY *Ice Cream* $
☎ 212-608-4170; www.chinatown icecreamfactory.com; 65 Bayard St; ☼ 11am-10pm; Ⓔ J, M, N, Q, R, W, Z, 6 to Canal St; Ⓥ ♿

Ask the servers here and they'll tell you that ice cream was invented in China during the Tang dynasty,

Decisions, decisions – shopping on Mott St

SWEET TREATS

Chinese bakeries are ubiquitous in Chinatown, as hardworking patrons stop by for a quick, filling treat. Many of the delicacies aren't found in the American pastry lexicon, but are delicious nonetheless. Cash-only **Tai Pan Bakery** (☎ 212-732-2222; 194 Canal St near Mott St; ⏰ 7:30am-8:30pm; ⊜ J, M, N, Q, R, W, Z, 6 to Canal St) carries most of these.

> Cock tail buns *(gai mei bao)*: shaped vaguely like a rooster's tail, and stuffed with sweet coconut filling.
> Coconut tarts *(ye tot)*: bright yellow tarts flavored with coconut and usually sporting a cherry or berry on top.
> Custard egg tart *(dan tot)*: every Chinatown bakery has these egg custards baked into a dry, flaky crust.
> Hot dog buns *(cheung zai bao)*: only found in NYC's Chinatown, these treats feature a hot dog in a sweet, fluffy bun and covered in a honey glaze.
> Pineapple buns *(bo lo bao)*: they look like pineapples on the outside, but the filling is usually custard or coconut.
> Red bean paste buns *(hong dau sa bao)*: a popular dessert made of sweet bread and red beans crushed into a semi-sweet paste.
> Roast pork buns *(char siu chan bao)*: sometimes steamed, other times baked, these sweet bread buns contain Chinese-style BBQ pork.

and based on the flavors the Factory can produce, you might just believe them. Sorbets and more in flavors such as avocado, durian, sesame and peppermint, plus the standards like vanilla and chocolate.

🍴 PEKING DUCK HOUSE
Chinese $$
☎ 212-227-1810; 28 Mott St; ⏰ lunch & dinner; ⊜ J, M, N, Q, R, W, Z, 6 to Canal St; ♿ 🅅 👶

You already know what the specialty of the house is – big, brown, crispy glazed duck, served with sides of pancakes and *hoisin* sauce

for tearing, rolling and dipping. There are plenty of other dishes to choose from, all bearing imprints of Peking, Shanghai and Szechuan flavors, mixed expertly together. Peking Duck is slightly fancier than other Chinatown spots, but not at all stuffy; it's a popular choice for local families celebrating a big event.

🍸 DRINK
🍸 GOLD BAR *Bar*
☎ 212-274-1568; 389 Broome St near Mulberry St; ⏰ 6pm-4am Tue-Sat; ⊜ 6 to Spring St, J, M, Z to Bowery

The interior of this bar could have served as a backdrop to the 1960s James Bond flick *Goldfinger*. Not only is the bar dripping in gold (including gold skulls on the walls, gold chains between rooms and gold ceilings), it's also full of 1960s kitsch and an aura of faux-exclusivity. Still, it's a funny and strange little place, great for a late-night drink (beware, it carries the gold theme even into the libations – many drinks feature honey, of course), and when the right crowd comes in, it's actually kind of fun.

PLAY

EXPERIENCE CHINATOWN
Tour

☎ 212-619-4785; www.moca-nyc.org; tours adult $15, senior & child $12; ⏱ weekly May-Dec

To truly penetrate the layers that make up bustling Chinatown, you'll need a guide. And trusting one from the Chinatown-based Museum of Chinese in America (p56) is definitely a good move. The tours are led by museum docents with family roots in the community, and they give you a sense of Chinatown's past and present.

>LOWER EAST SIDE

Signs of a louche, lush past abound in the Lower East Side (LES). Its slightly seedy streets are now dotted with trendy restaurants and cafés, but it's difficult to erase centuries of grit and grime. The LES was once a ghetto slum, full of Jewish and Eastern European immigrants who lived cramped, dank lives in crowded tenements and worked in nearby factories. They also built beautiful synagogues and neighborhood markets, and enjoyed a vibrant street life full of theater, music and art. Later came waves of Latinos, who wove their own traditions into the fluid neighborhood.

Now that condos and hotels have replaced many of the tenements, and expensive restoration projects have returned many cultural gems to their original beauty, the LES is hipster central, offering some of the best nightlife and dining in the city. Its flashy mix of modern and old – the stalwart Lower East Side Tenement Museum, for example, contrasts nicely with the innovative New Museum of Contemporary Art – give this nabe a unique allure.

LOWER EAST SIDE

Please see over for map

👁 SEE

👁 ELDRIDGE STREET SYNAGOGUE

☎ 212-219-0888; www.eldridgestreet
.org; 12 Eldridge St btwn Canal & Division
Sts; 🕐 tours 11am-4pm Sun, Tue, Thu or
by appt; 🚇 F to East Broadway

Shining like a new penny, this landmarked house of worship (built in 1887) was once the center of LES Jewish life. It fell into squalid condition in the 1920s, but today, thanks to a decades-long restoration effort, some of its original grandeur is back. It also hosts concerts, art exhibits, educational lectures and readings.

👁 ESSEX STREET MARKET

☎ 212-312-3603; www.essexstreet
market.com; 120 Essex St btwn Delancey
& Rivington Sts; 🕐 8am-6pm Mon-Sat;
🚇 F, J, M, V, Z to Delancey St-Essex St

Fantastic food shopping and people-watching make it a pleasure to meander through this 80-year-old market, which still has old-fashioned pickle stalls right next to gourmet cheese shops. Just like the neighborhood, Essex St Market is a mix of Jewish and Latino vendors.

👁 GALLERY ONETWENTYEIGHT

☎ 212-674-0244; www.onetwentyeight
.com; 128 Rivington St; 🕐 call for appt;
🚇 F to Lower East Side-Second Ave

Like its opening hours, the art at this gallery is eclectic and hit or miss. You never know what you'll find – or when – and that's what keeps people coming back for more. Check out the website to see what's on display and call in advance to make sure someone will be there when you stop by.

HIDDEN LOWER EAST SIDE

There's a lot of history to discover in the Lower East Side. If you want to take a few hours to really get to know the nabe, try a tour with the **Lower East Side Jewish Conservancy** (☎ 212-374-4100; nycjewishtours.org; 235 East Broadway; tours $18-30; 🕐 office 10am-5pm Mon-Thu, to 2pm Fri; 🚇 F, J, M, Z to Delancey St-Essex St). Tours are by appointment. A public tour also takes place every month, and there's an annual nosh-tour extravaganza on Christmas day. The professional guides will take you in and out of every major historic site within walking distance, with frequent stops for a nosh on the way. As you stroll the streets, keep an eye out for **St Augustine's Episcopal Church** (☎ 212-673-5300; 290 Henry St), near the Abrons Art Center. Originally the All Saints Free Church, this landmark Greek Revival was finished in 1828. Recalling a bit of the city's past that doesn't often get acknowledged, the church is currently renovating its two original 'Slave Galleries,' where slaves who helped build parts of the city had to sit during services.

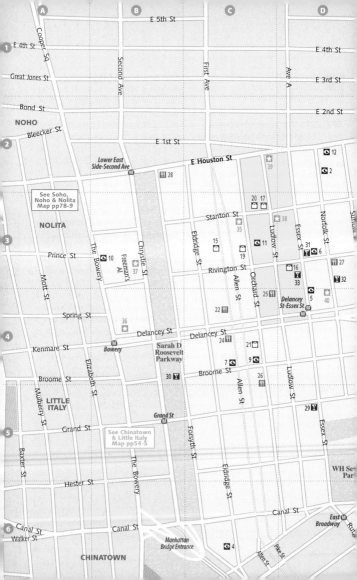

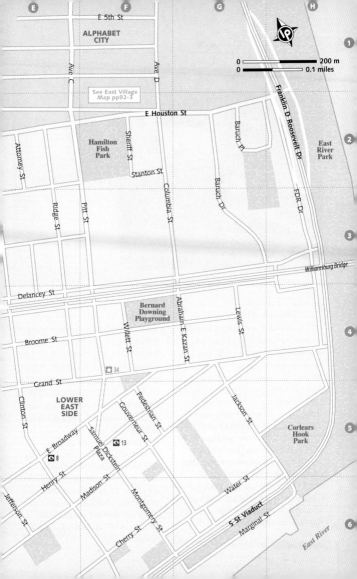

A window into yesteryear, the Lower East Side Tenement Museum

⊙ KEHILA KEDOSHA JANINA SYNAGOGUE AND MUSEUM

☎ 212-431-1619; www.kkjsm.org; 280 Broome St at Allen St; ⏲ 11am-4pm Sun, worship service 9am Sat; ⊖ F, J, M, Z to Delancey St-Essex St

This small synagogue is home to an obscure branch of Judaism, whose people, known as Romaniotes, come from ancestors who were slaves sent to Rome but rerouted to Greece. Their only synagogue in the Western Hemisphere is here, and includes a small museum that bears artifacts like hand-painted birth certificates, an art gallery, a Holocaust memorial for Greek Jews and costumes from Janina, the Romaniote capital of Greece.

⊙ LOWER EAST SIDE TENEMENT MUSEUM

☎ 212-431-0233; www.tenement.org; 90 Orchard St at Broome St; adult $17, senior & student $13, child under 5 free, discounts available for combo-tour tickets; ⏲ visitor center 11am-5:30pm, museum tours every 40min from 1pm & 1:20pm until 4:30pm & 4:45pm Tue-Fri (reservations suggested); ⊖ B, D to Grand St, F, J, M, Z to Delancey St-Essex St; ⧖

Get a firsthand look at the crowded conditions endured by Jewish and Eastern European immigrants at the turn of the century. The tours through restored and refurbished apartments raise poignant feelings about early settlers' enthusiasm for a future in the USA. You'll get to know the German-Jewish Gumpertz family, who lived in the LES in the 1870s, and the Sicilian-Catholic Baldizzi family from the 1930s, plus many others.

◉ NEW MUSEUM OF CONTEMPORARY ART

☎ 212-219-1222; www.newmuseum .org; 235 Bowery near Prince St; adult/ senior/student $12/8/6; ⏱ noon-6pm Wed-Fri, to 10pm Sat, to 6pm Sun; ◉ 6 to Spring St, N, R to Prince St

New York's newest museum is an off-kilter stack of seven white, ethereal boxes, creating a seven-story structure designed by Tokyo-based architects Kazuyo Sejima and Ryue Nishizawa. The city's sole museum dedicated to contemporary art features edgy works in new forms, like seemingly random, discarded materials fused together and displayed in the middle of a vast room. Founded in 1977 by Marcia Tucker and moved to five different locations over the years, the museum's mission statement is simple: 'New art, new ideas.' The museum also houses a small and

ART INVASION

Creativity is no stranger to the Lower East Side. Long before uptown galleries starting arriving, the LES was home to artists, musicians, writers and painters who often shared space and resources in order to do their work. Many of those collectives are still around today, and are open to the public for browsing.

ABC No Rio (☎ 212-254-3697; www.abcnorio.org; 156 Rivington St; admission price varies; ⏱ hours vary; ◉ F, J, M, Z to Delancey St-Essex St) Founded in 1980, this internationally known art and activism center features weekly hard-core/punk and experimental music shows, as well as regular fine-arts exhibits, poetry readings and more.

Angel Orensanz Foundation (☎ 212-529-7194; www.orensanz.org; 172 Norfolk St; admission price varies; ⏱ hours vary; ◉ F to Delancey St-Essex St) Inside one of the oldest synagogues in the city, this artist-run foundation hosts art and photography exhibits and various live music events.

Artists Alliance (☎ 212-420-9202; www.artistsai.org; 107 Suffolk St; admission price varies; ⏱ hours vary; ◉ F, J, M, Z to Delancey St-Essex St) A nonprofit artists' collective with more than 40 members, Artists Alliance has a rotating list of exhibits and contributors on its website.

Clemente Soto Velez (☎ 212-260-4080; www.el.net/csv; 107 Suffolk St; admission price varies; ⏱ hours vary; ◉ F, J, M, Z to Delancey St-Essex St) Inside the AAI building, this collective focuses on the work of Puerto Rican poet Velez, but also brings in theater, music, art and film from artists across the world.

healthy café, and has the added treat of a city viewing platform, which provides a unique perspective on the constantly changing architectural landscape.

ORCHARD STREET BARGAIN DISTRICT

Orchard, Ludlow & Essex Sts btwn Houston & Delancey Sts; ⏲ **Sun-Fri;** ⓞ **F, J, M, Z to Delancey St-Essex St**

Back in the day, this large intersection was a free-for-all, as Eastern European and Jewish merchants sold anything that could command a buck from their pushcarts. The 300-plus shops you see now aren't as picturesque, but it's a good place to pick up some cheap shirts, tees and jeans. If you like to haggle, take a shot at bargaining over the price.

PARTICIPANT INC

☎ **212-254-4334; 253 East Houston St;** ⏲ **noon-7pm Wed-Sun;** ⓞ **F to Lower East Side-Second Ave**

Part gallery, part performance-art space, Participant Inc uses its 2nd floor for all sorts of innovative fun. Opened in 2002 by founder Lia Gangitano, it's stayed afloat even as many other galleries disappear. It has a rotating roster of international artists, and also makes a point of showcasing LES-based work.

SHOP

ALIFE RIVINGTON CLUB

Fashion & Accessories, Footwear

☎ **212-375-8128; www.rivingtonclub .com; 158 Rivington St near Clinton St;** ⏲ **11am-7pm Mon-Sat, noon-6pm Sun;** ⓞ **J, M, Z to Delancey St-Essex St**

Unmarked doors and discreet buzzers put the 'club' in Alife Rivington's name. This temple to sneaker and T-shirt consumption has all the latest and hippest styles, in all the coolest colors, of course.

BLUESTOCKINGS *Books*

☎ **212-777-6028; www.bluestockings .com; 172 Allen St;** ⏲ **1-10pm;** ⓞ **F, V to Lower East Side-Second Ave**

It's run-down and ramshackle, but full of history and fueled by the alternative attitude that once permeated the Lower East Side. A holdover from the freewheeling '70s, Bluestockings offers books on a range of radical topics, including gender studies, black liberation theory and plenty more.

ECONOMY CANDY

Food & Drink

☎ **212-254-1531; www.economycandy .com; 108 Rivington St at Essex St;** ⏲ **9am-6pm Mon-Fri, 10am-5pm Sat;** ⓞ **F, J, M, Z to Delancey St-Essex St**

Known as the 'Nosher's Paradise of the Lower East Side,' this second-generation family store has a

LOWER EAST SIDE

jaw-dropping selection of old- and new-style nibbles. Jelly beans, halvah, Pez, Swedish Fish and so much more grace the shelves of this corner candy shop.

☐ FOLEY + CORINNA
Fashion & Accessories
☎ 212-529-5042; 143 Ludlow St at Stanton St; ⏰ noon-8pm; ☻ F, V to Lower East Side-Second Ave
This vintage store with a few of its own unique designs is pure girly romance. Delicate dresses, and tees, tanks and blouses matched with flirty skirts are the signature

style, along with Corinna's unique shoe and jewelry designs.

☐ HONEY IN THE ROUGH
Fashion & Accessories
☎ 212-228-6415; http://honeyinthe rough.com; 161 Rivington St near Clinton St; ⏰ noon-8pm Mon-Sat, to 6pm Sun; ☻ F, J, M, Z to Delancey St-Essex St
Stocking colorful variations on the always-popular little black dress, Honey in the Rough is all about the party frock – vivid, youthful and still sophisticated. You won't miss your basic black once you try on one of these.

Foley + Corinna – who doesn't love flirty skirts?

Enlarge your mind at radical, ramshackle and historical Bluestockings (p68)

REED SPACE
Fashion & Accessories, Footwear

☎ 212-253-0588; http://thereedspace
.com; 151 Orchard St; 🕑 1-7pm Mon-Fri,
noon-7pm Sat & Sun; 🚇 F to Delancey
St-Essex St

Sneakers, accessories, youthful
tees, pants and jackets for both
sexes line the bright and varied
shelves at Reed Space. Designer
Jeff Ng has found a blueprint for
the urban casual lifestyle.

SEPTEMBER WINES &
SPIRITS *Food & Drink*

☎ 212-388-0770; http://september
wines.com; 100 Stanton St at Ludlow St;
🕑 11am-10pm Mon-Thu, to 11pm Fri,
noon-11pm Sat, 1-8pm Sun; 🚇 F, J, M, Z
to Delancey St-Essex St

A boutique wine shop that has
lots of unique bottles on display,
including a section on women
vintners, hard-to-find wines,
specialty drinks and big-budget
classics.

STILL LIFE
Fashion & Accessories

☎ 212-575-9704; www.stilllifenyc.com;
77 Orchard St near Delancey St; 🕑 noon-
7pm; 🚇 B, F, J, M, V, Z to Delancey
St-Essex St

The cool tones of Mobb Deep and
Quiet Village will likely greet you
inside Still Life, a haven for hat
lovers. Check out styles like the

Mingus and the Langston – it takes hats to a whole new level of hip.

🍴 EAT

🍴 ALLEN & DELANCEY
American $$

☎ 212-253-5400; http://allenand delancey.net; 115 Allen St near Delancey St; 🕑 dinner; 🚇 F, J, M, Z to Delancey St-Essex St

Red velvet curtains and a sea of votive candles set the mood at this romantic joint. The menu claims to be American nouveau, but chef Neil Ferguson's British background plays a role in savory dishes like sea scallops in parsnip cream with bacon and onion compote, roasted duck foie gras with pears and celery root, bone marrow caviar, and rabbit terrine with French fingerling potatoes.

🍴 BONDI ROAD *Australian* $

☎ 212-253-5311; 153 Rivington St near Suffolk St; 🕑 dinner Mon-Fri, lunch & dinner Sat & Sun; 🚇 J, M, Z to Delancey St-Essex St; 🆅 🅰

What it lacks in width it makes up for in height. Still, Bondi Road is a tight squeeze on weekend nights. Slide onto one of the big barstools at the tables, check out the huge montages of Bondi Beach running down each wall, then take a stab at filling out your menu with the little stub pencils handed out. You

pick a fish (mackerel or cod, for example), a cooking method (like grilled, fried or sautéed) and a side dish (french fries, usually). Then drink as much Aussie beer as you can with the rowdy crowd till your food comes.

🍴 FRIED DUMPLING *Chinese* $

☎ 212-941-9975; 99 Allen St near Delancey St; 🕑 7:30am-9pm; 🚇 F, J, M, Z to Delancey St-Essex St; 🆅 🅰

Underneath the hanging Chinese sign rimmed in garish yellow is the entrance to the cheapest dumplings in town – and they actually taste delicious. For $1 you can get five pork-and-chive, mixed-veggie or Chinese-cabbage stuffed dumplings. One dollar will also buy you four fried pork buns or two sesame pancakes (beef costs an extra 50 cents), and for $2 you can get hearty, flavorful noodle soups.

🍴 KUMA INN *Pan-Asian* $$

☎ 212-353-8866; 113 Ludlow St btwn Delancey & Rivington Sts; 🕑 dinner Tue-Sun; 🚇 F, J, M, Z to Delancey St-Essex St

Reservations are a must at this strikingly popular spot in a secretive 2nd-floor location that's a headache to find (look for a small red door next to a Chinese deli with 113 painted on the concrete side). The Filipino- and Thai-inspired tapas run the gamut, from vegetarian summer rolls (with the unique addition of chayote) and edamame (soybean) drizzled with basil-lime oil to an oyster omelette and grilled salmon with mung beans and pickled onions. Pair anything with some chilled sake or mango nectar.

🍴 LITTLE GIANT
Seasonal American $$

☎ 212-226-5047; www.littlegiantnyc .com; 85 Orchard St; ☯ dinner daily, brunch Sat & Sun; 🚇 F to Delancey St-Essex St; ♿ Ⓥ

Fresh ingredients from organic farmers in upstate New York pepper Little Giant's revolving menu, which can carry dishes like chicken-liver mousse, maple-roasted brussel sprouts, sticky toffee pudding and a 'swine of the week' dish featuring pork. The 80-bottle wine list proudly offers only local vintners.

🍴 SCHILLER'S LIQUOR BAR
Bistro Cuisine $$

☎ 212-673-0330; www.schillersny.com; 131 Rivington St at Norfolk St; ☯ 11am-midnight Mon-Thu, to 2am Fri-Sun; 🚇 F, J, M, Z to Delancey St-Essex St; ♿ 🚻

The combination of eclectic bistro fare and warm, brassy decor is a large part of Schiller's allure – the other element is the Rivington St location, a great place to sit with a cold beer on a hot day. The wine carafes are generous, portions

ample, and the food – steak *frites*, Cuban sandwiches, baked chicken and glazed cod – reliably good.

🍴 YONAH SCHIMMEL KNISHERY *Knishes* $

☎ 212-477-2858; 137 E Houston St btwn Eldridge & Forsyth Sts; ☯ 9:30am-7pm; 🚇 F, V to Lower East Side-Second Ave; Ⓥ 🚻

Here's how to make a living the old-school way: buy a pushcart c 1890, sell your wife's knishes on Coney Island, save up for a mini storefront on the LES, and turn it into a 96-year-old family business that still follows the original recipe and uses a century-old dumb-waiter to haul potato, cheese, cabbage and kasha knishes up from your wood-burning stove in the cellar. One bite of a Yonah Schimmel knish and you'll be hooked.

🍸 DRINK

🍸 EAST SIDE COMPANY BAR
Bar

☎ 212-614-7408; 49 Essex St at Grand St; ☯ 7pm-4am Mon-Sat; 🚇 F, J, M, Z to Delancey St-Essex St

If you prefer a stiff martini over a cold beer, step into this establishment, where 'mixologists' will craft you an adult libation. You don't need a reservation, just keen eyes to spot the doorway; it's covered in plywood, next to the Pickle

Guys store. Walk through and step down into a low, tin-ceiling bar. There are cozy booths and DJ action in back, and an inviting industrial bar in front.

☿ HAPPY ENDING *DJ Bar*
☎ 212-334-9676; www.happyending lounge.com; 302 Broome St; ⏱ 10pm-4am Tue, 7pm-4am Wed-Sat; ⊕ B, D to Grand St, J, M, Z to Bowery

Ignore the hideous pink, purple and spangled decor at Happy Ending – it used to be a 'massage parlor,' and the new owners clearly didn't feel the need to refurbish. Focus instead on the groove, hip-hop, funk and electronica. Tuesday nights are 'We Bite' and 'Shit Hammered' events; Wednesday nights feature literary readings (before the dancing starts); there are gay, goth and punk nights, and the 'Human Jukebox' DJ on Saturdays. Note that the entrance awning says 'Xie He Health Club' – the owners apparently didn't feel the need to change that, either.

☿ MAGICIAN *Bar*
☎ 212-673-7851; 118 Rivington St btwn Essex & Norfolk Sts; ⏱ 5pm-4am; ⊕ F, J, M, Z to Delancey St-Essex St

Pick out an old classic on the jukebox, take your pick of microbrewed beers or specialty cocktails (mixed with a generous hand) and enjoy the spacious,

never-crowded bar at Magician, a low-key neighborhood joint that hasn't been discovered by the 'in' crowd.

☿ NURSE BETTIE *Bar*
☎ 917-434-9072; 106 Norfolk St btwn Delancey & Rivington Sts; ⏱ 6pm-2am Sun-Tue, 6pm-4am Wed-Sat; ⊕ F, J, M, Z to Delancey St-Essex St

Something a bit new is going on with this pint-sized charmer: plenty of roaming space between slick '00s-modern lounges and '50s-style ice-cream-shop stools and painted pin-ups on the brick walls. Cocktails get freaky: fruity vodka and brandies, plus bubble-gum martinis. You can bring food in, and many won-over locals do.

☿ WHISKEY WARD *Bar*
☎ 212-477-2998; www.thewhiskey ward.com; 121 Essex St; ⏱ 5pm-4am; ⊕ F, J, M, Z to Delancey St-Essex St; ⏱

Once upon a time, city officials divided Manhattan into wards, and the Lower East Side was the 'Whiskey Ward,' courtesy of its many drinking establishments. Modern owners of the Whiskey Ward apparently appreciate history as much as they adore single malts, rye whiskey, blended Scotch, Irish whiskey and bourbon. Patrons enjoy the single-mindedness of this brick-walled bar.

NEIGHBORHOODS

LOWER EAST SIDE

⭐ PLAY

⭐ ABRONS ART CENTER
Theater, Arts

☎ 212-598-0400; www.henrystreet.org; 466 Grand St; 🕒 hours vary; 🚇 F, J, M, Z to Delancey St-Essex St; ♿

This venerable cultural hub has three theaters, the largest being the Harry de Jur Playhouse (a national landmark), with its own lobby, fixed seats on a rise, a large, deep stage and good visibility. A mainstay of the downtown Fringe Festival, Abrons Art Center is also your best bet to catch experimental and community productions – including avant garde jazz brought to you by the former Tonic nightclub, which was driven out of the LES by rising rents. Not afraid of difficult subjects, Abrons sponsors plays and dance and photography exhibits that don't get much play elsewhere.

⭐ ARLENE'S GROCERY
Live Music, Karaoke

☎ 212-358-1633; www.arlenesgrocery .net; 95 Stanton St; cover charge for bands Tue-Sun $8-10; 🕒 6pm-4am; 🚇 F, V to Lower East Side-Second Ave

Formerly a bodega and butcher shop, Arlene's Grocery now serves up heaping portions of live talent with shows every night. Drinks are cheap and the crowd is good looking – make an impression

on Monday night with Rock 'n' Roll Karaoke. It's free, and you're backed by a live band. Probably your best shot at getting a groupie.

⭐ BOWERY BALLROOM
Live Music

☎ 212-533-2111; www.boweryball room.com; 6 Delancey St; ticket price varies; 🕒 performance times vary; 🚇 F to Delancey St-Essex St, J, M to Bowery

The clue to the Bowery's success, besides its cool location and look, is that it's the kind of place you want to hang in before and after the show, as well as during. Drinks are long and strong, acoustics are grand, and the list of talent is phenomenal. Dirty Pretty Things and Ziggy Marley play regularly, and the Losers Lounge nights (the Cure vs the Smiths) sell out instantly.

⭐ LIVING ROOM
DJ Bar, Live Music

☎ 212-533-7235; www.livingroomny .com; 154 Ludlow St; no cover charge, 1 drink minimum; 🕒 6:30pm-2am Sun-Thu, to 4am Fri & Sat; 🚇 F, V to Lower East Side-Second Ave, J, M, Z to Delancey St-Essex St

There's never a cover charge at this intimate space, which recently hosted Jealous Girlfriends and the Kidrockers. Most acts are acoustic, but the occasional amplifier will slip in. If the live music doesn't thrill you, the upstairs lounge – known as Googie's – features a DJ.

MERCURY LOUNGE
Live Music

☎ 212-260-4700; www.mercurylounge nyc.com; 217 E Houston St; cover charge $8-15; ☾ 4pm-4am; ⓞ F, V to Lower East Side-Second Ave

Featuring local, indie and up-and-coming talent, Mercury Lounge is a good place to catch bands just before they hit it big. The owners have an ear for talent, so don't be surprised to hear high-quality sounds – in all genres but heavy on rock – coming from the unassuming space.

PIANOS *Live Music*

☎ 212-505-3733; www.pianosnyc.com; 106 Norfolk St; cover charge $8-17; ☾ noon-4am; ⓞ F, V to Lower East Side-Second Ave

Nobody's bothered to change the sign at the door, a leftover from the location's previous incarnation as a piano shop. Now it's a musical mix of genres and styles, leaning more toward pop, punk and new wave, but throwing in some hip-hop and indie bands for good measure. Sometimes you get a double feature – one act upstairs and another below. Happy hour is a good time to visit.

>SOHO, NOHO & NOLITA

It's amazing that so much hipster coolness can be packed into three such comparatively small corners of Manhattan. Long before it became celebrity central, Soho (the area south of Houston St) was an industrial hole that gradually filled up with artists who loved the old factory lofts.

Now it's awash with luxury shops and million-dollar condos, and two other former triangles of depression have followed suit: Nolita, which is North of Little Italy, and Noho, just north of Houston St.

Of the three, Soho is still the most visually stunning, with massive, soaring cast-iron-facade buildings and a picturesque skyline. Nolita now has a similar concentration of pretty shops and eclectic designers but it moves at a slightly slower pace. Where Soho has its galleries and big stores, Nolita has its boutiques and rustic eateries.

On the north side of Houston St, below Astor Pl, is the triangle of Lafayette and Bond Sts. You couldn't pack more treats into a two-block radius. There are so many standout stores it looms large for shoppers in Manhattan.

SOHO, NOHO & NOLITA

◉ SEE

◉ ARTISTS SPACE

☎ 212-226-3970; www.artistsspace
.org; 3rd fl, 38 Greene St; admission free;
🕑 11am-6pm Tue-Sun; ◉ A, C, E, J, M,
N, R, 1, 6 to Canal St

One of the first alternative spaces
in New York, Artists Space was
founded in 1972 to support
contemporary artists working in
the visual arts, including video,
electronic media, performance,
architecture and design. It offers
an exhibition space for new art
and artists, and tries to foster an
appreciation for the role artists
play in communities.

◉ CHILDREN'S MUSEUM OF THE ARTS

☎ 212-274-0986; www.cmany.org; 182
Lafayette St btwn Broome & Grand Sts;

admission $6, suggested donation from
4-6pm Thu; 🕑 noon-5pm Fri-Sun & Wed,
to 6pm Thu; ◉ 6 to Spring St, N, R to
Prince St; ♿

Trained artists run this interactive museum, which is more like
a playhouse for kids than a stuffy
institution. Kids are free to touch,
run, pepper docents with ques-
tions and have a good time. Warn-
ing: children will leave knowing
how to make Flubber at home.

◉ DRAWING CENTER

☎ 212-219-2166; www.drawingcenter
.org; 35 Wooster St; admission free;
🕑 10am-6pm Tue-Fri, 11am-6pm Sat;
◉ A, C, E, 1 to Canal St

It's been around for ages, and the
Drawing Center remains one of
the city's premiere nonprofits. It's
dedicated exclusively to drawings,
with examples from Michelangelo,

For almost four decades, Artists Space has been showcasing emerging artists

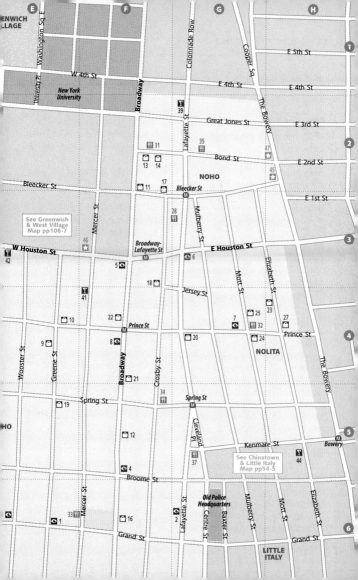

SOHO, NOHO & NOLITA

James Ensor and Marcel Duchamp, as well as Richard Serra, Ellsworth Kelly and Richard Tuttle.

HAUGHWOUT BUILDING
488 Broadway; 6 to Spring St
Look past the glaring red Staples facade and try to imagine this building c 1880. The Haughwout (pronounced 'how-out') was the first to put in an unheard of new contraption – the steam elevator, developed by Elisha Otis.

MUSEUM OF COMIC & CARTOON ART
☎ 212-254-3511; www.moccany.org; 594 Broadway; adult/child $3/free; noon-5pm Fri-Mon, by appt Tue-Thu; R, W to Prince St
Cartoon aficionados can't get enough of this museum and its wealth of graphic novels, comic lore and long-lost posters. Special exhibits include both well-known cartoonists and up-and-coming artists, with frequent opening parties and various festivals. Check the website for online exhibits and upcoming lecture series.

PUCK BUILDING
☎ 212-274-8900; www.thepuckbuild ing.com; 295 Lafayette St; 6 to Bleecker St
The southeast corner of Lafayette and Houston Sts is dominated by Albert Wagner's round-arched bit

of architectural genius. Wagner designed the building in 1885 as the printing facility for the German-language magazine *Puck* (now defunct, obviously). The building's dotted with little gold statues – Wagner's version of Puck the fairy – and he's a jolly, round-bellied, top-hatted fellow.

ST PATRICK'S OLD CATHEDRAL
260-264 Prince St at Mott St; rectory 8am-5pm Mon-Fri; R, W to Prince St
Before St Patrick's on Fifth Ave stole its thunder, this graceful 1809 Gothic Revival church was the seat of the Catholic arch-diocese in New York. Built by new immigrants mainly from Ireland, it continues to service its diverse community by giving liturgies in English, Spanish and Chinese. There are masses just about every hour on weekends and at least one every weekday. The brick-walled courtyard hides an ancient cemetery, and the mausoleum of many a famous New York family.

SINGER BUILDING
561-563 Broadway; R, W to Prince St
An example of why this area was once known as the Cast Iron District, the Singer building's got all the signature touches of a post–Civil War factory building. Designers will recognize Singer as the manufacturer of sewing

Nicole Pozzetti
Skin-care specialist

Is New York bad for the complexion? It's pretty good if you're talking about air quality – not much will hurt your complexion here. But there's too much temptation. That's where I come in – you can overindulge and I still make your skin look good. **Where do you go for fun?** I really enjoy Soho for a relaxing day. It's great to check out shops and galleries and, of course, have a couple of espressos. **What about at night?** Oh, I go to Chelsea and hang out with boys! It's so much fun. Gay bars are the best for dancing, drinking, and just getting your groove on. **Do you have any favorite books about New York?** Not really books, but I like to listen to tango music when riding the subway. Any kind of tango goes great with the city. **Do you dance tango here?** I do; there's a big tango community here. I sometimes go to Central Park (p180) or Lincoln Center (p195) and dance there.

machines; this building was the company's main warehouse.

🛍 SHOP

🏠 ANNA SUI
Fashion & Accessories

☎ 212-941-8406; www.annasui.com; 113 Greene St; 🕙 11:30am-7pm Mon-Sat, noon-6pm Sun; 🚇 R, W to Prince St

Boutique designer Anna Sui has a devoted following of *soigné* New Yorkers who trek to her downtown shop for the frilly, flirty dresses that skim the body in all the right places.

🏠 APPLE STORE SOHO
Computers & Accessories

☎ 212-226-3126; www.apple.com /retail/soho; 103 Prince St; 🕙 10am-8pm Mon-Sat, 11am-7pm Sun; 🚇 N, R, W to Prince St

The flagship Apple Store is always packed with curious tech heads and trend seekers who must have the latest in Mac accessories. Its gleaming, translucent decor still looks trendy. There is free email service at the store, and seminars on computer tips are given for free.

🏠 ATRIUM
Fashion & Accessories, Footwear

☎ 212-473-9200; 644 Broadway at Bleeker St; 🕙 10am-8pm; 🚇 B, D, F, V to Broadway-Lafayette St

Atrium has an excellent selection of funky designer wear, including

shoes and accessories, for both men and women from Diesel, G-Star, Miss Sixty and other popular labels. Best, though, is the grand range of high-end denim, from folks including Joe's, Seven, Blue Cult and True Religion.

🏠 BLOOMINGDALE SOHO
Fashion & Accessories

☎ 212-729-5900; 504 Broadway; 🕙 10am-9pm Mon-Fri, 10am-8pm Sat, 11am-7pm Sun; 🚇 R, W to Prince St

A little more avant garde than the 'real' Bloomies uptown, this Soho offshoot skews to the young, covering everything from beachwear to club duds.

🏠 BOND 07
Eyewear, Fashion & Accessories

☎ 212-677-8487; 7 Bond St; 🕙 11am-7pm Mon-Sat, noon-7pm Sun; 🚇 6 to Bleecker St

Selima Salaun's graceful glasses are the big draw, although Bond 07 also doubles as a chic boutique. Many a celebrity hides their orbs behind her perfectly tinted, boho chic styles. With more than 100 in stock, she can fit a pair to any face.

🏠 BOND 09 *Perfume*

☎ 212-228-1940; 9 Bond St; 🕙 11am-7pm Mon-Sat; 🚇 6 to Bleecker St

If you visit New York, you gotta smell like New York – that's the rule at Bond 09. It makes custom perfumes named after local nabes, like Eau de Noho, Chinatown and Chelsea Flowers. Don't worry – the fragrances actually smell good.

CHELSEA GIRL
Fashion & Accessories
☎ 212-343-1658; www.chelsea-girl.com; 63 Thompson St btwn Spring & Broome Sts; ⏰ noon-7pm; ⊖ C, E to Spring St
Get in there and dig – you never know what you'll find in this small, eclectic shop – sometimes vintage Pucci prints and Dior dresses are sitting casually on a back rack.

DAFFY'S
Fashion & Accessories, Homewares
☎ 212-334-7444; www.daffys.com; 462 Broadway at Grand St; ⏰ 10am-8pm Mon-Sat, noon-7pm Sun; ⊖ A, C, E to Canal St
Two floors of designer duds and accessories for men, women and children (as well as a random handful of housewares), with prices that can be shockingly low. And the tags – like those at most discount shops – show you the item's suggested retail price, which, at an average of 50 percent off, just gives you more incentive to buy.

EDGE NY NOHO
Fashion & Accessories
☎ 212-358-0255; http://edgeny.com; 65 Bleecker St near Crosby St; ⏰ noon-8pm Wed-Sat, to 6pm Sun; ⊖ 6 to Bleecker St, B, D, F, V to Broadway-Lafayette St

The latest Mac-cessories at Apple Store Soho

The favorite word of fashionistas is how best to describe Edge NY – it is 'fierce.' A collective dedicated to up-and-coming talent in clothes, jewelry and accessory designs, its many members are passionate, dedicated and very willing to engage with customers. Fans of cutting-edge looks will find much to rave about.

HOUSING WORKS USED BOOK CAFE *Books*
☎ 212-334-3324; www.housingworks .org/usedbookcafe; 126 Crosby St; ⏰ 10am-9pm Mon-Fri, noon-9pm Sat; ⊖ B, D, F, V to Broadway-Lafayette St
Relaxed, earthy and featuring a great selection of fabulous books

you can buy for a good cause (proceeds go to the city's HIV-positive and AIDS homeless communities), this spacious café is a great place to head to if you're looking to while away a few quiet afternoon hours.

🏠 JOHN VARVATOS
Fashion & Accessories
☎ 212-965-0700; 122 Spring St; ⏱ 11am-7pm Mon-Sat, noon-6pm Sun; 🚇 R, W to Prince St
One of the city's most coveted menswear designers, John Varvatos creates a classic, timeless look – with a rock 'n' roll soul – in his stylish and handsome-fitting sports coats, jeans, footwear and accessories. Head downstairs for JV's younger, edgier persona.

🏠 MCNALLY ROBINSON
Books, Magazines
☎ 212-274-1160; www.mcnallyrobinson.com; 52 Prince St; ⏱ 10am-10pm Mon-Sat, to 8pm Sun; 🚇 R, W to Prince St
Zone out in the cozy café (with wi-fi) inside this fully-stacked indie store that has books on every conceivable subject – food, fiction, travel, architecture, LGBT, to name a few – as well as magazines and newspapers from around the world.

🏠 ORIGINAL LEVI'S STORE
Fashion & Accessories
☎ 646-613-1847; 536 Broadway at Spring St; ⏱ 10am-8pm Mon-Sat, 11am-7pm Sun; 🚇 R, W to Prince St
Stock up on all your favorite Levi's jeans here – 501 button-fly, super-low boot-cut, zip-fly straight-leg cords – plus check out the great selection of Western shirts, tees, sweaters, jackets and always-evolving new styles for both men and women.

🏠 PRADA *Fashion & Accessories*
☎ 212-334-8888; 575 Broadway; ⏱ 11am-7pm Mon-Sat, noon-6pm Sun; 🚇 N, R, W to Prince St
Don't come just for the shoes: check out the space. Dutch architect Rem Koolhaas has transformed the old Guggenheim into a fantasy land full of elegant hardwood floors and small dressing spaces. Don't be afraid to try something on – those translucent changing-room doors do fog up when you step inside.

🏠 SEIZE SUR VINGT
Fashion & Accessories
☎ 212-343-0476; www.16sur20.com; 243 Elizabeth St; ⏱ 11am-7pm Mon-Sat, noon-6pm Sun; 🚇 F, V to Broadway-Lafayette St, 6 to Spring St
A Nolita secret, this store turns out stern, classic shirts and suits

(they're brightened by high-quality material in flashy and fancy colors). It even custom fits shirts to make sure you get just the right silhouette.

◻ SIGERSON MORRISON *Footwear*

☎ 212-941-5404; www.sigersonmorrison .com; 242 Mott St & 28 Prince St; 🕐 11am-7pm Mon-Sat, noon-6pm Sun; ◉ 6 to Spring St, N to Prince St

Innovation combined with surprising practicality (who would have thought we could have high-heeled flip-flops, or designer rubber boots to wear in the rain?), plus a love of splashy colors, have made Sigerson a hit. The store also carries Belle, a lower-priced line of its signature high-heeled, glamorous styles.

◻ TE CASAN *Footwear*

☎ 212-584-800; 382 W Broadway; 🕐 11am-8pm Mon-Sat, noon-7pm Sun; ◉ C, E to Spring St

There are three full stories to this lovely boutique, all full of artfully displayed footwear. The stylish heels, flats and boots are the product of seven emerging designers who aren't afraid of innovation, like Zulu beadwork, organic dyes and innumerable ways to make stiletto heels sky-high. Mind you don't trip on the luminous, shimmering staircase that anchors the room.

◻ UNIS *Fashion & Accessories*

☎ 212-431-5533; 226 Elizabeth St; 🕐 noon-7pm; ◉ N, R, W to Prince St

Unis remains a Nolita favorite for its fashionable but functional basics. You'll find slim, nicely cut jeans, soft button-downs and well-made jackets for the men, with feminine dresses and slender tops for the ladies.

◻ EAT

🍴 BITE *Organic Snacks* $

☎ 212-431-0301; 333 Lafayette St at Bleecker St; 🕐 7am-5pm; ◉ 6 to Bleecker St; ♿ Ⓥ ♟

Bite specializes in vegan, vegetarian and carnivore-friendly fare perfect for a quick breakfast or lunch. Roll up to the window and get your salad or sandwich to go, or step into the tiny, triangle-shaped shop for a seat.

🍴 BLUE RIBBON BRASSERIE *American Comfort* $$

☎ 212-274-404; 97 Sullivan St near Spring St; 🕐 dinner; ◉ C, E to Spring St; ♿ Ⓥ ♟

Going strong since 1992, this comfort-food mecca is still a standout, especially for late-night dining, and the founding Bromberg Brothers have multiple offshoots: **Blue Ribbon Sushi** (119 Sullivan St), just a few doors away, **Blue Ribbon Bakery** (Map pp106–7; 35 Downing St) and

Blue Ribbon Downing Street Bar (Map pp106–7; 34 Downing St). Blue Ribbon Brasserie's best-known dishes are the succulent, cheesy appetizers and sides; fresh, tangy salads; and delectable seafood, such as sweet and spicy catfish and red trout.

BOND ST *Japanese* $$$
☎ 212-777-2500; 6 Bond St; ⏰ 6-10:30pm Sun-Mon, to 11:30pm Tue-Sat; ⊕ 6 to Bleecker St; ♿ Ⓥ ♨

Move over Nobu, this is the new kid in town. Actually, Bond St has been around awhile, but it's been kept a secret by sushi lovers. A la carte rolls range from spicy yellowtail with red-pepper miso, spicy tuna with chili mayonnaise, sesame-crusted shrimp with orange curry dressing and hot eel with diced almond. There are also mains, nigiri and sashimi plates, and a full-on tasting *omakase* (chef's choice) menu.

CAFÉ GITANE
Moroccan Bistro $
☎ 212-334-9552; 242 Mott St; ⏰ 5:30-11:30pm; ⊕ N, R, W to Prince St

Clear the Gauloise smoke from your eyes and blink twice if you think you're in Paris – Gitane has that louche vibe. Label-conscious shoppers love this authentic bistro, with its dark, aromatic coffee and dishes such as yellowfin tuna ceviche, spicy meatballs in tomato

turmeric sauce with a boiled egg, Greek salad on focaccia and a heart-of-palm salad, with plenty of lusty wines.

CENDRILLON
Filipino Fusion $$
☎ 212-343-9012; 45 Mercer St btwn Broome & Grand Sts; ⏰ lunch & dinner Tue-Sun, weekend brunch; ⊕ J, M, Z, N, Q, R, W, 6 to Canal St

Filipino food gets a wonderful twist at this loft-like space with exposed brick, wood booths and a semi-open kitchen. Dishes range from chicken adobo braised in rice vinegar, udon and shrimp swimming in a Malaysian curry sauce, Chinese smoked spare ribs with mashed taro root, and spicy black-rice paella bursting with morsels of seafood.

FR.OG *Eclectic French* $$
☎ 212-966-5050; http://frognyc.com; 71 Spring St near Lafayette St; ⏰ lunch & dinner; ⊕ 6 to Spring St, N, R, W to Prince St

The name is short for France Origine, and it's a clue to the food you'll be eating – French, by way of North Africa, Vietnam and other colonial outposts of the old empire. Tagines, stews, ragouts, spring and summer rolls and more are on the menu, and the two-level location is done in shimmering pinks and silvers – a strangely alluring combo.

IL BUCO *Italian* $$$

☎ 212-533-1932; 47 Bond St btwn Bowery & Lafayette St; ✆ lunch & dinner Tue-Sun; ⊕ B, D, F, V to Broadway-Lafayette St, 6 to Bleecker St

This magical nook is a real charmer – it boasts hanging copper pots, kerosene lamps and antique furniture, plus a stunning menu and wine list. Sink your teeth into seasonal and ever-changing highlights like white polenta with braised broccoli rabe and anchovies, homemade pappardelle with a mélange of mushrooms, and a succulent Dijon-crusted lamb chop.

IVO & LULU *Caribbean* $

☎ 212-226-4399; 558 Broome St near Varick St; ✆ dinner; ⊕ C, E to Spring St, 1 to Canal St; ⑤ Ⓥ ⓑ

A tiny storefront shop run by two French Caribbean natives, featuring organic products, quick and simple veggie-friendly dishes and some duck, chicken and seafood specialties. There's no liquor license but you can bring a bottle of whatever you want and they'll uncork it for no fee.

LA ESQUINA *Mexican* $$

☎ 646-613-1333; 106 Kenmare St; ✆ 24hr; ⊕ 6 to Spring St

This mega-popular and quirky little spot is housed in a former greasy spoon that sits within the neat little triangle formed by Cleveland Pl and Lafayette St. It's three places really: a stand-while-you-eat taco window, a casual Mexican café and, downstairs, a cozy, overly hip cave of a dining room that requires reservations. Standouts include chorizo tacos, rubbed pork tacos and mango and jicama salads, among other authentic and delicious options (most of which are also available upstairs at the anyone-welcome area).

TURKS AND FROGS TRIBECA *Turkish* $$

☎ 212-966-4774; www.turksandfrogs.com; 458 Greenwich St near Desbrosses St; ✆ lunch & dinner; ⊕ A, C, E, 1 to Canal St; ⑤

A tongue-in-cheek name that refers to the Turkish and French antiques that decorate this winsome bistro (run by the same folks who own the Turks and Frogs wine bar in the West Village). While the decor is mixed, the food's unabashedly Turkish: meze appetizers, endless varieties of hummus, eggplant and olives, plus great mains such as ground lamb dumplings, red mullet with arugula, thinly sliced oregano lamb, or chunks of lamb in tomato sauce with baby eggplant.

⛉ DRINK

⛉ CHINATOWN BRASSERIE *Bar*

☎ 212-533-7000; http://chinatown brasserie.com; 380 Lafayette St near Great Jones St; 🕙 lunch & dinner; 🚇 6 to Bleecker St, N, R, W to Astor Pl; ♿ Ⓥ

The dining areas are huge and sprawling and marked by pagoda decor and hanging Chinese lanterns, and diners can nosh for hours on the dim sum delights. The bar is just as beautiful (and much less taxing on wallet and patience), and the crowd is eclectic and fun.

⛉ EAR INN *Bar*

☎ 212-226-9060; 326 Spring St btwn Greenwich & Washington Sts; 🕙 11:30am-4am; 🚇 C, E to Spring St

Weekly reading series, live music and history are the main features of this 1817 neighborhood bar. It's in the James Brown House (the James Brown, aide to George Washington, not Soul Brother No 1), and is the preferred dive of sanitation workers, stressed-out Wall Streeters and local folk in need of a drink.

⛉ MERCBAR *Bar*

☎ 212-966-2727; 151 Mercer St btwn W Houston & Prince Sts; 🕙 5pm-2am Sun-Tue, to 4am Wed-Sat; 🚇 R, W to Prince St

An intimate hideaway where you can actually hold a conversation without having to scream over the soundtrack is a big draw for the after-work publishing crowd, who likes to sip martinis and rub tweedy elbows.

⛉ PEGU CLUB *Bar*

☎ 212-473-7348; www.peguclub.com; 77 W Houston St near Wooster St; 🕙 5pm-2am; 🚇 B, D, F, V, 6 to Broadway-Lafayette St

Head on up to the 2nd floor and step inside this naval-themed bar, which prides itself on its out-of-this-world cocktails. Try a Gin Gin Mule, Pisco Sour, Lemon Drop, or any number of martinis, manhattans and vodka mixes.

⛉ TOAD HALL *Bar*

☎ 212-431-8145; 57 Grand St near W Broadway; 🕙 noon-2am; 🚇 A, C, E, J, M, N, Q, R, W, Z, 1, 6 to Canal St

Old-fashioned hospitality is the norm at Toad Hall (hence the sign in the door: 'Be nice or leave'). There's plenty of wine, beer and good cheer to be had, and if you get hit with the munchies, bartenders have a handy supply of takeout menus on hand to order in.

⛉ XICALA *Bar*

☎ 212-219-0599; 151 Elizabeth St; 🕙 5pm-2am; 🚇 6 at Spring St; ♿

There's a Cuban trio on Wednesday nights who add to the already-festive atmosphere at this quaint, tiny tapas and wine bar. The strawberry sangria is the house signature drink, but the Riojas and Jerez sherries are just as delicious.

PLAY

AMATO OPERA HOUSE
Opera

☎ 212-228-8200; www.amato.org; 319 Bowery; ⏱ hours vary; ⊕ 6 to Astor Pl; ♿ ♾

After 59 years of no-nonsense opera, Amato still has what it takes to pack in the crowds. Classic shows like *Falstaff, Madame Butterfly, La Forza del Destino* and *Die Fledermaus* are put on without any of the glitz found in uptown opera houses, but plenty of passion.

ANGELIKA FILM CENTER
Cinema

☎ 212-995-2000; www.angelikafilm center.com; 18 W Houston St at Mercer St; tickets $10-14; ⏱ daily; ⊕ B, D, F, V to Broadway-Lafayette St; ♿ ♾

Angelika specializes in foreign and independent films and has some quirky charms (the rumble of the subway, long lines and occasionally bad sound). But its roomy café is a great place to meet and the beauty of its Stanford White–designed, beaux-arts building undeniable.

BOUWERIE LANE THEATER
Theater

☎ 212-677-0060; www.jeancocteaurep .org; 330 Bowery; ⏱ noon-6pm Mon-Fri (1hr before curtain for shows); ⊕ 6 to Bleecker St

An off-Broadway theater venue that is presently inhabited by the Jean Cocteau Review, the Bouwerie was designed more than 100 years ago by Henry Engelbert. Its cast-iron facade is a rare standing example of the French Second Empire style. Before it was converted into a theater in the 1960s, the Bouwerie was occupied by a bank, but it has great sight lines nonetheless.

HERE *Theater*

☎ 212-647-0202; www.here.org; 145 Sixth Ave btwn Spring & Broome Sts; ⊕ C, E to Canal St

An acclaimed and perpetually underfunded theater group that supports the independent, the innovative and the experimental, Here helped develop Basil Twist's *Symphonie Fantastique,* Hazelle Goodman's *On Edge* and Trey Lyford and Geoff Sobelle's *all wear bowlers*. Production times and prices vary, but the on-site café offers a great opportunity to check things out.

>EAST VILLAGE

Anarchy still reigns in the East Village, but now the tension is over rents and housing instead of civil rights. Full of punks, NYU students and Wall St brokers, professors, philosophers, poets, hustlers, dancers and ditch-diggers – there are layers of class struggle, class-consciousness and revolutionary leanings. If the cause that everyone rallies behind has more to do with individual survival than universal issues, that's just how it goes in today's East Village, which has traded its hard-core activist roots for some kick-ass nightlife.

But not all is lost: amid the nightly limo crawls up and down Second Ave, the crazy dancing, drinking and dishing, people still step into KGB Bar (former Socialist headquarters) for its weekly reading series, they still attend sit-ins and walk-outs and protest rent hikes, and they still fight against high-rise development with all their might. It's refreshing to know that facades may change, but at least in the East Village, the collective spirit remains the same.

EAST VILLAGE

📷 SEE
6th and B Garden	1	G4
Colonnade Row	2	B4
Gallery 440	3	B4
Grace Church	4	B3
Merchant's House Museum	5	B5
Russian and Turkish Baths	6	E3
St Mark's in the Bowery	7	D3
Tompkins Square Park	8	F3
Ukrainian Museum	9	C4

🛍 SHOP
Cadillac Castle	10	D3
John Derian	11	C6
John Derian's Dry Goods	12	C6
MoMo Falana	13	F5
Odin	14	D2
Other Music	15	B5
Tokio 7	16	D4
Trader Joe's	17	B1
Underdog East	18	E4

🍴 EAT
Artichoke Basille's Pizza	19	D1
B & H Dairy	20	D4
Caracas Arepas Bar	21	E4
EU	22	F5
Kanoyama	23	D2
Lavagna	24	G4
Momofuku Ko	25	E3
Momofuku Noodle Bar	26	E3
Momofuku Ssam	27	D2
S'Mac	28	D2
Tuck Shop	29	E6

🍸 DRINK
11th Street Bar	30	F2
Angel's Share	31	C3
Bowery Wine Company	32	C6
DBA	33	E5
In Vino	34	F5
KGB Bar	35	C5
Louis 649	36	G3
Nublu	37	H5

⭐ PLAY
Baraza	38	H3
Easternbloc	39	F4
Joseph Papp Public Theater	40	B5
La MaMa ETC	41	C5
Nuyorican Poets Café	42	G5
Orpheum Theater	43	D4
Webster Hall	44	B2

Please see over for map

👁 SEE

🎯 6TH AND B GARDEN

www.6bgarden.org; E 6th St & Ave B;
🕙 **1-6pm Sat & Sun;** 🚇 **6 to Astor Pl**
Nature reigns supreme at this quiet corner lot, once a squalid, infested tangle of dirt and roots. Residents turned it into a 17,000-sq-ft section of neat plots, vines, sculptures and flowers. Garden members fought long and hard to keep the city from selling the land out from under them, and now it's a city oasis everyone enjoys.

🎯 COLONNADE ROW

428-434 Lafayette St btwn Astor Pl & E 4th St; 🚇 **6 to Astor Pl**
Once there were nine Greek Revival mansions in this row; now there are four. All were built in 1833, out of stone, the work done by prisoners from the upstate Sing Sing prison, and all have ornate, detailed touches on their classic facades. Some of the other great buildings you'll see around Colonnade Row are part of Cooper Union, including its great hall, where Abraham Lincoln once made an anti-slavery speech and Barack Obama gave a major economic speech during the 2008 presidential primary.

🎯 GALLERY 440

☎ **212-979-5800; www.gallery440 .com; 440 Lafayette St; admission free;**
🕙 **10am-6pm Mon-Fri, by appt Sat;** 🚇 **6 to Bleecker St**
One-stop shopping for art lovers or art browsers. Located above the famed Wooster Gallery, Gallery 440 has an eclectic roster of artists that it represents, and always has something fresh hanging in its front room.

👁 GRACE CHURCH

800-804 Broadway at E 10th St;
🕙 **10am-5pm, services daily;** 🚇 **R, W to 8th St-NYU, 6 to Astor Pl**
Nestled into a surprisingly verdant patch of land not far from Astor Pl, Grace Church's ethereal Gothic Revival design is quite an eye-catcher. Designed by James Renwick Jr, it's made of marble quarried by inmates in the upstate Sing Sing prison. Grace Church is also a much-sought-after school, and students love the Harry Potter–esque feel of its hidden nooks, stained-glass windows and old libraries.

👁 MERCHANT'S HOUSE MUSEUM

☎ **212-777-1089; www.merchants house.com; 29 E 4th St btwn Lafayette St & Bowery; adult/child $8/5;** 🕙 **noon-5pm Thu-Mon;** 🚇 **6 to Bleecker St**
Get a glimpse of how wealthy businessmen lived in New York in the 1800s at this local museum. Drug importer Seabury Tredwell lived in this house (built in 1831),

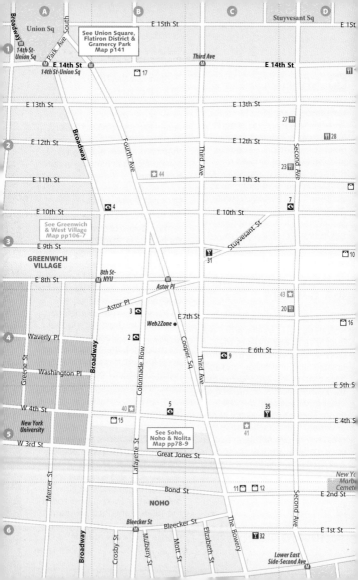

Union Sq

A
B
C
D

E 15th St

Stuyvesant Sq

E 15t

See Union Square,
Flatiron District &
Gramercy Park
Map p141

14th St-
Union Sq

1

Third Ave

E 14th St

E 14th St

14th St-Union Sq

17

E 13th St

E 13th St

Broadway

27

E 12th St

28

E 12th St

E 12th St

Fourth Ave

Second Ave

23

E 11th St

44

E 11th St

E 11th St

Broadway

7

E 10th St

4

E 10th St

See Greenwich
& West Village
Map pp106-7

3

E 9th St

Stuyvesant St

10

**GREENWICH
VILLAGE**

8th St-
NYU

31

Astor Pl

E 8th St

Astor Pl

43

Astor Pl

20

3

E 7th St

16

4

Waverly Pl

2

Web2Zone

Colonnade Row

E 6th St

9

Greene St

Washington Pl

Cooper Sq

Third Ave

E 5th S

Broadway

40

W 4th St

5

35

15

E 4th St

5

New York
University

41

W 3rd St

See Soho,
Noho & Nolita
Map pp78-9

Great Jones St

Mercer St

Lafayette St

Bond St

New Yo
Marbl
Cemete

11

12

NOHO

E 2nd St

Second Ave

6

Broadway

Bleecker St

Bleecker St

32

Crosby St

Mulberry St

Mott St

Elizabeth St

The Bowery

E 1st St

Lower East
Side-Second Ave

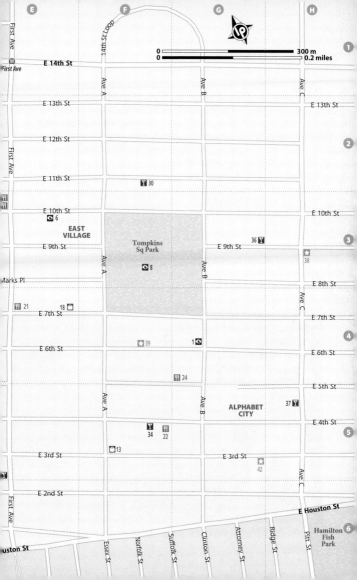

and his family has preserved the original furnishings and clothing, and even his kitchen sink. It's a remarkable glimpse into the past.

🌀 RUSSIAN AND TURKISH BATHS
☎ 212-473-8806; www.russianturkish baths.com; 268 E 10th St btwn First Ave & Ave A; per visit $30; 🕙 11am-10pm Mon, Tue, Thu & Fri, 9am-10pm Wed, 7:30am-10pm Sat & Sun; 🚇 L to First Ave, 6 to Astor Pl
Since 1892 this has been the place to go for a romp in steam baths, an ice-cold plunge pool, a sauna and on a sundeck. All-day access includes the use of lockers, locks,

robes, towels and slippers, and an on-site Russian café has fresh juices, potato-olive salad, blintzes and borscht. The spas are women only from 10am to 2pm on Wednesdays and men only from 8am to 2pm Saturdays.

🌀 ST MARK'S IN THE BOWERY
☎ 212-674-6377; www.stmarkschurch -in-the-bowery.com; 131 E 10th St at Second Ave; 🕙 10am-6pm Mon-Fri; 🚇 6 to Astor Pl, L to Third Ave
Still a working Episcopal church, St Mark's was built in 1799 on farm land owned by Dutch governor Peter Stuyvesant – he's buried in the crypt below. Sunday services

Tompkins Square Park is a leafy spot with a feisty history

are a big draw, but St Mark's is also revered for its cultural contributions. Regular poetry readings such as **Poetry Project** (☎ 212-674-0910) and dance events like **Danspace** (☎ 212-674-8194) culminate every New Year's Day in a 24-hour nonstop orgy of poetry, song and performance.

☢ TOMPKINS SQUARE PARK
www.nycgovparks.org; E 7th & 10th Sts btwn Aves A & B; 🕙 6am-midnight; 🚇 6 to Astor Pl; ♿
In 1874, 7000 angry workers took on 1600 police in this leafy enclave, and history's been repeated many times since then – Tompkins Square Park lies at the heart of every East Village rebellion. This wide, pretty, green spot is pastoral by day, communally welcoming at night, and still a bit sketchy in the wee hours.

☢ UKRAINIAN MUSEUM
☎ 212-228-0110; www.ukrainian museum.org; 222 E 6th St btwn Second & Third Aves; admission adult $8, senior & student $6, child under 12 free; 🕙 11:30am-5pm Wed-Sun; 🚇 F, V to Lower East Side-Second Ave, L to First Ave
Eastern Europeans have a long history in the East Village, and Ukrainians in particular staked a claim here. The Ukrainian Museum documents that history and

showcases its collection of folk art, ceramics, metalwork, woven textiles and traditional Ukrainian Easter eggs.

🛍 SHOP

🛍 CADILLAC CASTLE
Fashion & Accessories
☎ 212-475-0406; 333 E 9th St; 🕙 noon-8pm; 🚇 6 to Astor Pl, L to First Ave
Vintage shoes, bags, dresses and accessories at fantastic prices are the big draw at Cadillac Castle (as well as the owner's winsome dog). Lots of big-name merchandise – modern designers as well as the classics like Chanel – to be found.

🏠 JOHN DERIAN
Homewares, Curios
☎ 212-677-3917; 6 E 2nd St; 🕙 noon-7pm Tue-Sun; 🚇 F, V to Lower East Side-Second Ave
Looking for one-of-a-kind plates, paperweights, coasters, lamps, bowls and vases? Swing by John Derian's shop. The atmospheric store hides many other curiosities, such as T-shirts with roguish 19th-century graphics, handmade terracotta pottery, linoleum cut prints and papier-mâché figurines. For eclectic bed linens and such, visit the nearby **John Derian's Dry Goods** (☎ 212-677-8408; 10 E 2nd St; 🕙 noon-7pm Tue-Sun).

MOMO FALANA *Fashion & Accessories*

☎ 212-979-9595; http://momofalana.com; 43 Ave A at E 3rd St; ⏲ 12:30-8:30pm Mon & Wed-Sun, to 7pm Tue; ◉ F, V to Lower East Side-Second Ave

Indie, bohemian, girly looks rule at MoMo Falana, an eccentric-looking shop with a vine-covered entrance painted purple. The owner hand-dyes the delicate silks she later turns into flowy, attractive dresses that can fit – and flatter – women of many different sizes.

ODIN *Fashion & Accessories*

☎ 212-475-0666; http://odinnewyork .com; 328 E 11th St; ⏲ noon-8pm; ◉ L to First Ave, L, N, Q, R, W, 4, 5, 6 to 14th St-Union Sq

Fashion-forward men flock to cheery, chippy Odin, full of artistic T-shirts and avant-garde designs that are sure to turn heads. Although the atmosphere is definitely downtown chic, you can find anything here, from hippy head gear to Monday-morning suits.

OTHER MUSIC *Music*

☎ 212-477-8150; www.othermusic.com; 15 E 4th St; ⏲ noon-9pm Mon-Fri, to 8pm Sat, to 7pm Sun; ◉ 6 to Bleecker St
An indie-run store that carries new and used offbeat lounge, psych-edelic, electronica, indie-rock and more, staffed with helpful, friendly music geeks.

TOKIO 7 *Fashion & Accessories*

☎ 212-353-8443; 64 E 7th St; ⏲ noon-8:30pm Mon-Sat, to 8pm Sun; ◉ 6 to Astor Pl

This revered, hip consignment shop, down a few steps on a shady stretch of E 7th St, has good-condition designer labels for men and women at some fairly hefty prices. Best of all is the selection of men's suits – there's nearly always something tip-top in the $100 to $150 range that's worth trying on.

TRADER JOE'S *Food & Drink*

☎ 212-529-4612; 142 E 14th St; ⏲ 9am-10pm; ◉ L, N, Q, R, W, 4, 5, 6 to 14th St-Union Sq

Most people love Trader Joe's, it seems. It's a slightly smaller version of Whole Foods with fair-trade coffee, organic produce, beef and poultry, and an odd smattering of exotic goods not normally stocked in stores. In fact, so many people love the Trader Joe's on E 14th St that shopping there takes enormous patience; the store is small and awkwardly laid out, and crowds quickly form.

UNDERDOG EAST *Fashion & Accessories*

☎ 212-388-0560; 117 E 7th St btwn First Ave & Ave A; ⏲ 2-8pm Tue-Sun; ◉ 6 to Astor Pl

East Village is full of punks, poets, professors and philosophers, and hats too

Most East Village boutiques are all about women but, here, men take center stage. The low-key, exposed-brick space features high-end denim, sweaters, shirts and accessories (including some delicious cashmere hats) from designers like Earnest Sewn, Steven Alan, Filippa K and La Coppola Storta.

🍴 EAT

🍴 ARTICHOKE BASILLE'S PIZZA *Pizza* $

☎ 212-228-2004; 328 E 14th St btwn First & Second Aves; 🕑 lunch & dinner;

🚇 L, N, Q, R, W, 4, 5, 6 to 14th St-Union Sq; 🚭 Ⓥ 🚼

Some say this pizzeria is in the East Village, others Union Sq but, hey, wherever Artichoke Basille's is, count yourself lucky to be there. Run by two Italian guys from Staten Island, the pizza here is authentic, tangy and piled high with all sorts of toppings. The signature pie is a rich, cheesy treat with artichokes and spinach; the plain Sicilian is thinner, with emphasis solely on the crisp crust and savory sauce. Hours are from around noon to about midnight, but sometimes it doesn't open until 3pm. Lines usually form fast.

B & H DAIRY
Kosher Dairy $

☎ 212-505-8065; 127 Second Ave btwn St Marks Pl & E 7th St; ☽ breakfast, lunch & dinner; ❻ 6 to Astor Pl; ♿ Ⓥ ♿

Fresh, vegetarian, homemade Kosher fare, including six types of soups on offer daily with a big knot of challah bread. Join the crowd at the bar and try to grab someone's attention – you've got to speak up here, or you'll go hungry!

CARACAS AREPAS BAR
Arepas, South American $

☎ 212-228-5062; www.caracasarepas bar.com; 93 1/2 E 7th St btwn First Ave & Ave A; ☽ noon-10pm Mon-Sat, to 11pm Sun; ❻ 6 to Astor Pl; ♿ Ⓥ ♿

Cram in to this tiny joint and order a crispy, hot *arepa* (corn tortilla stuffed with veggies and meat) such as the Pepi Queen (chicken and avocado) or La Pelua (beef and cheddar). You can choose from 17 types of *arepas* (plus empanadas and daily specials like oxtail soup), served in baskets with a side of *nata* (sour cream) and fried plantains.

EU
Pan-European Pub Food $$$

☎ 212-254-2900; 235 E 4th St btwn Aves A & B; ☽ lunch & dinner Mon-Fri, brunch & dinner Sat & Sun; ❻ F, V to Lower East Side-Second Ave

The gastro-pub craze has come to the East Village, but with a minimalist twist (in terms of decor) EU (yes, that stands for European Union) has old-world comfort food such as gnocchi with braised capon, boar with Swiss-chard

YO, MOMOFUKU

A strange madness has descended on the East Village in the form of chef David Chang. His Momofuku empire now consists of three Asian-focused restaurants – and getting into his most popular incarnation, **Momofuku Ko** (www.momofuku.com; 163 First Ave near E 10th St; ☽ lunch & dinner; ❻ L to First Ave, 6 to Astor Pl) is almost impossible. Bookings are taken online only and are done a week in advance; if you aren't logged on and typing by 10am exactly seven days ahead of the day you want to dine, forget it. There's also **Momofuku Ssam** (207 2nd Ave near E 13th St; ❻ 6 to Astor Pl) and **Momofuku Noodle Bar** (171 First Ave near E 10th St; ❻ L to First Ave, 6 to Astor Pl). They're open daily for lunch and dinner, but there are no reservations except for the bar at Ssam. What's all the hype about? The fantastic raw bars, the ramen noodles, crispy sweetbreads, grilled octopus salads, grilled beef tongue and those delicious *bib bim bap* (rice dish with veggies) lunch boxes.

fondue, and grilled octopus with braised quince. There's plenty of choice beyond the hearty mains, too – like a small tapas menu, a raw bar and a range of charcuterie plates.

KANOYAMA *Sushi* $

☎ 212-777-5266; http://kanoyama.com; 175 Second Ave near E 11th St; 🕙 dinner; 🚇 L to Third Ave, L, N, Q, R, W, 4, 5, 6 to 14th St-Union Sq; ♿ Ⓥ

No fuss, no muss sushi with fresh daily specials in the heart of the East Village, Kanoyama is a local favorite that so far has been overlooked by the city's big name food critics (that might explain its unpretentious air). You can order sushi a la carte or in rolls, or choose from the many tempura plates.

LAVAGNA *Italian* $$

☎ 212-979-1005; http://lavagnanyc .com; 545 E 5th St near Ave B; 🕙 dinner; 🚇 F, V to Lower East Side-Second Ave; ♿ Ⓥ

Dark wood, flickering candles and a fiery glow from a somewhat open kitchen help make homey Lavagna a late-night hideaway for lovers. But it's laid-back enough to make it appropriate for children, at least in the early hours before the smallish space fills up. Delicious pastas, thin-crust pizzas and a

few eclectic mains, such as rabbit ragout, are standard fare.

S'MAC *American* $

☎ 212-358-7912; www.smacnyc.com; 345 E 12th St at First Ave; 🕙 1-10pm Mon, 11am-11pm Tue-Thu & Sun, 11am-1am Fri & Sat; 🚇 6 to Astor Pl; Ⓥ ♿

If you're only going to do one thing, you've got to do it well – and S'Mac hits the spot with mac 'n' cheese lovers. The all-American has cheddar and Vermont jack cheese, with bacon if you like. Or, try the Gruyère mac 'n' cheese and the Manchego cheese and Cajun macs.

TUCK SHOP *Australian* $

☎ 212-979-5200; http://tuckshopnyc .com; 68 E 1st St near First Ave; 🕙 8am-2am Mon-Thu, 8am-5am Fri & Sat, noon-10pm Sun; 🚇 F, V to Lower East Side-Second Ave; ♿ Ⓥ ♿

Homemade pasties, sausage rolls and sandwiches of all sorts are the rule at Tuck, where everything's done organic and fresh. Daily pie specials include a chook curry pie, shepherd's pie, vegan pie, tiger prawn pie, a chili pie, and more. Desserts are a treat, including the Dame Edna delight and Peter Allen pie, but perhaps the best is the early morning breakfast: lashings of meat with fresh eggs and cheese, served with steaming cups of fair-trade organic coffee.

Y DRINK

Y 11TH STREET BAR Bar

☎ 212-982-3929; 510 E 11th St btwn Aves A & B; 🕐 noon-2am; ◉ F, V to Lower East Side-Second Ave

Couches, a big bar and a crazy, rowdy clientele made up of East Village hippies and young students make 11th Street Bar the de facto community hangout.

Y ANGEL'S SHARE Bar

☎ 212-777-5415; 2nd fl, 8 Stuyvesant St near Third Ave & E 9th St; 🕐 5pm-midnight; ◉ 6 to Astor Pl

Show up early and snag a seat at this hidden gem, behind a Japa-nese restaurant on the same floor. It's quiet and elegant with creative cocktails, but you can't stay if you don't have a table, and they tend to go fast.

Y BOWERY WINE COMPANY Bar

☎ 212-614-0800; www.bowerywineco.com; 13 E 1st St; 🕐 5pm-1am Mon-Thu, 5pm-2am Fri, noon-2am Sat, noon-1am Sun; ◉ F, V to Lower East Side-Second Ave

Low-key and trendy with good wines, the Bowery Wine Company has been targeted by locals upset by increasing gentrification in the area. Occasional protests are held outside, but why this bar gets singled out above all others is a bit unclear.

Y DBA Pub

☎ 212-475-5097; www.drinkgoodstuff.com; 41 First Ave; 🕐 1pm-4am; ◉ F, V to Lower East Side-Second Ave

While you're here, see if you can get owner Ray Deter to tell you if the name stands for 'doing business as,' 'don't bother asking' or 'drink better ale.' The third choice is the most obvious, since Deter specializes in British-style ales in casks. He's got more than 150 at hand, including microbrews like 'High and Mighty Ale.' Other standouts are the single malts and smooth tequilas. A garden

DBA stands for...

in the back doubles as a beer garden.

▼ IN VINO *Bar*

☎ 212-539-1011; www.invino-ny.com; 215 E 4th St; ⏱ 5-11pm Sun-Thu, to midnight Fri & Sat; ◉ F, V to Lower East Side-Second Ave

Step off the hectic streets for a second and chill out at In Vino, a cavelike little space with hundreds of Italian wines to choose from and a calm, tranquil atmosphere. Jazzy music is the norm, sometimes live, sometimes piped in, and small plates of Italian snacks – paninis, olives, anchovies – are readily available.

▼ KGB BAR *Bar*

☎ 212-505-3360; 2nd fl, 85 E 4th St near Second Ave; ⏱ 5pm-1am; ◉ 6 to Astor Pl, F, V to Lower East Side-Second Ave

Back in the 1940s, this space housed the local headquarters of a Ukrainian socialist party; its dingy red walls and bright yellow propaganda banners are the real thing. KGB reinvented itself as a literary bar a few years ago and hasn't looked back; its readings are marquee events, and the crowd laps up the vodka.

▼ LOUIS 649 *Bar*

☎ 212-673-1190; http://louis649.com; 649 E 9th St near Ave C; ⏱ 6pm-4am; ◉ L to First Ave

Bronx-born Zachary Sharaga's bar is a local standout in the East Village, beloved by its patrons for the excellent live jazz as well as the affordable prices and quaint, no-frills decor. Hamsa is Sharaga's pit bull and she's often prowling around the space, making sure you don't ask for a Budweiser in this European-import friendly place. Sharaga's got a fine hand for cocktails, too – check out the special of the day.

▼ NUBLU *Bar, Club*

62 Ave C; ⏱ 8pm-4am; ◉ 6 to Astor Pl, F, V to Lower East Side-Second Ave

Don't back away from the graffiti-scarred exterior – you're at the right place if you see the blue light at the door. Nublu doesn't believe in signage (or paint jobs, apparently), but inside you'll quickly adjust to the hardwood floors, wide open French doors to a back patio, and chilled out crowds. On weekends, things get hot and sweaty at night, as the whole club starts to get a little dance happy.

★ PLAY

▣ BARAZA *Club*

☎ 212-539-0811; http://barazany.com; 133 Ave C near E 9th St; ⏱ 8pm-3am; ◉ F, V to Lower East Side-Second Ave

Kitschy and upbeat, Baraza's got some bizarre decor, including an odd wooden duck and a gaggle of dismembered Barbie dolls. Check the website for DJ schedules; the rotation is heavy with French and Latin funk designed to get you dancing.

★ EASTERNBLOC *Club*
☎ 212-420-8885; 505 E 6th St btwn Aves A & B; ⏱ 7pm-4am; ◎ F, V to Lower East Side-Second Ave
The Red Scare is still among us – at least at Easternbloc, which boasts a kitschy iron-curtain theme replete with Bettie Page videos, Communist-era posters and ador-able Eastern European–looking bartenders. The go-go dancers ap-pear Thursday through Saturday.

★ JOSEPH PAPP PUBLIC THEATER *Theater*
☎ 212-260-2400; www.publictheater .org; 425 Lafayette St; ⏱ hours vary; ◎ N, R to 8th St-NYU, 6 to Astor Pl
Every summer the Papp presents its fabulous, and eagerly awaited, Shakespeare in the Park productions at Central Park's Delacorte Theater – one of its many contributions to the city's cultural tapestry. Established by a wealthy progressive more than 50 years ago, Joseph Papp Theater continues to help actors, both novice and veteran, develop their craft through its groundbreaking productions.

★ LA MAMA ETC *Theater*
☎ 212-475-7710; www.lamama.org; 74A E 4th St; ⏱ hours vary; ◎ F, V to Lower East Side-Second Ave
A longstanding home for onstage experimentation (the ETC stands for experimental theater club), La MaMa is now a three-theater complex with a café, an art gallery and a separate studio building that features cutting-edge dramas, sketch comedy and readings of all kinds.

★ NUYORICAN POETS CAFÉ *Arts*
☎ 212-505-8183; www.nuyorican.org; 236 E 3rd St; ⏱ 6pm-1am Tue-Sun; ◎ F to Lower East Side-Second Ave
A legendary club started in 1973 by Miguel Algarin, a Puerto Rican poet, the Nuyorican is home to hip-hop performances, poetry slams, plays and film and video events. It's a piece of East Village history, but also a vibrant and still-relevant nonprofit arts organiza-tion (supported by proceeds from the café).

★ ORPHEUM THEATER *Theater*
☎ 212-477-2477; www.stomponline .com; 126 Second Ave at E 8th St; ⏱ hours vary; ◎ F to Lower East Side-Second Ave; ♿ 🚻
A Yiddish theater in the beginning of the 20th century, the Orpheum feeds off creative East Village

energy. Currently it's home to 'Stomp,' a dance-happy beat fest.

☆ WEBSTER HALL *Club*
☎ 212-353-1600; 125 E 11th St near Third Ave; ⏲ 10pm-4am Thu-Sat; Ⓜ L, N, Q, R, W, 4, 5, 6 to 14th St-Union Sq
The granddaddy of dance halls, Webster Hall has been around so long it's being considered for landmark status. Following the old 'if it ain't broke, don't fix it' adage, what you'll get here are cheap drinks, eager young things ready to dance, pool tables for the self-conscious and enough room to really work up a sweat.

>GREENWICH & WEST VILLAGE

Still charming after all these years, Greenwich Village holds a special place in New Yorkers' hearts. This once flamboyant and progressive toehold became a gentle old lady, albeit one with a decidedly unladylike past.

There's no pleasure equal to exploring this twisty little enclave on a sunny afternoon. Its quaint and quirky streets create oddly shaped storefronts and misshapen cafés, and many of its brick buildings are historic landmarks. Edna St Vincent Millay lived at 75½ Barrow St for a while; her neighbor was William S Burroughs. They'd sometimes stop for a pint at Ear Inn (p88).

There are a few old-style cabaret bars and comedy clubs lining Seventh Ave, and some gay icons – the Duplex, the Monster and Stonewall – are still standing. It's easily the most romantic part of Manhattan.

GREENWICH & WEST VILLAGE

⊙ SEE
Christopher Street Piers/
  Hudson River Park.......1 A5
LGBT Community
  Center.....................2 C1
New York University......3 G4
Sheridan Square...........4 C3
Washington Mews.........5 F3
Washington Square
  Park.......................6 F4
West 4th Street
  Basketball Courts......7 E4

🛍 SHOP
CO Bigelow Chemists....8 D3
Duane Reade...............9 D3
Environment 337.........10 G2
Hus..........................11 D3
Marc Jacobs...............12 B3
Marc Jacobs...............13 B3

Murray's Cheese..........14 D5
Oscar Wilde Memorial
  Bookshop................15 D3
Owl's Lab..................16 F1
Ricky's.....................17 D2

🍴 EAT
Annissa.....................18 D4
Babbo......................19 E3
Blue Hill New
  American................20 E4
Blue Ribbon Bakery......21 D5
Blue Ribbon Downing
  Street Bar...............22 D6
Cru.........................23 F2
Gus's Place................24 E5
Mas........................25 D5
Pearl Oyster..............26 D4
Soy Luck Club............27 B1
Spotted Pig...............28 A3

🍸 DRINK
Art Bar....................29 B1
Bar Next Door............30 E4
Employees Only..........31 B4
Fat Cats...................32 C3
Little Branch.............33 C1
Sullivan Room............34 E5

★ PLAY
55 Bar.....................35 C3
Cherry Lane Theater.....36 C5
Comedy Cellar...........37 E4
Duplex.....................38 C3
Film Forum...............39 D6
Le Poisson Rouge........40 E5
SOBs.......................41 D6
Village Vanguard.........42 C2

Please see over for map

SEE

CHRISTOPHER STREET PIERS/HUDSON RIVER PARK

Christopher St & West Side Hwy; ⊕ 1 to Christopher St-Sheridan Sq

Like so many places in the Village, the extreme west side was once a derelict eyesore used mostly as a cruising ground for quick, anonymous sex. Now it's a pretty waterside hangout, bisected by the Hudson River Park's slender bike and jogging paths, with great sunset views. It's still a place to cruise; now it's just much less dangerous.

NEW YORK UNIVERSITY

☎ 212-998-4636; www.nyu.edu; 50 W 4th St (information center); ⊕ N, R, W to 8th St-NYU, 6 to Astor Pl

In 1831 Albert Gallatin (buried in the Trinity Church cemetery, p47), Secretary of Treasury under President Thomas Jefferson, founded an intimate center of higher learning open to all students, regardless of race or class. Now it's a mammoth urban campus filled with 50,000 students. Check out the main buildings around Washington Sq Park.

SHERIDAN SQUARE

Christopher St & Seventh Ave; ⊕ 1 to Christopher St-Sheridan Sq

The shape of a triangle, Sheridan Sq isn't much more than a few park benches and some trees surround-ed by an old-fashioned wrought-iron gate. But its location (the heart of gay Greenwich Village) has meant that it's witnessed every rally, demonstration and uprising that has contributed to New York's gay rights movement. It also holds two sets of slender white statues: a male couple and a female couple, holding hands and talking. Known as Gay Liberation, they are a tribute to the normalcy of gay life.

WASHINGTON MEWS

btwn Fifth Ave & University Pl & btwn E 8th St & Washington Sq Park; ⊕ R, W to 8th St-NYU; ⚷

Private stables converted into homes line one side of the picturesque Washington Mews. Gaslights and horses have disappeared, but the tiny alley still embodies the essence of old New York. Famous residents have included writers Sherwood Anderson and Walter Lippman, and artist Gertrude Vanderbilt Whitney, founder of the Whitney Museum. It's surrounded now by New York University, which owns some of the properties.

WASHINGTON SQUARE PARK

www.washingtonsquareparkcouncil.org; Fifth Ave at Washington Sq N; ⊕ A, B, C, D, E, F, V to W 4th St, R, W to 8th St-NYU, 6 to Astor Pl

This crazy place is the heart of what's left of bohemian life in

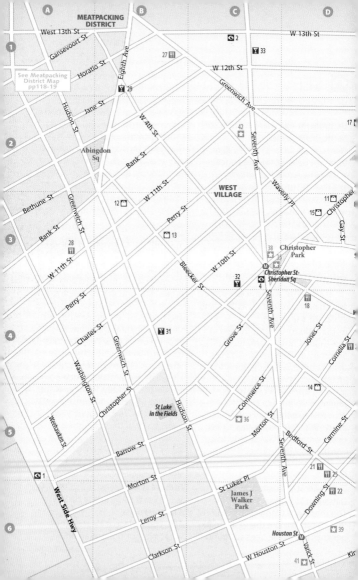

Greenwich Village. But, if the city has its way, the park will undergo a radical redesign: it will have a 4ft fence around it; the famed Garibaldi fountain where, rumor has it, Bob Dylan sang his first folk song will be relocated; and the entire site will be raised 4ft to ground level, disturbing those who were buried underneath it when it was a cemetery and a hanging spot (check out the hanging elm on the northwest corner). Community groups filed a lawsuit and won a stay; the city has appealed, and it will be years before a decision is made. Enjoy it while you can. Regular events are listed on the website.

The one not to miss? Quiet Disco on weekend afternoons – 300 people dancing to iPod tunes only they can hear.

☑ WEST 4TH STREET BASKETBALL COURTS

Sixth Ave at W 4th St; ☽ **hours vary;** ☯ **A, C, E, F, V to W 4th St**

Don't step into 'the Cage,' as this fenced-in court is called, without bringing your A game; these guys play to win in fierce competitive games. You can have just as much fun watching in the 10-deep crowds that gather, especially on weekends. In summer the W 4th St Summer Pro-Classic League hits the scene.

Washington Square Park: formerly cemetery, execution site and concert venue – and still an NYC must-see

SHOP

CO BIGELOW CHEMISTS
Drugstore

☎ 212-473-7324; 414 Sixth Ave btwn W 8th & W 9th Sts; ⏲ 7:30am-9pm Mon-Fri, 8:30am-7pm Sat, 8:30am-5pm Sun; ⊕ A, B, C, D, E, F, V to W 4th St

There are cheaper and more efficient drugstores all over the city, but none have the charm of Bigelow's, America's 'oldest apothecary' if you believe the managers. It's still got a working pharmacy, but it's most famous for its organic beauty products such as witch-hazel salves and honey-bee balms.

ENVIRONMENT 337
Homewares

☎ 212-254-3400; 56 University Pl near E 10th St; ⏲ 11am-8pm Mon-Fri, noon-6pm Sat & Sun; ⊕ L, N, Q, R, W, 4, 5, 6 to 14th St-Union Sq

An offbeat and environmentally aware home-furnishings store full of unique, one-of-a-kind designs, Environment 337 is a great place to shop for those who have everything – or think they do.

HUS
Fashion & Accessories, Homewares

☎ 212-620-5430; www.husliving.com; 11 Christopher St near Waverly Pl; ⏲ 11am-8pm Mon-Fri, noon-6pm Sat & Sun; ⊕ 1 to Christopher St-Sheridan Sq

Rotating art exhibits hang next to the latest in Scandinavian outdoor wear in this gallery/shopping center. Hus (a home in Scandinavia) also has some sleek furnishings and jewelry for sale.

MARC JACOBS
Fashion & Accessories

☎ 212-924-0026; www.marcjacobs.com; 403, 405 & 385 Bleecker St; ⏲ noon-8pm Mon-Sat, to 7pm Sun; ⊕ 1 to Christopher St-Sheridan Sq

Marc Jacobs' monster stores dominate Bleecker St. Bags and accessories at 385, menswear at 403, and his celebrated women's collection holds court at 405.

MURRAY'S CHEESE
Food & Drink

☎ 212-243-3289; www.murrayscheese.com; 254 Bleecker St; ⏲ 8am-8pm Mon-Sat, 9am-6pm Sun; ⊕ 1 to Christopher St-Sheridan Sq, A, B, C, D, E, F, V to W 4th St

Founded in 1914, this is repeatedly hailed as the best cheese shop in the city. Owner Rob Kaufelt is, to put it kindly, obsessed with finding the best *fromage* from all over the world, be it runny, firm, mild, sharp or full of holes. There's a Murray's at Grand Central Terminal, too.

OSCAR WILDE MEMORIAL BOOKSHOP *Books*

☎ 212-255-8097; 15 Christopher St; ⏲ 11am-7pm; ⊕ 1 to Christopher St-Sheridan Sq

The world's oldest bookshop geared to gay and lesbian

literature (open since 1967) lives in a lovely red-brick townhouse and stocks new and used books, and a fine range of magazines, rainbow flags, bumper stickers and other gifts. Its founder went on to create the Gay Liberation Movement after the 1969 Stonewall Riots.

☐ OWL'S LAB
Fashion & Accessories

☎ 212-633-2672; 20 E 12th St near Fifth Ave; ☼ noon-7pm Mon-Sat, to 5pm Sun; ⊕ L, N, Q, R, W, 4, 5, 6 to 14th St-Union Sq

A trendy little boutique popular with the NYU crowd. Shopping in Owl's Lab is like browsing through someone else's walk-in closet (someone who has unlimited money and impeccable taste). The Alicia + Olivia frocks, Kooba bags and Rebecca Minkoff totes get snapped up pretty quickly here.

☐ RICKY'S *Drugstore*

☎ 212-924-3401; 466 Sixth Ave at W 11th St; ☼ 9am-11pm Mon-Sat, to 10pm Sun; ⊕ A, C, E to 14th St, L to Eighth Ave-14th St

This is one of the few times in life that stocking up on mundane essentials like toothpaste and hair gel is actually fun – Ricky's is a drugstore that likes to think it's a nightclub – expect pounding music, hot-pink toothpaste tubes and lots of glitter, faux-color, and

outrageous hair and wardrobe selections. In the back you'll find sex toys, of course.

🍴 EAT

🍴 ANNISA
American Nouveau $$

☎ 212-741-6699; http://annisarestaurant .com; 13 Barrow St near W 4th St; ☼ dinner; ⊕ A, B, C, D, E, F, V to W 4th St, 1 to Christopher St-Sheridan Sq; ♿ Ⓥ

Chef and owner Anita Lo likes to mix things up in the kitchen, but you'd never know it from the quiet, almost one-note decor. Annisa's gray storefront entrance leads to a soothing (slightly boring) glossy interior, but the excitement level kicks up several notches when you get the menu. Smoked roe, roesti potatoes and sorrel; pan-roasted chicken in sherry, white truffles and pig feet; smoked Berkshire pork with millet and Gruyère; and oxtail, bone marrow and more are on the menu.

🍴 BABBO *Italian* $$$

☎ 212-777-0303; www.babbonyc.com; 110 Waverly Pl; ☼ dinner; ⊕ A, B, C, D, E, F, V to W 4th St, 1 to Christopher St-Sheridan Sq; ♿

Celebrity chef Mario Batali has multiple restaurants in Manhattan, but everyone has a sneaking suspicion that this two-level split townhouse is his favorite. Whether you order mint love letters, lamb's brain *francobolli* (small, stuffed ravioli) or pig's foot *milanese,* you'll find Batali at the top of his innovative, eclectic game. Reservations are in order.

🍴 CRU *French* $$$
☎ 212-777-0303; http://cru-nyc.com; 24 Fifth Ave at 9th St; 🕒 dinner Mon-Sat; 🚇 1 to Christopher St–Sheridan Sq; ♿

A big hit with the Euro crowd, Cru has more than 150,000 bottles of wine and happily helps you make a good match to dishes like cod with Castelluccio lentils, roasted broccoli ribbons and sautéed cauliflower in lingonberry–red wine jus, and roasted duck-breast braised Romanesco, duck pancetta, maitake mushroom and sweet-potato puree port wine–natural jus. A quick tip: the handsome mahogany bar out front has the same wines and better views to the street, and lets you order a la carte off the menu.

🍴 GUS'S PLACE *Greek* $
☎ 212-777-1660; http://gusplacenyc .com; 192 Bleecker St near MacDougal St; 🕒 lunch & dinner; 🚇 A, B, C, D, E, F, V to W 4th St, 1 to Houston St; ♿ Ⓥ 🍴

Channeling Greek food by way of Crete, Gus's Place is like an old-fashioned taverna, minus the wavy blue Mediterranean out front. As airy and light as a restaurant can get

on a busy street, Gus's has tangy feta salads, crisp calamari, spanakopita, souvlakis, mezes and more.

🍴 MAS
New American, French $$$
☎ 212-255-1790; www.masfarmhouse .com; 39 Downing St; 🕒 dinner & late-night dinner Mon-Sat; 🚇 A, B, C, D, E, F, V to W 4th St; ♿

Chef Galen Zamarra draws heavily from the South of France (in old Provençal a 'mas' is a traditional stone farmhouse), from the solid and ornate oak front door to the earthy menu featuring *beau soleil* oysters, braised ribs, flying pig pork belly and wild nettle risotto. A great option for late-night dining.

🍴 PEARL OYSTER
American Seafood $$

☎ 212-691-8211; 18 Cornelia St near Bleecker St; ✨ lunch & dinner Mon-Fri, dinner Sat; ⊕ A, B, C, D, E, F, V to W 4th St; ♿

People line up for the lobster rolls and oyster rolls and the crowds keep getting bigger, even though Pearl Oyster has now expanded its space twice. The wine list is more detailed than the menu, which consists of fresh fish (catch of the day), Maine lobsters, clams, shrimp and scallops and thick hearty New England chowder.

🍴 SOY LUCK CLUB
Healthy Café $

☎ 212-229-9191; 115 Greenwich Ave at Jane St; ✨ 7am-10pm Mon-Fri, 9am-10pm Sat & Sun; ⊕ A, C, E, L to Eighth Ave-14th St; Ⓥ

Many menu items are indeed soy-based – the soy chicken and fontina (wheat-free) crepe, the tofu salad and avocado sandwich, and the mesclun, edamame (soybean) and soy-nut salad, just for starters – but there's plenty here too for the soy-phobic. *Panini* (sandwiches), salads and brunch items (some even containing meat), abound.

🍴 SPOTTED PIG
Pub Fare $$

☎ 212-620-0393; www.thespottedpig .com; 314 W 11th St; ✨ lunch & dinner

to 2am; ⊕ A, C, E, L to Eighth Ave-14th St; ♿ Ⓥ ♿

When you belly up for a drink at this bar, don't expect bowls of peanuts. Pub fare here means chicken-liver toast, mozzarella with fava-bean bruschetta, duck egg with tuna *bottarga* (salted tuna roe) and much, much more. Busy at night, much better for children in the day, and with at least two vegan options daily, the Spotted Pig's got something for everyone.

🍸 DRINK

🍸 ART BAR *Bar*

☎ 212-727-0244; 52 Eighth Ave near Horatio St; ✨ 4pm-4am, happy hour 4-7pm; ⊕ L to Eighth Ave-14th St, A, C, E to 14th St

A decidedly bohemian crowd favors Art Bar, which doesn't look like much up front (oval booths crowded too close to the wooden bar) but it has a bit more going on in the back. Grab your beer or one of the house specials (usually martinis) and head for the couches, placed under a huge *Last Supper* mural featuring Hollywood hotties Jimmy Dean and Marilyn Monroe, among others.

🍸 BAR NEXT DOOR *Bar*

☎ 212-529-5945; 129 MacDougal St btwn W 3rd & W 4th Sts; ✨ 6pm-2am Sun-Thu, to 3am Fri & Sat; ⊕ A, B, C, D, E, F, V to W 4th St

One of the loveliest boîtes in the neighborhood, the basement of this restored townhouse is all low ceilings, exposed brick and romantic lighting. You'll find mellow, live jazz nightly, as well as the tasty Italian menu of the restaurant next door, La Lanterna di Vittorio.

▼ EMPLOYEES ONLY *Bar*
☎ 212-242-3021; 510 Hudson St near Christopher St; ⏱ 6pm-4am; ⊕ 1 to Christopher St-Sheridan Sq

The entrance is sometimes blocked by a tarot-card reader, but once you navigate your way inside you'll find a big fireplace, old-style bartenders (some with mustaches) and a relaxed, hard-drinking crowd. It can get packed on busy weeknights and weekends as crowds flock in for the perfectly balanced cocktails.

▼ FAT CATS *Pub*
☎ 212-675-6056; http://fatcatmusic .org; 75 Christopher St near Seventh Ave; ⏱ 2pm-2am Mon-Fri, noon-2am Sat & Sun; ⊕ 1 to Christopher St-Sheridan Sq, A, B, C, D, E, F, V to W 4th St

Crappy and run down, Fat Cats is the place to go for those who want to hang out, shoot some pool, play a little chess, scrabble or backgammon, and maybe even get a Ping-Pong game going. Serious gamers and amateurs get a kick out of this quasi-pool-hall locale, with its live music, cheap

beers and no-holds-barred approach to life.

▼ LITTLE BRANCH *Bar*
☎ 212-929-4360; 20 Seventh Ave; ⏱ 7pm-3am Mon-Fri, 9pm-3am Sun; ⊕ 1, 2, 3 to 14th St, L to Eighth Ave-14th St

You might have heard of Milk & Honey, an unmarked Lower East Side bar that famously makes patrons call ahead using a secret phone number to gain entry. The same owner, Sasha Petraske, a West Village native whose mother worked at the *Village Voice* newspaper alongside famed photographer

The Spotted Pig – something for everyone

Sylvia Plachy (mother of actor Adrien Brody), now has three bars, including this one. The homey, welcoming Little Branch serves perfectly mixed cocktails; be nice to the bartender and maybe you'll get the secret digits to Sasha's other bars.

▼ SULLIVAN ROOM *DJ Bar*
☎ 212-252-2151; 218 Sullivan St btwn Bleecker & W 3rd Sts; ☒ 9pm-5am Wed-Sat; ⊚ A, B, C, D, E, F, V to W 4th St
You'll have to look hard to find the entrance to this below-ground hangout, which attracts its share of the beautiful people with DJ-hosted dance parties, a foreign beer collection and generous mixed cocktails. Best after 1am.

UNDER THE RADAR
Some live music venues are so hip they're hidden. Find them, and try them on for size.
Brooklyn Masonic Temple (www .masonicboom.com; 317 Clermont Ave, Brooklyn) Local hip-hop artists do their thing in the huge, high-ceilinged hall.
Le Poisson Rouge (http://lepoisson rouge.com; 158 Bleecker St, West Village) Artists like Baby Dee frequent this hip downtown spot.
Santos Party House (Map pp54–5; www.santospartyhouse.com; 100 Lafayette St, Chinatown) Be prepared to wait to get into this brand-new megaclub.

⭐ PLAY
⭐ 55 BAR *Jazz Music*
☎ 212-929-9883; www.55bar.com; 55 Christopher St; cover charge $3-15, 2-drink minimum; ☒ 1pm-4am; ⊚ 1 to Christopher St-Sheridan Sq, A, B, C, D, E, F to W 4th St
It's not one of the big players of the jazz scene, but 55 Bar is well known among aficionados who want to hear great music without paying a hefty cover charge. Next to the famous Stonewall Bar (the location of the infamous Stonewall Riot), 55 Bar attracts top-shelf players but doesn't take itself too seriously.

⭐ CHERRY LANE THEATER *Theater, Arts*
☎ 212-989-2020; www.cherrylane theater.com; 38 Commerce St; ☒ hours vary; ⊚ 1 to Christopher St-Sheridan Sq
A theater with a distinctive charm hidden in the West Village, Cherry Lane has a long and distinguished history. It was started by poet Edna St Vincent Millay and has given a voice to numerous play-wrights and actors over the years. It remains true to its mission of creating 'live' theater that's accessible to the public. Readings, plays and spoken-word performances rotate frequently.

⭐ COMEDY CELLAR *Comedy*
☎ 212-254-3480; www.comedycellar .com; 117 MacDougal St; cover charge

$15; ⏱ shows start at 9pm Sun-Fri, 7:30pm Sat; ⊕ A, C, E, F, V, S to W 4th St
A Greenwich Village staple for decades, the Comedy Cellar has seen quite a few careers come and go over the years, and is still filled nightly with wannabes, has-beens and hot-for-the-moment comics.

⭐ DUPLEX *Cabaret, Karaoke*
☎ 212-255-5438; www.theduplex.com; 61 Christopher St; cover charge $10-20; ⏱ 4pm-4am; ⊕ 1 to Christopher St-Sheridan Sq
Cabaret, karaoke and campy dance moves are par for the course at the legendary Duplex. Pictures of Joan Rivers line the walls and the performers like to mimic her sassy form of self-deprecation, while getting in a few jokes about audience members as well. It's fun and unpretentious place, and certainly not for the bashful.

⭐ FILM FORUM *Film*
☎ 212-727-8110; www.filmforum.com; 209 W Houston St; tickets $12; ⏱ daily; ⊕ 1 to Houston St; ♿ 🚻
The best foreign and domestic films in the history of cinema get star treatment at the Film Forum, which often devotes weeks at a time to one director or artist's best

works. Buy tickets early, as shows tend to sell out.

⭐ SOBS *Club*
☎ 212-243-4940; www.sobs.com; 204 Varick St; cover charge $10-20; ⏱ 6:30pm-3am; ⊕ 1 to Houston St; ♿
Shake your hips at SOBs – aka Sounds of Brazil. Aside from samba and the lambada, you'll find Afro Cuban rumba, salsa, reggae and more. The cheery (if kitschy) decor and decent food make it a popular choice for after-work parties; real dancing doesn't start until 2am. Sometimes a cover charge applies.

⭐ VILLAGE VANGUARD *Jazz Music*
☎ 212-255-4037; www.villagevanguard .com; 178 Seventh Ave; cover charge $15-40, 2-drink minimum; ⏱ 7pm-1am; ⊕ 1 to Christopher St-Sheridan Sq
Possibly the city's most prestigious jazz club, the Vanguard has hosted literally every major star of the past 50 years. It started as a home to spoken word performances and occasionally returns to its roots, but most of the time it's just smooth, sweet jazz all night long. Mind your step on the steep stairs, and close your eyes to the signs of wear and tear – acoustically, you're in one of the greatest venues in the world.

>MEATPACKING DISTRICT

The Meatpacking District is all about shopping, eating and drinking – and if you enjoy all three, this neighborhood will be nirvana for you.

As you explore this district's wide cobblestone streets, check out two hotels that helped move this part of town from stodgy to fabulous: the Hotel Gansevoort and the Maritime Hotel near Chelsea. At research time, a third – the Standard – was set to open. Be sure to stroll the nabe's most famous byway, Gansevoort St, which was a Dutch market, and then a slaughterhouse. It also did a brisk business in prostitution, mostly plied by transsexual or gay men. A holdover from that time is the LGBT Community Center (Map pp106–7), which played a crucial role in forcing discussion of the AIDS epidemic in the 1980s and '90s.

The district's far less rough-and-ready these days. With the coming of the long-awaited High Line, and more incursions from restaurants, galleries and high-end boutiques, this is one neighborhood that's not looking back.

MEATPACKING DISTRICT

☉ SEE
Hotel Gansevoort	........**1** D3
Maritime Hotel	........**2** D1
White Columns	........**3** E3

🛍 SHOP
Adam	........**4** D3
Alexander McQueen	....**5** C2
An Earnest Cut & Sew	...**6** C4
Apple Store	........**7** D2
Balducci's	........**8** F2
Buckler	........**9** E3

Carlos Miele	........**10** D2
Catherine Malandrino	....**11** D3
Chocolate Bar	........**12** F3
Helmut Lang	........**13** C4
Iris	........**14** C3

🍴 EAT
5 Ninth	........**15** D3
Mi Cocina	........**16** E4
Paradou	........**17** C3
STK	........**18** D3

🍸 DRINK
Brass Monkey	........**19** C3
Buddha Bar	........**20** D3
Plunge	........**21** D3

⭐ PLAY
Cielo	........**22** C3
Kiss & Fly	........**23** D3
Level V	........**24** D2
Tenjune	....(see 18)

Please see over for map

◉ SEE

◉ WHITE COLUMNS

☎ 212-924-4212; http://whitecolumns
.org; 320 W 13th St; admission free;
◷ noon-6pm Tue-Sat; ◉ A, C, E, L to
Eighth Ave-14th St

Geographically, White Columns is part of the Meatpacking District, but aesthetically speaking, it's in Chelsea. The sedate, four-room space has ample installations and exhibits, many of which are by fairly well-known names like Andrew Serrano, Alice Aycock, Lorna Simpson and a White Columns founder, Gordon Matta-Clark. One of its most successful recent installations came from South London's Studio Voltaire, which presented different works all somehow related to the public persona of singer Michael Jackson.

▢ SHOP

▢ ADAM *Fashion & Accessories*

☎ 212-229-2838; www.shopadam.com;
678 Hudson St btwn W 13th & W 14th Sts;
◷ 11am-7pm Mon-Wed & Fri, 11am-
8pm Thu, 10am-7pm Sat, noon-6pm Sun;
◉ A, C, E to Eighth Ave-14th St

Oscar de la Renta protégé Adam Lippes' Meatpacking store is full of the smart, modern clothes that have made him a rising star. There's something for men and women (on the left and right sides of the store, respectively) amid the casually hung chic separates, polos, T-shirts and sweaters. Emphasis is on unusual and sensuous materials, like buttery suede and plump quilting.

▢ ALEXANDER MCQUEEN
Fashion & Accessories

☎ 212-645-1797; www.alexander
mcqueen.com; 417 W 14th St; ◷ 11am-
7pm Mon-Sat, noon-6pm Sun; ◉ A, C, E,
L, 1, 2, 3 to Eighth Ave-14th St

McQueen's rambunctious outfits are shown to perfection in his massive MPD store, and his edgy creations seem made to be worn in this fashion-forward district.

▢ AN EARNEST CUT & SEW
Tailor

☎ 212-242-3414; www.earnestsewn
.com; 821 Washington St; ◷ 11am-7pm
Mon-Fri, to 8pm Sat, to 7pm Sun; ◉ A, C,
E, L, 1, 2, 3 to Eighth Ave-14th St

Get your jeans custom made at this ranchero-style store, where denim is cut, hemmed, shaped, trimmed and studded to fit your specific contours.

▢ APPLE STORE
Computers & Accessories

☎ 212-444-3400; 401 W 14th St at Ninth
Ave; ◷ 11am-8pm Mon-Fri, noon-7pm
Sat & Sun; ◉ A, C, E, F, V to Eighth
Ave-14th St

A gleaming glass-and-chrome presence in an already stylish 'hood, this Apple Store has all the

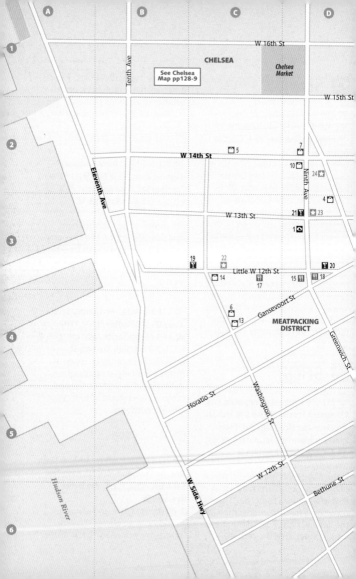

A

B

C

D

1

W 16th St

CHELSEA

Tenth Ave

See Chelsea
Map pp128-9

Chelsea
Market

W 15th St

2

W 14th St 5

7

10

Ninth Ave

24

4

W 13th St 21 23

1

3

19 22

20

Little W 12th St

14 15 18

17

6

13

Gansevoort St

MEATPACKING
DISTRICT

4

Greenwich St

Horatio St

Washington St

5

Hudson River

W 12th St

Bethune St

W Side Hwy

6

Eleventh Ave

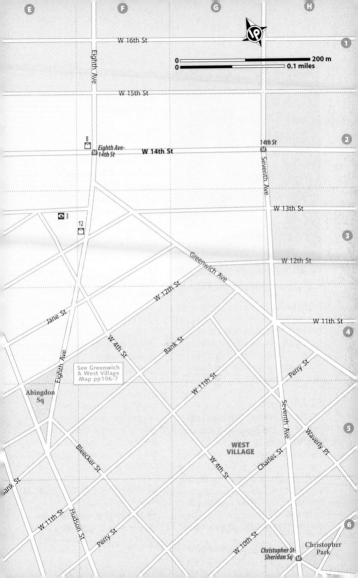

Carlos Miele – adding a little Brazil to NYC

latest tech accessories and trendy Mac products. You can play games or check your email on the Mac-Books on the 1st floor, or sweep up the curving staircase to the iPods and 'genius bar' on floors two and three.

BALDUCCI'S *Food & Drink*
☎ 212-741-3700; 81 Eighth Ave at W 14th St; ⏰ 9am-10pm; ⊕ A, C, E, L to Eighth Ave-14th St
Heavenly aromas fill this landmark, turn-of-the-century bank building that now houses a Balducci's, one of New York's toniest gourmet stores. Just like the Balducci's in Greenwich Village, you'll find here the highest-quality gourmet pro-

duce, international cheeses, olives, bakery goods, fresh roasted coffee and packaged items from around the globe.

BUCKLER
Fashion & Accessories
☎ 212-255-1596; www.bucklershow room.com; 13 Gansevoort St; ⏰ 11am-7pm Mon-Sat, noon-6pm Sun; ⊕ A, C, E, L, 1, 2, 3 to Eighth Ave-14th St
Producing cult menswear that blends 'roguish American icons with British edge,' Buckler's famous for its selection of brash and boyish denim designs. If you like the way Lenny Kravitz and Iggy Pop dress, you've found the perfect store.

CARLOS MIELE
Fashion & Accessories
☎ 646-336-6642; www.carlosmiele.com .br; 408 W 14th St; ⏰ noon-7pm; ⊕ A, C, E, L to Eighth Ave-14th St
A bright store for bold shoppers, the cut-out design of Miele's flagship boutique is almost as eye-catching as his sexy, sultry, Carnaval-inspired Brazilian dresses. This is a great place for glamorous gowns that leave you room to dance.

CATHERINE MALANDRINO
Fashion & Accessories
☎ 212-929-8710; www.catherine malandrino.com; 652 Hudson St;

⏰ 11am-8pm Mon-Sat, noon-6pm Sun;
Ⓜ A, C, E, L, 1, 2, 3 to Eighth Ave-14th St
A favorite of curvy girls, Maland-rino's city-smart creations are af-fordable and chic, sort of a slightly younger, hipper version of Donna Karan's sleek, working-woman's clothes.

🏠 **CHOCOLATE BAR**
Confectionary
☎ 212-367-7181; 48 Eighth Ave at W 13th St; ⏰ 11am-8pm Tue-Sun; Ⓜ A, C, E, L to Eighth Ave-14th St
It's all chocolate all the time at this diminutive storefront. You can create custom gift boxes of fancy artistic chocolates (flavors include chocolate mint tea and pistachio marzipan) by Brooklyn Willy Wonka Jacques Torres, stock up on rich bricks of the stuff or simply hover over a steaming cup of some of the best hot cocoa you'll ever find.

🏠 **HELMUT LANG**
Fashion & Accessories
☎ 212-242-3240; www.helmutlang.com; 819 Washington St; ⏰ 11am-7pm Tue-Sun; Ⓜ A, C, E, L to Eighth Ave-14th St
Lang's latest outpost is this brick-walled wonder near Little W 12th St, full of dashingly cut men's and women's clothes that have all the style you'd expect but at a some-what more affordable price than you'll find in his other stores.

🏠 **IRIS** *Footwear*
☎ 212-645-0950; 827 Washington St;
⏰ 11am-7pm Tue-Fri, 10am-7pm Sat, noon-6pm Sun; Ⓜ A, C, E, L to Eighth Ave-14th St
All the fine Italian footwear you could ever dream of owning is on display at Iris. Strap on some strappies from Chloe, Viktor & Rolf, Galliano, Marc Jacobs and Bran-quinho and break out the plastic to pay for it all.

🍴 **EAT**

🍴 **5 NINTH**
American Nouveau $$
☎ 212-929-9460; http://5ninth.com; 5 Ninth Ave near Gansevoort St; ⏰ lunch & dinner; Ⓜ A, C, E, L to Eighth Ave-14th St; Ⓥ ♿
A freestanding three-story brown-stone, complete with back porch and pocket-sized garden, makes

NOSHWALKS
Check out the best that New York has to offer in street food on a culinary tour through the city's most delicious neighborhoods. **Noshwalks** (www .noshwalks.com) will take you through the Meatpacking District, Lower East Side, Harlem, and even into truly ad-venturous territory in Brooklyn and Queens, where you'll likely get tasty Indian, Chinese and Latino food over Jewish and Italian.

NEIGHBORHOODS

MEATPACKING DISTRICT

for a gorgeous dining experience. The menu is inventive and rotates often; you'll find things like roasted black-pepper pork belly braised in garlic, chili jam and anchovy dressing on bib lettuce, a root-vegetable terrine, butternut-squash ravioli, sturgeon, Angus sirloin and Korean-style pork.

MI COCINA Mexican $$
☎ 212-627-8273; 57 Jane St at Hudson St; ☽ dinner daily, lunch Sat & Sun; ☉ A, C, E, L to Eighth Ave-14th St; Ⓥ ♿

Stop by for some corn tamales stuffed with guajillo chili sauce and Mexican white cheese; empanadas plumped up with beef, raisins

and olives; corn tacos with salsa, goat cheese, cilantro and onion; or sautéed shrimp in spicy adobo sauce with steamed spinach. Other usuals like grilled chicken get jazzed up with Mexican oregano, white wine and artistic dabs of guacamole and sour cream. Top-shelf tequilas make for amazing cocktails, and sinful desserts make for dreamy endings.

PARADOU French Bistro $$
☎ 212-463-8345; 8 Little W 12th St btwn Ninth Ave & Washington St; ☽ dinner; ☉ A, C, E, L to Eighth Ave-14th St; Ⓥ

This is indeed paradise, which is the literal translation of Paradou

Treat yourself to fine food in a gorgeous setting at 5 Ninth (p121)

in the Provençal dialect. The hydrangea-heavy garden out the back is a mini-miracle in springtime and is the perfect place to share the antipasto plate with artisanal hams, salamis, pâtés, asparagus and haricot verts, or the herbed seared tuna, sardines and smoked trout with baby veggies and saffron aioli. Traditionalists will lick their fingers over the frog's legs with wild mushrooms, fingerling potatoes and paprika crème fraîche.

🍽 STK *Steakhouse* $$$
☎ 646-624-2444; www.stkhouse.com; 26 Little W 12th St near Ninth Ave; ⏰ dinner until 2am; 🚇 A, C, E, L to Eighth Ave-14th St; ♿

An oddly stylized restaurant, with sleek banquettes, metallic and black decor and one kitschy pair of horns protruding from over the bar, STK bills itself as 'not your daddy's steakhouse.' That's why you'll find salads filled with green melon, avocado, mâche greens and kefir lime, or blue cheese, vine-ripe tomatoes and smoked bacon, plus organic roast chicken, tuna tartare with roasted pineapple, crispy shallots and plantain chips, and scallop ceviche. But there's still plenty of what you'd expect: T-bones, skirt steaks, filet mignon, and so on. Portion sizes can be petite, medium or large, and you can add toppings such as black truffles.

HIGH LINE
An old elevated train track has been turned into a bucolic city park, with walkways surrounded by flowers, delicate pathways and leafy trees, 14ft above street level. Slated to open in 2009, the High Line has been a long-awaited addition to the city's already fabulous reclaimed green spaces.

🍸 DRINK

🍸 BRASS MONKEY *Pub*
☎ 212-675-6686; 55 Little W 12th St at Washington St; ⏰ 11:30am-4am; 🚇 A, C, E, L to Eighth Ave-14th St

An appealing, down-at-the-heels straightforward pub in a neighborhood of over-the-top 'cocktail bars,' Brass Monkey's for patrons who like to shoot pool, hook their heels over worn out bar stools, and put more thought into their brew choice than their wardrobe.

🍸 BUDDHA BAR *Bar*
☎ 212-647-7314; www.buddhabarnyc .com; 25 Little W 12th St; ⏰ 6pm-4am; 🚇 A, C, E, L to Eighth Ave-14th St

An Asian-themed bar complete with 17ft Buddhas, bamboo pagodas and a Zen-like atmosphere in the back garden, this MPD favorite gets busy on weekend nights. Besides Buddha-inspired cocktails, you'll find a sushi bar and other snacks.

NEIGHBORHOODS

MEATPACKING DISTRICT

ⓨ PLUNGE *Bar*
☎ 212-206-6700; Gansevoort Hotel, 18 Ninth Ave at W 13th St; ⏱ 11am-3am; ⓐ A, C, E, L to Eighth Ave-14th St

Head to the top of the Gansevoort Hotel and grab a drink in time to watch the sun go down over the Hudson. Although the bright-blue pool is for guests only, the hoi polloi are allowed to enjoy the views and imbibe freely on the rooftop deck.

⭐ PLAY
✪ CIELO *Club*
☎ 212-645-5700; 18 Little W 12th St; admission $15-25; ⏱ 10:30pm-5am Mon-Sat; ⓐ A, C, E, L to Eighth Ave-14th St

The demise of this house-heavy dancehall has been imminent for years, but so far, Cielo is holding on. The club has still got its 'Deep House' Monday nights and brings in its DJs from Europe who spin entrancing, seductive sounds that pull everyone to their feet.

✪ KISS & FLY *Club*
☎ 212-255-1933; 409 W 13th St near Ninth Ave; cover charge $10-25; ⏱ 11pm-4am Wed-Sat; ⓐ A, C, E, L to Eighth Ave-14th St

A heavily European crowd moves and grooves to French electronica and pop into the wee hours at Kiss & Fly, a unique club designed to look a bit like a Roman bathhouse.

At Plunge you can imbibe at altitude

The circular room flows around a central bar, and arches pull the eye upward to elaborately decorated walls and ceilings.

⭐ LEVEL V *Club*
☎ 212-699-2410; 675 Hudson St; cover charge $15; 🕐 8pm-4am; Ⓔ A, C, E, L to Eighth Ave-14th St

Waaay underground, in all senses of the word, Level V is another subterranean Meatpacking District club. If you can manage to get past the doorman, you'll descend into a super-cool, dungeon-like space, with beckoning bright-red puffy couches, sexy bartenders (men and women) and a DJ that works the dance floor all night long.

⭐ TENJUNE *Club*
☎ 646-624-2410; 26 Little W 12th St near Ninth Ave; cover charge $10-20; 🕐 dinner until 2am; Ⓔ A, C, E, L to Eighth Ave-14th St

Hotter than hot (for the moment), Tenjune's horseshoe-shaped dance floor is like a magnet for celebrities, models and the men who love them. Hidden underneath the STK restaurant, Tenjune's got three basic areas to hang in: a cushion-covered main room, a gallery area and a VIP section. The door policy is tough; dress accordingly.

>CHELSEA

Few neighborhoods are as distinctive as edgy, arty Chelsea – home to New York's club scene, gallery scene and a large part of its gay scene.

Once a wasteland of empty factories and derelict dumps on the far west side of Manhattan, Chelsea has been transformed over the last 10 years and is now filled almost completely with art galleries, studios and artist collectives. Where once it was hard to find a decent cup of coffee, Chelsea now overflows with cafés, bistros and high-end shops.

It can still feel like a remote region – with its long, sweeping blocks and brisk westerly winds coming off the Hudson River – but most days you'll find crowds on the streets. If not to see the art, then to hit the clubs – Chelsea's famous for its nightlife, especially from 26th St to around 29th St.

CHELSEA

◉ SEE
Andrea Rosen Gallery	**1**	C3
Chelsea Art Museum	**2**	B3
Chelsea Hotel	**3**	F3
Chelsea Piers Complex	**4**	B4
Dia Center for the Arts	**5**	C3
Gagosian	**6**	B3
Greene Naftali	**7**	C2
Maritime Hotel	**8**	E5
Matthew Marks Gallery	**9**	C3
Matthew Marks Gallery	**10**	C3
Museum at FIT	**11**	F2
Paul Kasmin	**12**	C2
Paul Kasmin	**13**	C2
Rubin Museum of Art	**14**	F5
White Box	**15**	C2

🛍 SHOP
17th Street Market	**16**	G5
192 Books	**17**	C4

Antiques Garage Flea Market	**18**	G2
Authentiques Past & Present	**19**	F5
Balenciaga	**20**	B3
Barney's Co-op	**21**	F5
Chelsea Market	**22**	D5
Giraudon	**23**	E5
Housing Works Thrift Shop	**24**	G5
Loehmann's	**25**	G5

🍴 EAT
202	(see 22)	
Buddakan	(see 22)	
El Quinto Pino	**26**	D3
Empire Diner	**27**	C3
F&B	**28**	F3
Green Table	(see 22)	
Klee Brasserie	**29**	D3

Omai	**30**	D4
Tia Pol	**31**	C3

🍸 DRINK
Bar Veloce	**32**	F4
Chelsea Brewing Company	**33**	A4
Glass	**34**	C2
Half King	**35**	C3
Park	**36**	C5

⭐ PLAY
10ak	**37**	D5
Cain	**38**	B2
Eagle NYC	**39**	B1
Home	**40**	C2
Joyce Theater	**41**	E4
Marquee	**42**	C2
Pink Elephant	**43**	C2

Please see over for map

⊙ SEE

◎ ANDREA ROSEN GALLERY

☎ 212-637-6000; www.andrearosen gallery.com; 525 W 24th St; admission free; ⏱ 10am-6pm Tue-Sat; ⊖ C, E, 1 to 23rd St; ♿

Oversized installations are the norm at this spacious gallery, where curators fill every inch of space (and the annex Gallery 2 next door) in interesting ways. Rosen opened her gallery in 1990 and quickly made a name for herself. She's showcased John Currin's 'pale portraits,' Felix Gonzalez-Torres's 'Vultures' and Tetsumi Kudo's oil paintings, to name just a few of her artists.

◎ CHELSEA ART MUSEUM

☎ 212-255-0719; www.chelseaart museum.org; 556 W 22nd St; admission free; ⏱ noon-6pm Tue, Wed, Fri & Sat, to 8pm Thu; ⊖ C, E to 23rd St; ♿

Set inside a three-story, redbrick building dating from 1850, and standing on land once owned by writer Clement Clarke Moore, this museum's focus is on post-war abstract expressionism, by both national and international artists. The permanent collection includes works by Antonio Corpora, Laszlo Lakner and sculptor Bernar Venet. It's also the headquarters of the Miotte Foundation, dedicated to archiving the works of Jean Miotte, a Soho-based artist who has played a big role in the genre of Informel (Informal Art).

◎ CHELSEA HOTEL

☎ 212-243-3700; 222 W 23rd St btwn Seventh & Eighth Aves; ⊖ 1, 2, C, E to 23rd St

The prime sight on noisy 23rd St is a redbrick hotel with ornate iron balconies and no fewer than seven plaques declaring its literary landmark status. Even before the infamous onsite death of Sid Vicious' girlfriend, Nancy Spungeon, the hotel was famous as a hangout for the likes of Mark Twain, Thomas Wolfe, Dylan Thomas and Arthur Miller. Jack Kerouac allegedly crafted *On the Road* during one marathon session here. Musicians have long favored the Chelsea, and it counts many local eccentrics among its permanent residents. Now under new ownership, it seems the hotel's 'art before profit' attitude is in for a change.

◎ CHELSEA PIERS COMPLEX

☎ 212-336-6000; www.chelseapiers .com; Hudson River at end of W 23rd St; ⊖ C, E to 23rd St

This massive waterfront sports center caters to the athlete in everyone. You can set out to hit a bucket of golf balls at the four-level driving range, ice skate

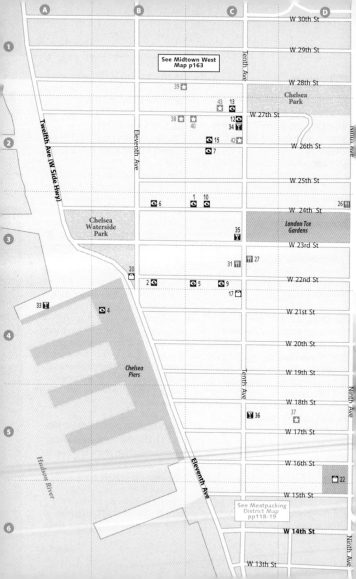

A

B

C

D

1

See Midtown West
Map p163

W 30th St

W 29th St

W 28th St

39 ★

Chelsea
Park

43 13
★ ⏱

38 ★ ★
40

12 ⏱
34 🍴

W 27th St

⏱ 15

42 ★

W 26th St

Ninth Ave

2

Twelfth Ave (W Side Hwy)

Eleventh Ave

⏱ 7

W 25th St

⏱ 6

1 10
⏱ ⏱

W 24th St

26 🍴

3

Chelsea
Waterside
Park

35
🍴

London Tce
Gardens

W 23rd St

31 🍴

27 🍴

20
📷

2 ⏱

⏱ 5

⏱ 9

W 22nd St

17 📷

33 🍴

⏱ 4

W 21st St

4

Chelsea
Piers

W 20th St

Tenth Ave

W 19th St

W 18th St

🍴 36

37
★

W 17th St

5

Hudson River

W 16th St

Eleventh Ave

W 15th St

📷 22

Ninth Ave

See Meatpacking
District Map
pp118-19

W 14th St

6

W 13th St

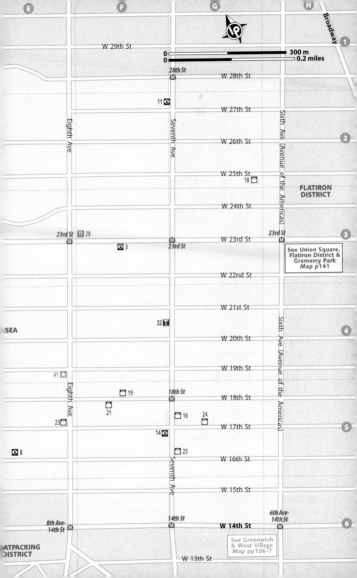

E

F

G

H

Broadway

1

W 29th St

0   300 m

0   0.2 miles

28th St

W 28th St

11

W 27th St

Eighth Ave

Seventh Ave

W 26th St

2

Sixth Ave (Avenue of the Americas)

W 25th St

18

W 24th St

FLATIRON
DISTRICT

W 23rd St

23rd St   28

23rd St

3

23rd St

See Union Square,
Flatiron District &
Gramercy Park
Map p141

W 22nd St

W 21st St

32

W 20th St

4

Sixth Ave (Avenue of the Americas)

SEA

W 19th St

41

W 18th St

19

18th St

W 18th St

21

Eighth Ave

16   24

23

14

W 17th St

5

8

25

W 16th St

Seventh Ave

W 15th St

8th Ave-
14th St

14th St

W 14th St

6th Ave-
14th St

6

ATPACKING
DISTRICT

See Greenwich
& West Village
Map pp106-7

W 13th St

NEIGHBORHOODS

CHELSEA

International art at Gagosian

in the complex's indoor rink or rent in-line skates to cruise down to Battery Park along the new Hudson Park waterfront bike path. There's a jazzy bowling alley, Hoop City for basketball, a sailing school for kids, batting cages, a huge gym facility with an indoor pool – the works. Kayaks are loaned out free at the Downtown Boathouse just north of Pier 64.

DIA CENTER FOR THE ARTS
☎ 212-989-5566; www.diaart.org; 548 W 22nd St; admission free; 🕚 11am-6pm Mon-Fri; 🚇 C, E to 23rd St
As of press time the Dia Center was looking for a new site to

house its contemporary art collection in Chelsea and had closed its W 22nd St location temporarily. Check the website for information while in town to see if it has reopened or relocated, as the Dia Center is not something you want to miss if you can avoid it. Aside from its own fantastic collections, Dia often runs screenings and lecture series from filmmakers and other artists. The Dia Beacon offshoot in upstate New York remains open to the public.

GAGOSIAN
☎ 212-741-1111; www.gagosian.com; 555 W 24th St; admission free; 🕚 10am-6pm Sat; 🚇 C, E to 23rd St; ♿
International works dot the walls at both the Gagosian in Chelsea and the gallery **uptown** (Map p183; ☎ 212-741-1111; 980 Madison Ave; 🕚 10am-6pm Tue-Sat; 🚇 6 to 77th St-Lexington Ave; ♿). The ever-revolving exhibits feature greats like Julian Schnabel, William de Kooning, Andy Warhol and Basquiat.

GREENE NAFTALI
☎ 212-463-7770; www.greenenaftali gallery.com; 526 W 26th St; admission free; 🕚 10am-6pm Tue-Sat; 🚇 C, E to 23rd St; ♿
Sharp, edgy and youth-oriented Greene Naftali has an ever-rotating display of art in all kinds of mediums: film/video, installation, paint-

ing, drawing and performance art. Check out the column running through the gallery's center; it's often used to display pieces.

☉ MATTHEW MARKS GALLERY

☎ 212-243-0200; www.matthewmarks .com; 522 W 22nd St at Tenth Ave; admission free; ⏲ 10am-6pm Mon-Fri; ⊕ C, E to 23rd St; ♿

The trendsetter that started the push into Chelsea, Matthew Marks' two galleries (the second is at 523 W 24th St) were once factories. Now they are high-falutin' art houses with shows by the likes of Nan Goldin and Andreas Gursky.

☉ MUSEUM AT FIT

☎ 212-217-5800; www.fitnyc.edu; Seventh Ave at W 27th St; admission free; ⏲ noon-8pm Tue-Fri, 10am-5pm Sat; ⊕ 1 to 28th St

The Fashion Institute of Technology is a fashion, design and fine-arts school located on the edge of Manhattan's Fashion District. The best way for a visitor to access its unique riches is to visit its museum, which showcases rotating exhibits on fashion and style, including works by students. Its new permanent collection, opened in late 2005, is the country's first gallery of fashion and textile history; it displays rotating items from its collection of more than 50,000 garments and accessories dating from the 18th century to the present.

☉ PAUL KASMIN

☎ 212-563-4474; www.paulkasmin gallery.com; 293 Tenth Ave at W 27th St; admission free; ⏲ 10am-6pm Tue-Sat, 9am-5pm Mon-Fri Jul & Aug; ⊕ C, E to 23rd St; ♿

Expect the unexpected at Paul Kasmin. After all, the gallery does represent the legendary Frank Stella. All media are accepted here: collages, paintings, photography, sculptures and more. Shows at this gallery are wide-ranging, expansive and thought-provoking. There's a second branch at 511 W 27th St.

☉ RUBIN MUSEUM OF ART

☎ 212-620-5000; www.rmanyc.org; 150 W 17th St at Seventh Ave; admission free; ⏲ 11am-7pm Mon & Sat, to 5pm Wed, to 9pm Thu & Fri, to 6pm Sun; ⊕ 1 to 18th St

The first museum in the Western world dedicating itself to art of the Himalayas and surrounding regions, Rubin's got an impressive collection. You'll see embroidered textiles from China, metal sculptures from Tibet, Pakistani stone sculptures, intricate Bhutanese paintings and ritual objects and dance masks from various Tibetan regions, spanning from the 2nd to 19th centuries.

WHITE BOX
☎ 212-714-2347; www.whiteboxny.org; 525 W 26th St; admission free; ⏰ 11am-6pm Tue-Sat; ◎ C, E to 23rd St

White Box is an artists' collective that prides itself on showing socially relevant contemporary art. It features emerging artists as well as established creative types, and also runs the neighboring Annex, an internship program for young artists from all over the world. Expect to see diverse works in a range of mediums from international as well as local artists. Inside the same building are the Sara Meltzer Gallery and the George Adams Gallery.

SHOP

192 BOOKS Books
☎ 212-255-4022; 192 Tenth Ave btwn W 21st & W 22nd Sts; ⏰ 11am-7pm Tue-Sat, noon-6pm Sun & Mon; ◎ C, E to 23rd St

This small indie bookstore is located right in the gallery district, with sections on literature, history, travel, art and criticism. The

rotating art exhibits – during which the owners organize special displays of books which relate, thematically, to the featured show or artist – are a special treat.

AUTHENTIQUES PAST & PRESENT
Vintage Homewares, Curios
☎ 212-675-2179; 255 W 18th St btwn Seventh & Eighth Aves; ⏰ noon-6pm Wed-Sat, 1-6pm Sun; ◎ 1 to 18th St

Tucked on a quiet side street is this thoroughly dramatic and kitsch-filled vintage shop. Find groovy and colorful lamps from the '50s and '60s, pastel vases and cache pots, quirky barware, nostalgic cartoon figurines, glasses and flashy costume jewelry.

BALENCIAGA
Fashion & Accessories
☎ 212-206-0872; 522 W 22nd St at Eleventh Ave; ⏰ 10am-7pm Mon-Sat, noon-5pm Sun; ◎ C, E to 23rd St

Come and gaze at this cool, gray, Zen-like space. It's the gallery

---

ANTIQUES GARAGE FLEA MARKET

The weekend **Antiques Garage Flea Market** (112 W 25th St; ⏰ 7am-5pm Sat & Sun; ◎ 1 to 23rd St) is set in a two-level parking garage, with more than 100 vendors spreading their wares. Antique lovers shouldn't miss a browse here, as you'll find clothing, shoes, records, books, globes, furniture, rugs, lamps, glassware, paintings, artwork and many other relics from the past. If there's not enough here to keep you happy, catch the $1 shuttle to the affiliated Hell's Kitchen Flea Market in Midtown. Or head to the **Chelsea Outdoor Market** (Map p141; 29 W 25th St btwn Fifth & Sixth Aves; ⏰ 7am-5pm Sat & Sun; ◎ L, N, R, 4, 5, 6 to Union Sq) or the **17th Street Market** (W 17th St; ⏰ 7am-5pm Sat & Sun; ◎ L, N, R, 4, 5, 6 to Union Sq).

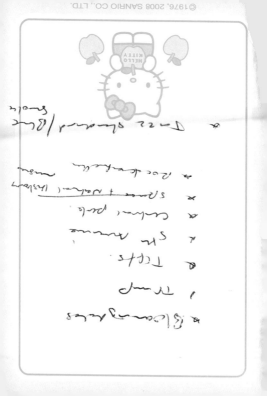

district's showcase, appropriately enough, for the artistic, post-apocalypse avant-garde styles of this French fashion house. Expect strange lines, goth patterns and pants for very skinny (and deep-pocketed) gals.

🛍 BARNEY'S CO-OP
Fashion & Accessories

☎ 212-593-7800; 236 W 18th St; ⏱ 11am-8pm Mon-Fri, to 7pm Sat, noon-6pm Sun; 🚇 1 to 18th St

The edgier, younger, less expensive version of Barneys (p187) has (relatively) affordable deals. At this expansive, loftlike space, with a spare, very selective inventory of clothing for men and women, plus shoes and cosmetics, the biannual warehouse sale (February and August) packs the place, both with endless merchandise and mobs of customers.

🍴 CHELSEA MARKET
Food & Drink, Market

www.chelseamarket.com; 75 Ninth Ave btwn W 15th & W 16th Sts; ⏱ 7am-9pm Mon-Sat, 10am-8pm Sun; 🚇 A, C, E, L to Eighth Ave-14th St

Gourmet-food fans will think they've died and entered the pearly gates once they've stepped into this 800ft-long shopping concourse bursting with some of the freshest eats in town. But Chelsea Market is part of a larger, million-sq-ft space that occupies a

Knead bread? Visit Amy's Bread at Chelsea Market

full city block, home to the Nabisco cookie factory in the 1930s (which created the Oreo cookie), and current home to the Food Network, Oxygen Network and the local NY1 news channel. There are more than 25 market food shops, including Amy's Bread, Fat Witch Brownies, the Lobster Place, Hale & Hearty Soup, Ronnybrook Farm Dairy and Frank's butcher shop. These shops are the prime draw for locals.

👞 GIRAUDON *Footwear*

☎ 212-633-0999; 152 Eighth Ave btwn W 17th & W 18th Sts; ⏱ 11:30am-7:30pm Mon-Wed & Fri-Sun, to 11pm Thu; 🚇 A, C, E, L to Eighth Ave-14th St

This small shoe boutique has been selling finely made leather foot >

NEIGHBORHOODS

CHELSEA

sculptures since way before the 'hood was hip. The designs are classic and have a touch of edginess, with both casual and glamorous options. It's a tiny space, but rarely crowded. The staffers are friendly and encouraging.

🏠 HOUSING WORKS THRIFT SHOP *Fashion & Accessories, Bric-a-Brac*

☎ 212-366-0820; 143 W 17th St; ⏲ 10am-6pm Mon-Sat, noon-5pm Sun; ⊕ 1 to 18th St

This shop, with its swank window displays, looks more boutique than thrift, but its selections of clothes, accessories, furniture and books are great value. All proceeds benefit the charity serving the city's HIV-positive and AIDS homeless communities.

🏠 LOEHMANN'S *Fashion & Accessories*

☎ 212-352-0856; www.loehmanns.com; 101 Seventh Ave at W 16th St; ⏲ 9am-9pm Mon-Sat, 11am-7pm Sun; ⊕ 1 to 18th St

A starting point for local hipsters looking for designer labels on the cheap (though some may not admit it), Loehmann's is a five-story department store that, it is said, inspired a wee-young Calvin Klein to make clothes. The original store of the successful chain is in the

Bronx; see the website for other locations.

🍴 EAT

🍴 202 *Pub Food* $$

☎ 646-638-3508; 75 Ninth Ave; ⏲ lunch & dinner; ⊕ 1 to 18th St; ♿ V ♿

Now you can shop until you drop... right into a seat at 202, a quasi British/Irish pub set right in the middle of Nicole Farhi's Chelsea Market Store (it's named after Farhi's original London restaurant). Shoppers browse around as you eat your bubble and squeak, fish 'n' chips or full English breakfast. Lunchtimes are busiest, but you can also just swing by the 202 entrance inside the market for counter service and a quick cup of joe (that's coffee in New York).

🍴 BUDDAKAN *Asian* $$$

☎ 646-989-6699; www.buddakannyc .com; 75 Ninth Ave; ⏲ lunch & dinner; ⊕ 1 to 18th St; ♿ V ♿

Get in early if you want to dine without having to shout to be heard – this cavernous space fills up fast and the buzz starts to get *loud*. Another great find in the Chelsea Market, Buddakan's decor is beyond strange: half movie-set, half banquet hall. But put together they produce a jaw-dropping effect. The Asian-fusion cuisine is heavy on seafood infused with delectable flavors and spices.

🍴 EL QUINTO PINO
Tapas $$

☎ 212-206-6900; 401 W 24th St; 🕐 lunch & dinner; 🚇 C, E to 23rd St; ♿ Ⓥ ♨

Trolling for tapas is easy enough in small-plate-crazy New York, but true aficionados of the Spanish treats are often disappointed. Not anymore. Now there's El Quinto Pino, a long narrow room ringed with 16 bar stools and no place else to sit; you'll have to lean on the bar like you're in Madrid and snack away on olives, anchovies, sautéed and garlicky shrimp, mini *paninis* (sandwiches), cod sticks, calamari and more. If you must sit down, the owners also run **Tia Pol** (205 Tenth Ave) around the corner; same great food, but with a wee bit more space.

🍴 EMPIRE DINER *Diner* $

☎ 212-243-2736; www.theempirediner .com; 210 Tenth Ave; 🕐 24hr; 🚇 C, E to 23rd St; Ⓥ ♨

Housed in a restored silver Pullman car, Empire Diner has a lot of wacky charm, mostly thanks to the occasional odd character who sits at the counter eating pie. Can't really blame 'em – the pie, burgers, salads and heaping, fat omelettes

are delicious, and all types swing by for a bite.

🍴 GREEN TABLE
Organic $$

☎ 212-741-9174; http://cleaverco.com; 75 Ninth Ave; 🕐 lunch & dinner daily, closed Sun Jun-Aug; 🚇 C, E, L, 1, 2, 3 to Eighth Ave-14th St; Ⓥ ♨

Another treat tucked inside the Chelsea Market, Green Table uses only organic, local fare trucked in daily from upstate Satur Farms. All the meat, eggs and dairy products are from grass-raised, free-range animals and the many veggie options studding the menu will seduce you with their fresh taste. Menus change daily.

FAST FOOD THAT'S GOOD FOOD

Fuel your night of dancing and drinking with some Belgian street snacks, made fresh and delicious at **F&B** (☎ 646-486-4441; 269 W 23rd St btwn Seventh & Eighth Aves; 🕐 lunch & dinner; 🚇 C, E to 23rd St). This sliver of a fast-food joint, with seating limited to high stools and brushed-steel counters, doles out steamed dogs in options including beef, pork, chicken and soy, and toppings that range from the classic relish and sauerkraut to cheese, bacon, salsa and coleslaw. Other perky menu items include lobster rolls, Swedish meatballs and, of course, the source of the name's acronym: *frites* and beignets.

🍽 KLEE BRASSERIE
Brasserie $$

☎ 212-633-8033; 200 Ninth Ave btwn W 22nd & W 23rd Sts; 🕙 dinner; 🚇 C, E to 23rd St; **V** ♿

As you'd expect from the name, this brasserie is whimsical and fun with a slight sparkle of romance – and decidedly low-fuss. The open kitchen dishes up wholesome, fresh ingredients: a starter salad matches crisp chicory and chanterelle mushrooms with a slow-poached egg, while chicken gets spiced with licorice, and risotto is studded with shrimp and lemon. The thoroughly unique herbivore option packs a wide-mouthed jelly jar with a cornucopia of seasonal veggies and a healthy heaping of quinoa.

🍽 OMAI *Vietnamese* $

☎ 212-633-0550; 158 Ninth Ave btwn W 19th & W 20th Sts; 🕙 dinner; 🚇 A, C, E to 14th St

Serving Vietnamese delights in a romantic cubbyhole, Omai has cultivated a following for its wok-seared monkfish with peanuts, chili and basil served over sesame rice crackers, crispy rice crepes with shrimp, chicken and bean sprouts, and unexpected combos like grilled shrimp on sugarcane with angel-hair pasta and peanut sauce.

Succumb to the wacky Pullman-car charms of Empire Diner (p135)

DRINK

BAR VELOCE *Bar*

☎ 212-629-5300; 176 Seventh Ave near W 20th St; ⏱ 5pm-3am; ⊕ C, E to 23rd St

Sip your wine, eat a few *paninis*, watch the well-dressed world walk by, or strike up a conversation with an interesting stranger (or two). What could be better than that? Small and friendly Bar Veloce caters to a fairly sophisticated crowd that likes wine and a few laughs at the end of a hard day.

CHELSEA BREWING COMPANY *Pub*

☎ 212-336-6440; Chelsea Piers, Pier 59, W Side Highway at W 23rd St; ⏱ noon-midnight; ⊕ C, E to 23rd St

Enjoy a quality microbrew, waterside, in the expansive outdoor area of this way-west beer haven – a perfect place to re-enter the world after a day of swimming, golfing or rock climbing as a guest at the Chelsea Piers Complex (p127).

GLASS *Bar*

☎ 212-904-1580; 287 Tenth Ave at W 26th St; ⏱ 9pm-4am Wed-Sat; ⊕ C, E to 23rd St

Lots of translucent tiles, bar stools and table tops edged with bright pinks and blues give this glassy bar its name – or maybe it's from the slick crowd. Either way, the cocktails are the big draw: strong

and varied, ranging from blue martinis to deep-green caipirinhas and pretty pink cosmos. It has a small dance floor and sometimes a $10 cover at the door, but the egalitarian entrance policy won't leave you waiting in line for hours.

HALF KING *Pub*

☎ 212-462-4300; 505 W 23rd St at Tenth Ave; ⏱ 11am-4am Mon-Fri, 9am-4am Sat & Sun; ⊕ C, E to 23rd St

A unique marriage of cozy pub and sophisticated writers' lair, you'll often experience top-notch literary readings in this wood-accented, candlelit watering hole. Its myriad seating-area options are bound to provide one that will seduce you – particularly during warm weather, when a front sidewalk café, main indoor room, cozy back section and mellow backyard patio are all open for business.

PARK *Bar*

☎ 212-352-3313; 118 Tenth Ave near W 17th St; ⏱ 11am-2am Mon-Wed, to 4am Thu-Sun; ⊕ A, C, E, L to Eighth Ave-14th St

There are plenty of places to get lost in the Park – a sprawling, old-fashioned hangout with a big front room, an even bigger back garden (open year round), an even more cavernous red room (filled with sexy red Chinese lanterns), an airy atrium to drink in, and even a glass-covered rooftop with a hot tub. The garden really looks like an urban park, and there are even a few pretend deer scattered about. The crowd is a varied mix of art-world professionals and fashionistas.

⭐ PLAY

⭐ 1OAK Club
☎ 212-242-1111; 453 W 17th St; cover charge $10-25; ☽ 10pm-4am Tue-Sat; ◉ A, C, E, L to Eighth Ave-14th St

Part Nordic hunting lodge and part Moroccan hookah lounge, this celebrity favorite has a DJ spinning house and techno tunes, a roaring corner fireplace and bottle service at tables, and it stays packed into the wee hours.

⭐ CAIN Club
☎ 212-947-8000; www.cainnyc.com; 544 W 27th St; cover charge $20; ☽ 10pm-4am Mon-Sat; ◉ C, E to 23rd St

Plenty of wanna-be partiers would commit fratricide for a glimpse of the safari-themed interior of Cain, known for its rather hoity-toity entrance policies as much as for its wild dancing, a DJ booth carved out of a boulder, and live drummers accompanying the funk, house and rock music. Don't miss a Tuesday night if you're a fan of celeb sightings, but be prepared

to work some magic at the door if you want to get in.

⭐ EAGLE NYC Club
☎ 646-473-1866; www.eaglenyc.com; 555 W 28th St btwn Tenth & Eleventh Aves; cover charge $10; ☽ 10pm-4am Mon-Sat; ◉ C, E to 23rd St

A bi-level club full of hot men in leather, the Eagle is the choice for out and proud fetishists. Its two levels plus roof deck leave plenty of room for dancing and drinking, which are done with abandon at the Eagle. Thursdays are 'code' nights, meaning everyone must meet the dress code (wear leather, or nothing at all). Located in a renovated 19th-century stable, the inside joke is that 'the studs keep coming.'

⭐ HOME Club
☎ 212-273-3700; 532 W 27th St near Tenth Ave; cover charge $20; ☽ 10pm-4am Tue-Sun; ◉ C, E to 23rd St, 1 to 28th St

Most homes aren't multilevel, cavernous spaces with dark leather couches lining nearly every wall and eerily lit passageways taking you from nook to nook, but maybe that's a growing trend. Either way, there's lots to make you feel comfortable at Home – ample seating and space, and deep electronic, funk and pop coming from the live DJ. Sometimes the doors between Home and the neighboring club Guesthouse are opened and you can pass from one to the other.

✪ JOYCE THEATER *Arts*
☎ 212-242-0800; www.joyce.org; 175 Eighth Ave; ⏰ hours vary; ⊙ C, E to 23rd St, A, C, E to Eighth Ave-14th St, 1 to 18th St

An offbeat, intimate venue in Chelsea with clean sight lines from every corner, the Joyce is blessed with annual visits from Merce Cunningham and Pilobolus dance companies, comfortably seen from any of the renovated theater's 470 seats.

✪ MARQUEE *Club*
☎ 646-473-0202; 289 Tenth Ave btwn W 26th & W 27th Sts; cover charge $20; ⏰ 11pm-4am Wed-Sat; ⊙ C, E to 23rd St

Glamorous masses and a fair share of A-listers try to slip past the vel-

vet ropes to get inside, where DJs spin electronica, house and funk all night long. Be prepared to wait to get in unless the doorman takes a shine to you or you are simply born lucky.

✪ PINK ELEPHANT *Club*
☎ 212-463-0000; 527 W 27th St; cover charge $20; ⏰ 5pm-4am Wed-Sat; ⊙ C, E to 23rd St

Low ceilings, pink and blue lighting and a dance-happy crowd mix well at the Pink Elephant. From the outside it doesn't appear like much (you'll know you're there when you spot a twirling pink elephant on the door, looking like a drug-crazed Disney character), but the inside's cozier, with benches and chandeliers sprouting everywhere.

>UNION SQUARE, FLATIRON DISTRICT & GRAMERCY PARK

A mid-sized public plaza that's the preferred location for community-led vigils, demonstrations and celebrations, busy, bustling Union Sq is the heartbeat of the city's activist movement. It's also home to the city's best-known greenmarket, a popular weekend shopping choice for New Yorkers.

Gramercy Park, a small stretch of neighborhood just northeast of Union Sq, couldn't be more different. Where Union Sq is egalitarian, Gramercy is exclusive. The tony, brownstone-filled nabe is full of old money and great restaurants, and is dominated by its own lush and beautiful gated park (to be used only by the wealthy few who live on its perimeter).

In contrast, the Flatiron District, directly north of Union Sq, has become a de facto shopping street, full of big-name department stores, such as Home Depot and ABC Carpet & Home.

These three enclaves together are a practical yet wealthy neighborhood that has more than its share of big and expensive restaurants.

UNION SQUARE, FLATIRON DISTRICT & GRAMERCY PARK

◉ SEE
Flatiron Building **1** B4
Madison Square Park **2** B3
Museum of Sex **3** B3
National Arts Club **4** C5
Union Square **5** C6
Union Square
   Greenmarket ....(see 5)

⌂ SHOP
ABC Carpet & Home **6** C5
Chelsea Outdoor
   Market **7** B3
Discorama Annex **8** C5

Filene's Basement **9** C6
Stardust Antiques **10** D4

⎘ EAT
15 East **11** B6
Blue Smoke **12** C3
Chocolate by the Bald
   Man **13** C6
Curry in a Hurry **14** D3
Hill Country **15** A3
Shake Shack **16** C4
Union Square
   Café **17** C5

▼ DRINK
Flatiron Lounge **18** B5
Gallery at the
   Gershwin **19** B3
Living Room at
   W Hotel **20** C5
Pete's Tavern **21** D5
Underbar ....(see 20)

★ PLAY
718 Sessions at Club
   Deep 22 A4
Irving Plaza 23 C6
Karaoke One 7 .... 24 C5

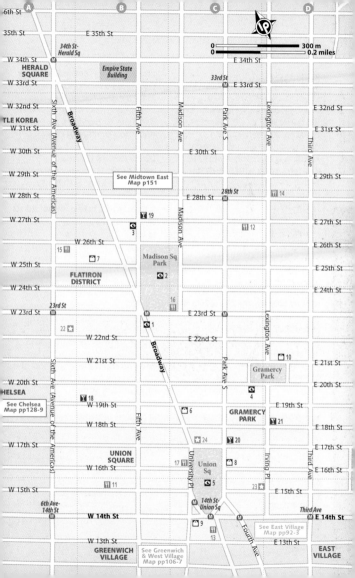

SEE

FLATIRON BUILDING
Broadway, cnr Fifth Ave & 23rd St; N, R, 6 **to 23rd St**
It's a three-dimensional triangle brought to life: the Flatiron building is a 22-story limestone and terra-cotta structure that was known as 'Burnham's Folly' when it was built in 1902 (after architect Daniel Burnham). Skeptical residents doubted that its odd ironlike shape would hold up. Six feet across at its narrowest point, it's now the defining landmark of the neighborhood.

MADISON SQUARE PARK
www.nycgovparks.org; 23rd to 26th Sts btwn Broadway & Madison Ave; 6am-1am; N, R, 6 **to 23rd St;**
You can visit this cute little spot in the Flatiron District for the elegant statues, free summer art programs and the playground for kids. Or you can be like everyone

else and come for the **Shake Shack** (☎ 212-989-6600; www.shakeshack.com; 23rd St & Madison Ave; 11am-11pm), an environmentally friendly food kiosk that's turned the park's south end into a dining hot spot.

MUSEUM OF SEX
☎ 212-689-6337; www.museumofsex.com; 233 Fifth Ave; **adult $14.50, senior & student $13.50;** 11am-6:30pm Sun-Fri, to 8pm Sat (last tickets sold 45min before closing); N, R, 6 **to 28th St**
You do have to be over 18 to visit this museum, but there's nothing particularly illicit about it (sorry, folks). Its mission is more to educate than to titillate, and permanent collections showcase America's various sexual revolutions, from burlesque to gay rights. Some of its visiting and online exhibits are a bit racier, and you can leave with a top-of-the-line sex toy, courtesy of the museum gift store.

GREENMARKETS
Also known as farmers markets, these open-air shopping sprees aim to increase awareness of locally grown produce, mostly from the Hudson Valley. The **Union Square Greenmarket** (17th St btwn Broadway & Park Ave S; Mon, Wed, Fri & Sat 10am-6pm) is arguably the most famous, and attracts many of the city's top chefs to its stalls to finger aromatic greens, fresh yellow corn and deep orange squashes. But there are many other greenmarkets around the city on any given day. For more information visit the website of the **Council of the Environment of New York City** (☎ 212-788-7476; www.cenyc.org), which has been organizing the greenmarkets since 1976.

The prow of the Flatiron Building seems set to sail up Broadway

NATIONAL ARTS CLUB

☎ 212-475-3424; 15 Gramercy Park S;
🚇 6 to 23rd St

Boasting a beautiful, vaulted, stained-glass ceiling above its wooden bar, this club was designed by Calvert Vaux, one of the creators of Central Park. The space holds free art exhibitions, ranging from sculpture to photography. These exhibitions are sometimes open to the public from 1pm to 5pm.

UNION SQUARE

17th St btwn Broadway & Park Ave S;
🚇 L, N, Q, R, W, 4, 5, 6 to 14th St-Union Sq

A former 'needle' park opened in 1831, Union Sq has become syn-onymous with protests – starting with the nation's first Labor Day gathering in 1882 and continuing into the present. But the little park was named not for its strong union activities (many labor groups, including the American Civil Liberties Union, Communist and Socialist parties and Ladies' Garment Workers Union set up offices on its outskirts), but because it was at the 'union' of Broadway and Bowery. It's now home to a fabulous greenmarket (see opposite), several statues (including George Washington *and* Mahatma Gandhi), public works of art, and – after a facelift on the north end – a new restaurant and playground.

Union Square (p143), a little park with a long history

🛍 SHOP

🛍 ABC CARPET & HOME
Homewares
☎ 212-473-3000; 888 Broadway;
🕙 10am-8pm Mon-Thu, to 6:30pm Fri &
Sat, noon-6pm Sun; Ⓜ L, N, Q, R, W, 4, 5,
6 to 14th St-Union Sq
North of Union Sq there is a
plethora of home-furnishing
stores: besides the museumlike
ABC Carpet & Home, there are
numerous other interior design/
furnishing options stretching all
the way up to 23rd St. ABC's six
stories are filled with home goods,
small and large, including easy-
to-pack knick-knacks, designer
jewelry, global gifts and more
bulky antique furnishings and
carpets. Come Christmas season,
the shop is a joy to behold, as the

decorators go all out with lights
and other wondrous touches.

🛍 DISCORAMA ANNEX *Music*
☎ 212-260-8616; 40 Union Sq E btwn
E 16th & E 17th Sts; 🕙 8:30am-6:15pm
Mon-Fri, 10am-6pm Sat, 11am-5:45pm
Sun; Ⓜ L, N, Q, R, W, 4, 5, 6 to 14th
St-Union Sq
Eschew the violent red glare of the
Virgin Megastore looming over
Union Sq's south end and instead
shop for your CDs and DVDs at
Discorama Annex, a self-professed
'CD and DVD store of the new mil-
lennium and beyond.'

🛍 FILENE'S BASEMENT *Mall*
☎ 212-348-0169; 4 Union Sq; 🕙 9am-
10pm Mon-Sat, 11am-8pm Sun; Ⓜ L, N,
Q, R, W, 4, 5, 6 to 14th St-Union Sq

This outpost of the Boston-based chain is not actually in a basement, but instead three flights up in the small strip mall that's sprouted up at the south end of Union Sq (around the Whole Foods supermarket). Fashionistas willing to conduct painstaking explorations could unearth treasures, including apparel from Dolce & Gabbana, Michael Kors and Versace, among others. On the floors below you'll find cheap chain stores, with the exception of Whole Foods, which is always packed.

🏛 STARDUST ANTIQUES
Antiques, Jewelry
☎ 212-677-2590; www.stardust antiques.com; 38 Gramercy Park; ⌚ noon-7pm Mon-Sat, to 6pm Sun; ◉ N, R, 6 to 23rd St

If you have found the perfect life partner, you need the perfect ring. Check out the antique collection of 19th-century, Edwardian and art deco wedding bands and engagement rings at Stardust. Even if you're not the marrying kind, a beautiful tear-drop sapphire bauble makes a nice memento. The rambling, eclectic shop with enchanting rooms, myriad paintings, furnishings and accessories is fun to visit, even if you're not ready to get hitched.

🍴 EAT

🍴 15 EAST *Sushi* $$
☎ 212-647-0015; www.15eastrestaurant .com; 15 E 15th St; ⌚ lunch & dinner Mon-Sat; ◉ L, N, Q, R, W, 4, 5, 6 to 14th St-Union Sq; Ⓥ

Traditional-sushi lovers rejoice: this is your spot. The large, geometric lights that look like massive paper lanterns and sleek, minimalist interior (done in dark brown and creamy white with red flourishes) will transport you right to Japan. Chef Masato Shimizu relies on daily shipments of fresh fish (such as silverfish, salmon, all sorts of yellowtail, mackerel and eel) flown in from his native island to make his delectable sushi and sashimi.

🍴 BLUE SMOKE
Southern, BBQ $$
☎ 212-447-7733; www.bluesmoke.com; 116 E 27th St; ⌚ lunch & dinner; ◉ 6 to 28th St; ♿ 👶

Lunchtime and early afternoon is your best chance of sneaking in without a wait; Blue Smoke gets busy at night. Downstairs is a bustling jazz club, but the upstairs – spacious and good for groups and children – is where most of the action is. Belly up for old-fashioned appetizers such as hush puppies or mac 'n' cheese, or go straight for the good stuff:

Texas beef brisket, organic grilled chicken, Kansas City spareribs (sweet), Memphis baby back ribs (lean), Texas salt-n-pepper ribs (smoky and hot) or try them all in the rib sampler.

🍴 CHOCOLATE BY THE BALD MAN *American Eclectic* $
☎ 212-388-0030; www.maxbrenner.com; 841 Broadway; ⏰ 8am-midnight Mon-Wed, to 2am Thu-Sat, 9am-midnight Sun; ⊕ L, N, Q, R, W, 4, 5, 6 to 14th St-Union Sq
Sweet-toothed Aussie Max Brenner brought his chocolate empire to Union Sq, and his wildly popular café-cum-chocolate-bar, looking from the outside like a gingerbread house, is all the rage.

CURRY HILL
It's not exactly politically correct, but a small four-block section north of Union Sq and Gramercy, traditionally known as Murray Hill, is sometimes also referred to as Curry Hill – a nod to the numerous Indian restaurants, shops and delis that proliferate here. Starting around E 28th St and flowing north on Lexington Ave to about E 33rd St, you'll find some of the finest Indian eateries in town – and most at bargain prices. The all-time local fave? **Curry in a Hurry** (☎ 212-683-0900; 119 Lexington Ave at E 28th St; ⏰ lunch & dinner; ⊕ 6 to 28th St). It's not fancy, but even Bono of U2 fame has been spotted having a nosh here.

Besides the sweets he's got a full menu (great breakfast) and also does low-cal variations mixed by hand on the spot. Divine!

🍴 HILL COUNTRY
American BBQ $$
☎ 212-255-4544; 30 W 26th btwn Broadway & Sixth Ave; ⏰ lunch & dinner; ⊕ N, R, W to 28th St
It's all about the sausage, fatty brisket, beef shoulder and pork ribs cooked Texas-style at Hill Country – named for the area between Austin and San Antonio. You can eat your meat – with sides of smoky baked beans and butter-drenched biscuits – in the large main room dotted with stacks of freshly split wood and brick walls, or drop into the basement for some live honky-tonk music. There are Sunday football games on the big screens and a hoppin' bar that stays open till 2am.

🍴 UNION SQUARE CAFÉ
American $$
☎ 212-243-4020; http://unionsquarecafe.com; 21 E 16th St; ⏰ lunch & dinner; ⊕ L, N, Q, R, W, 4, 5, 6 to 14th St-Union Sq; ♿ 🚹
Chef Danny Meyer, whose name has become synonymous with Union Sq, kicked off his career at this café 20 years ago, and hasn't looked back since. This trendy parkside café keeps pulling in

locals and visitors alike, thanks to stalwart dishes like seared foie gras on toasted brioche, fried calamari with spicy anchovy mayo, black bean soup with lemon sherry, braised rabbit with homemade pasta, caramelized onion risotto and a house favorite, spaghettini with flaked halibut, chili, garlic and white wine sauce.

DRINK

FLATIRON LOUNGE *Bar*
☎ 212-727-7741; 37 W 19th St btwn Fifth & Sixth Aves; ⏰ 5pm-2am Sun-Wed, to 4am Thu-Sat; ◉ F, N, R, V, W to 23rd St
A simple nook with a classic vibe, this mahogany bar from 1927 serves up specialty cocktails made with fresh, seasonal ingredients (pomegranate, Granny Smith apples, mint, lychee nuts) in a setting that's historic and retro, decorated with red-leather booths and stained-glass lamps. The dramatic entrance, a low-lit archway, only adds to the elegant excitement.

GALLERY AT THE GERSHWIN *DJ Bar*
☎ 212-447-5700; Gershwin Hotel, 7 E 27th St btwn Fifth & Madison Aves; ⏰ 6pm-midnight; ◉ F, N, R, V, W to 23rd St
A convenient perk for those bedding down at this hip, budget

hotel is that it's not only a cool destination, but also a sure bet for meeting other globetrotters, solo travelers especially. Either way, stop in and relax on one of the high-backed red banquettes and enjoy the vibe – artistic (huge paintings grace the walls), mellow (lounge DJs set the vibe) and clever (cocktails named after luminaries from Pablo Neruda to Jean-Michel Basquiat).

LIVING ROOM AT W HOTEL *Lounge Bar*
☎ 212-353-8345; 201 Park Ave S at E 17th St; ⏰ 7am-midnight; ◉ L, N, Q, R, W, 4, 5, 6 to 14th St-Union Sq
Mossy green walls, 16ft arch windows, fantastic Union Sq views and wavy metallic installations define the Living Room, a laid-back but well-heeled ground-floor lounge at W Hotel. Drinks are crisp and costly, and you can order nibbles from Todd English's on-site restaurant, Olives.

PETE'S TAVERN *Pub*
☎ 212-473-7676; 129 E 18th St at Irving Pl; ⏰ noon-2am; ◉ L, N, Q, R, W, 4, 5, 6 to 14th St-Union Sq
This dark and atmospheric watering hole has all the earmarks of a New York classic – all pressed tin and carved wood and an air of literary history. You can get a respectable burger here, and choose from more than 15 draft beers. The

NEIGHBORHOODS

UNION SQUARE, FLATIRON DISTRICT & GRAMERCY PARK

Beer for all at Pete's Tavern (p147)

pub draws in everyone from post-theater couples and Irish expats to no-nonsense NYU students. *Gift of the Magi* author O Henry used to drink here.

Y UNDERBAR *Bar*

☎ 212-358-1560; www.mocbars.com; 201 Park Ave S; ⏱ 4pm-2am; ⊕ L, N, Q, R, W, 4, 5, 6 to 14th St-Union Sq

Deep in the basement of the W Hotel Union Square is the Underbar, a dark and sexy hangout for wealthy youngsters and 30-somethings. There's so little light it's hard to know who you're talking to, but that doesn't seem to deter the friendly clientele.

⭐ PLAY

⭐ 718 SESSIONS AT CLUB DEEP *Club*

☎ 212-229-2000; 16 W 22nd St btwn Fifth & Sixth Aves; cover charge $20; ⏱ 11pm-4am Tue-Sat; ⊕ F, V, R, W to 23rd St (W Sat & Sun only)

Legendary DJ Danny Krivit has built quite a following with his traveling party known as 718 Sessions. It's a riot of old-school dancing as Krivit spins soulful house music. He moves from club to club; check out www.dannykrivit .net to catch his act while you're in town, or swing by Club Deep, where Krivit and house DJ Marc Anthony can be found rocking the dance floor.

⭐ IRVING PLAZA *Live Music*

☎ 212-777-6800; 17 Irving Pl at E 15th St; admission $12-35; ⏱ 7pm-midnight Tue-Sat; ⊕ L, N, Q, R, W, 4, 5, 6 to 14th St-Union Sq

An old-time hall, Irving Plaza has shows that run the gamut, from classic hard rock to emo to punk (sometimes in the same night, depending on who's opening for whom). U2, Prince, Rufus Wainwright and others have played here. A nonprofit organization hands out free condoms at the door, and some proceeds from ticket sales go toward AIDS initiatives in developing nations.

⭐ **KARAOKE ONE 7** *Karaoke*
☎ 212-675-3527; http://karaoke17.com; 29 W 17th St; 🕐 4pm-4am, happy hour 2-7pm; 🚇 L, N, Q, R, W, 4, 5, 6 to 14th St-Union Sq

If you can remember the song name, you can sing it at Karaoke One 7, which has more than 800,000 titles (and that includes songs in French, Spanish and Tagalog). Join the happy mix of Japanese businessmen, overstimulated NYU students and after-work corporate types blowing off steam. There's a limited bar menu, but you can also bring in food from outside.

>MIDTOWN EAST

Better pack a protein bar for any visit to Midtown East – this fluid space ranges from the Empire State Building at W 34th St to the edge of Central Park at W 59th St and is jam packed with classic New York sights.

Shoppers will revel in the opulence along Fifth Ave, where Prada, Ferragamo, Bulgari and more surround Trump Tower, and just a few blocks east, moneyed Park Ave brings you to the gilded door of a still stunning art deco masterpiece: the Waldorf Astoria Hotel.

You've also got the Chrysler Building, Grand Central Terminal, Rockefeller Center and the UN to explore, not to mention ritzy Sutton Pl, a mini-community of lucky New Yorkers who live along the East River Esplanade from 54th to 59th Sts. The views of the Queensboro Bridge and the East River are amazing – just make sure you've got the stamina to get there.

MIDTOWN EAST

☺ SEE

☐ SHOP

▥ EAT

▾ DRINK

▦ PLAY

◉ SEE

◉ CHRYSLER BUILDING

405 Lexington Ave at E 42nd St; ⏱ **lobby 9am-7pm;** ◉ **any train to Grand Central-42nd St**

Feast your eyes on the gorgeous silver spire that most New Yorkers identify as their favorite city symbol. No observation deck here, but the iconic Chrysler Building's art deco lobby and chic wood elevators are sights unto themselves.

◉ EMPIRE STATE BUILDING

☎ **212-736-3100; www.esbnyc.com; 350 Fifth Ave at W 34th St; adult/child under 12/under 18 $18/8/16;** ⏱ **9:30am-midnight;** ◉ **B, D, F, N, Q, R, V, W to 34th St-Herald Sq**

The tallest building in New York, this 102-floor steel and brick monster is a sight to behold – and its sunset views of the city are equally stunning. Be prepared to stand in line and expect tight security (hint: buy and print tickets online and you can cut your wait in half). Since 1976 the building's top 30 floors have been floodlit in seasonal and holiday colors (eg green for St Patrick's Day in March, black for World AIDS Day on December 1, red and green for Christmas, and lavender for Gay Pride weekend in June; visit the website for each day's lighting scheme and meaning). As of research time the 86th-floor Observatory tickets could be bought online, but tickets to the 102nd-floor deck could only be bought on site.

◉ GRAND CENTRAL TERMINAL

☎ **212-340-2210; www.grandcentral terminal.com; Park Ave at 42nd St;** ⏱ **5:30am-1:30am;** ◉ **any train to Grand Central-42nd St**

The world's largest and busiest train station (76 acres; 500,000 commuters and subway riders daily) is also a gorgeous feat of engineering and architecture. Take in the theatrical beaux-art facade from E 42nd St, particularly luminous at night, and then head inside to marvel at gold-veined marble arches and the bright blue domed ceiling, decorated with twinkling fiber-optic constellations. Don't miss the tiny unrenovated corner of the original ceiling, left alone to acknowledge the size of the job. For a glimpse of how the unfinished ceiling looks underneath all the celestial glitter, find the northwest corner amid the 88,000-sq-ft ceiling, at the very end of the meridian line, and you'll see a small black patch that designers deliberately left there for contrast. Grand Central has an upscale food market, stocked with luxurious delicacies and gourmet goodies like caviar, fine wine and cheese, fresh fish and organic produce.

☉ NEW YORK PUBLIC LIBRARY

☎ 212-930-0800; www.nypl.org; Fifth Ave at W 42nd St; ⏰ 11am-7:30pm Tue-Wed, 10am-6pm Thu-Sat; ⊕ any train to Grand Central-42nd St or Times Sq-42nd St; &

Visit this 1911 beaux arts beauty while you can – it will shortly kick off a massive renovation slated to end around 2014. Not much will change on the outside, but a new name will get carved into its stone facade when work is finished. The NYPL is slated to become the Stephen A Schwarzman Library, named after the billionaire hedge funder who made a $100-million donation toward renovations.

But the NYPL's molded ceilings, graceful bay windows and ancient staircases won't change, nor will its world-class exhibits of rare and out-of-print books. Patience and Fortitude, the two great lions who greet you at the library steps, aren't going anywhere either.

☉ RADIO CITY MUSIC HALL

☎ 212-247-4777; www.radiocity.com; W 51st St at Sixth Ave; admission to hall free, shows $15-40; ⊕ B, D, F, V to 47th-50th Sts-Rockefeller Center

This 6000-seat art deco movie palace had a triumphant restoration, returning the velvet seats and furnishings to their original 1932 state. Concerts here sell out

Creep past Patience and Fortitude at the New York Public Library

TOP OF THE ROCK OBSERVATION DECK

It's not quite as famous as the Empire State Building, but the views from the top of Rockefeller Center are equally dazzling. **Top of the Rock** (☎ 212-698-2000; www.topoftherocknyc .com; 30 Rockefeller Plaza, entrance on W 50th St btwn Fifth & Sixth Aves; ⏰ 8am-midnight, last elevator at 11pm; ◉ B, D, F to 47th-50th Sts-Rockefeller Center) also has a pre-show on the mezzanine level to entertain you between elevator rides (those elevators, by the way, are super fast and full of neon blue flashing lights, just for a little extra stimulation). The multimedia show talks about the center's history and the legacy of the Rockefellers, and gives you a chance to take a Beam Walk – a simulated example of the narrow steel beams the original Rockefeller construction workers trod every day without harnesses, even at 850ft above the city.

quickly, and tickets to the annual Christmas spectacular featuring the hokey but enjoyable Rockette dancers now cost up to $70. You can see the interior by taking a tour, which leaves every half-hour between 11am and 3pm Monday to Sunday. Tickets are sold on a first-come, first-served basis.

◉ ROCKEFELLER CENTER

☎ 212-632-3975; www.rockefeller center.com; btwn Fifth & Sixth Aves & 48th & 51st Sts; ⏰ 24hr, times vary for individual stores; ◉ B, D, F, V to 47th-50th Sts-Rockefeller Center

Built in the 1930s, during the height of the Great Depression in the USA, the 22-acre center gave jobs to 70,000 workers over nine years – and employed many artists who sculpted, painted and otherwise created the numerous works of public art that dot the space, making it an art deco delight. The

skating rink is a winter highlight, as is the annual Christmas-tree lighting, but summer sizzles too, as salsa, rock and pop bands take over the space for nightly shows. You can browse the shops and restaurants or take a guided tour of Rockefeller Center. Tours are also given of NBC studios, and you can join the throngs outside every morning if you want to be in the background of a *Today Show* taping.

◉ ST PATRICK'S CATHEDRAL

☎ 212-753-2261; www.ny-archdiocese .org/pastoral/cathedral_about.html; Fifth Ave btwn 50th & 51st Sts; ⏰ 7am-8:45pm; ◉ V to Fifth Ave-53rd St, 4, 6 to Lexington Ave-53rd St; ♿

Check out the 330ft spires that dwarf everything in the Midtown neighborhood surrounding St Patrick's, including nearby Rockefeller Center. This graceful cathedral, done in Gothic Revival style, is the seat of New York's Roman Catholic Archdiocese, and is used for every major city ceremony.

☉ UNITED NATIONS

☎ 212-963-8687; www.un.org; E 46th St & First Ave; tours adult/child $14/7; ☼ tours every 45min from 9:45am-4:45pm, call for tours in other languages; ☻ any train to Grand Central-42nd St; ♿ Like a time capsule dug up 40 years after it was buried, the UN is dated, a wee bit irrelevant, and yet somehow captivating. There are guided tours given daily, but you need to call to book ahead, as sales are limited and sometimes sell out early, and opening hours subject to change. Even in all its fusty, musty 1960s glory, there's no denying the aura of intrigue inside the green-glass Le Corbusier buildings that were built in 1953.

🛍 SHOP

🛍 BLOOMINGDALE'S
Department Store

☎ 212-705-2000; www.bloomingdales .com; 1000 Third Ave at E 59th St; ☼ 10am-8:30pm Mon-Thu, 9am-10pm Fri & Sat, 11am-7pm Sun; ☻ 4, 5, 6 to 59th St, N, R, W to 59th St-Lexington Ave It's big and brash and full of attitude – beloved Bloomie's is

Bloomingdale's is brash, beloved and BIG

where New Yorkers go to get a major shopping fix. While the store carries plenty of high-end names, it also likes to bring in new designers and right-off-the-runway collections that won't break the bank.

🏠 **CALVIN KLEIN**
Fashion & Accessories, Homewares
☎ 212-292-9000; www.calvinklein.com; 654 Madison Ave at E 60th St; 🕙 10am-6pm Mon-Sat, noon-6pm Sun; 🚇 4, 5, 6 to 59th St, N, R, W to 59th St-Lexington Ave

Calvin Klein's signature lines fill his flagship Madison Ave store from top to almost the bottom (the lower floor is dedicated to a surprisingly detailed collection of houseware items, from lamps to linens). On the other floors, you can outfit yourself from head to toe – Calvin Klein sells it all, in materials ranging from denim to lizard skin.

🏠 **DIOR** *Fashion & Accessories*
☎ 212-931-2950; www.dior.com; 21 E 57th St near Madison Ave; 🕙 10am-

TOP FIVE ON FIFTH AVENUE

Starting at 59th St and Fifth Ave and heading south, you'll immediately see names like **Trump Towers Galleries** (725 Fifth Ave), **Tiffany's** (727 Fifth Ave), **Louis Vuitton** (1 E 57th St at Fifth Ave) and **Prada** (724 Fifth Ave), but here are five standout shops you don't want to miss.

Bergdorf Goodman (☎ 212-753-7300; www.bergdorfgoodman.com; 754 Fifth Ave; 🕙 10am-7pm Mon-Wed & Fri, 10am-8pm Thu, noon-8pm Sun; 🚇 N, R, W to Fifth Ave, F to 57th St) An otherworldly experience, with separate floors for jewels, fragrance, handbags, menswear, shoes and more, gives you room to browse unhurriedly.

Henri Bendel (☎ 212-247-1100; www.henribendel.com; 712 Fifth Ave; 🕙 10am-7pm Mon-Wed & Fri-Sun, to 8pm Thu; 🚇 E, V to Fifth Ave-53rd St, N, R, W to 59th St-Lexington Ave) The lovely Lalique windows in Henri Bendel frame its quaint little tearoom perfectly; it makes you feel like you're shopping in someone's home.

Jimmy Choo (☎ 212-593-0800; www.jimmychoo.com; 645 Fifth Ave; 🕙 10am-6pm Mon-Sat, noon-5pm Sun; 🚇 E, V to Fifth Ave-53rd St, 6 to 51st St) Sky-high stilettos, sandals and boots galore.

Saks Fifth Ave (☎ 212-753-4000; www.saksfifthavenue.com; 611 Fifth Ave at 50th St; 🕙 10am-8pm Mon-Fri, 10am-7pm Sat, noon-7pm Sun; 🚇 B, D, F, V to 47th-50th Sts-Rockefeller Center, E, V to Fifth Ave-53rd St) A 10-story extravaganza stretching a whole block. Designer goods, casual wear, and an 8th-floor café to feed the weary.

Takashimaya (☎ 212-350-0100; www.nytakashimaya.com; 693 Fifth Ave; 🕙 10am-7pm Mon-Sat, noon-5pm Sun; 🚇 E, V to Fifth Ave-53rd St) Seven stories with beauty products, a day spa (top floor), clothes, accessories, home design, floral bouquets and a tea shop.

7pm Mon-Sat, noon-6pm Sun; ⓔ E,
V to Fifth Ave-53rd St, N, R, W to 59th
St-Lexington Ave
Stacks of signature Dior sunglasses, handbags and pumps line
the walls. Women's clothing and
high-end jewelry is in the back;
men should head next door to the
black-and-white space dedicated
to Dior *homme*.

⬛ MULBERRY
Fashion & Accessories
☎ 212-453-4722; www.mulberry.com;
605 Madison Ave near 57th St; ⏲ 10am-
6pm Mon-Wed, Fri & Sat, 10am-7pm
Thu, noon-5pm Sun; ⓔ 4, 5, 6 to 59th
St-Lexington Ave
High end but not uptight, the
friendly staff at Mulberry will help
you wade through the designer
bags, women's clothes, shoes
and other accessories with nary a
lifted eyebrow, and gift wrap your
purchase too.

⬛ SHANGHAI TANG
Fashion & Accessories
☎ 212-888-0111; www.shanghaitang
.com; 600 Madison Ave at E 57th St;
⏲ 10am-6pm Mon-Sat, noon-6pm
Sun; ⓔ 4, 5, 6 to 59th St, N, R, W to
59th St-Lexington Ave, N, R, W to Fifth
Ave-59th St
Asian powerhouse Shanghai
Tang is shaking up staid Madison
Ave with its bold, patterned and
visually arresting designs. Meant

to appeal to youthful buyers, this
store is as vivid as the clothes, and
just as entertaining. Pick up a silk
mandarin jacket, beautifully fitted
blouses, daring dresses and much
more here.

🍴 EAT

🍴 99 CENT PIZZA *Pizza* $
☎ 212-922-0257; 151 E 43rd St near
Third Ave; ⏲ breakfast, lunch & dinner;
ⓔ 4, 5, 6, 7, S to Grand Central-42nd St;
♿ V ⛄
Serving up quick and cheap pizza
in a city where most slices cost
about $2.50, 99 Cent Pizza does a
brisk business – always a sign that
you've found a good bargain. It's
not gourmet and doesn't claim
to have fancy toppings, but if
you like a good slice with a nice
balance of tangy tomato sauce
and creamy cheese, 99 Cent won't
disappoint. Just don't forget the
tax – that'll raise the final price to
about $1.10.

🍴 ABURIYA KINNOSUKE
Japanese $$$
☎ 212-867-5454; www.aburiyakinnosuke
.com/aburiya.htm; 213 E 45th St near Third
Ave; ⏲ lunch & dinner; ⓔ 4, 5, 6, 7, S to
Grand Central-42nd St; ♿ V
Fairly authentic Japanese cuisine
(a few nods to American can be
found here and there) dished up
amid paper lanterns and sleek
cheerywood tables tucked behind

private screens, or at the open Robata grill at the bar. Sashimi, sake and mains like salmon *harasu* (fatty salmon), dried horse mackerel, organic pork simmered with brown-sugar *soju,* and Japanese-style beef and veggie pot-au-feu dot the menu.

🍴 ARTISANAL
French $$$

☎ 212-725-8585; 2 Park Ave S; 🕑 lunch & dinner; ⊕ 6 to 33rd St; 🚻 🆅

For those who live, love and dream *fromage*, Artisanal is a must-eat. More than 250 varieties of cheese, from stinky to sweet, are on the menu. Along with classic French mains like steak au poivre, you can sample four types of fondue (including chocolate) and *gougères* (little servings) of everything from Brie to Ossau-Iraty.

🍴 GRIFONE
Northern Italian $$$

☎ 212-490-7275; www.grifonenyc.com; 244 E 46th St near Second Ave; 🕑 lunch & dinner Mon-Sat, closed 3-5pm; ⊕ 4, 5, 6, 7, S to Grand Central-42nd St; 🚻 🆅 🚹

An expensive secret not far from the UN, Grifone is a favorite diplomat hangout. The rich red decor goes hand in hand with the succulent, calorie-laden dishes, heavy on cheeses and sauces, but

so finely seasoned that they stop just short of gluttonous. Pasta lovers will swoon at the spaghetti carbonara, with fresh pancetta and parmigiano cheese, and the pesto sauces that are ground and flecked with garlic right under your eyes by chefs working in the open kitchen. There's also tender veal, beef and chicken dishes, and lots of seafood plates.

🍴 L'ATELIER DE JOEL ROBUCHON
Japanese, French $$$

☎ 212-350-6658; www.fourseasons .com/newyorkfs/dining.html; 57 E 57th St near Park Ave; 🕑 11:30am-2pm & 6-11pm; ⊕ 4, 5, 6 to 59th St-Lexington Ave; 🆅

If you've eaten at any of Robuchon's celebrated restaurants in Paris, Tokyo, London or Las Vegas, you know what to expect: a smorgasbord of flavors in tiny bites. Taking small plates and *omakase* (chef's choice) to a whole new level, L'Atelier's frog-legs croquettes, hangar steak, caramelized free-range quail stuffed with foie gras and served with potato puree, and litchi desserts are divine. Sit at the counter, if you can.

🍴 ROUGE TOMATE
Belgian $$

☎ 646-237-8977; www.rougetomate .com; 10 E 60th St btwn Madison & Fifth

Aves; 🕐 lunch & dinner; Ⓜ F to 57th St, 4, 5, 6 to 59th St-Lexington Ave

Midtown East, home to the five-course business lunch, desperately needed a high-end place that's as easy on the budget as it is on the waistline: voila Rouge Tomate. This sleek Belgian restaurant eschews french fries and waffles in favor of organic veggies and lean cuts of meat. All the meals – including the $72 prix-fixe with three courses plus dessert – come in at 550 calories or less, but with no sacrifice to flavor or presentation. The chef, formerly of Daniel Boulud's DB Bistro Moderne, works with a nutritionist to count calories (and cooks with olive oil and yogurt over butter and heavy cream), but you won't leave feeling hungry: portions are ample, as Americans like them, and desserts are every bit as decadent as one would hope.

🍴 **SIP SAK** *Turkish* $
☎ 212-583-1900; www.sip-sak.com; 928 Second Ave; 🕐 lunch & dinner; Ⓜ 6 to 51st St, E, V to Lexington Ave-53rd St; 🚫 Ⓥ 🚫

Owner Orhan Yeger can usually be found supervising the kitchen, just to make sure everything tastes authentically Turkish (to match the orangey ceiling, bright yellow walls and vivid blue tiles of his restaurant). Lamb and seafood

specials never disappoint, but the classic Turkish meze, with *borek filo* (dough stuffed with feta cheese), hummus and *cacik* (thick yogurt with garlic and cucumber) is also a winner.

🍴 **SOFRITO** *Puerto Rican* $
☎ 212-754-5999; www.sofrito.com; 400 E 57th St near First Ave; 🕐 dinner until 2am; Ⓜ 4, 5, 6 to 59th St; 🚫 Ⓥ 🚫

Pile in for late-night fun (and be prepared to wait) fueled by tasty Caribbean treats like *mo-fongo* (mashed plantain), *tostones* (mashed, deep-fried plantain), roasted pork with rice and peas, grilled fish dishes, succulent paella, yucca, calamari and more. The ambience is groovy, with the live Sofrito band from Monday to Thursday, and a DJ spinning salsa and hip-hop on other nights.

🍸 DRINK
🍸 **BILL'S GAY NINETIES** *Bar*
☎ 212-355-0243; 57 E 54th St near Madison Ave; 🕐 11am-1:30am Mon-Sat; Ⓜ E, V to Fifth Ave-53rd St, 6 to 51st St

Don't let the name fool you – the clientele at this bar are generally as straight as they come. It's all about the Roaring Twenties at Bill's, the decade when original owner Bill Hardy converted the ground floor of his brownstone into a speakeasy. Bill's still retains its illicit aura, in part because you have to traverse hand-carved swinging doors to reach the cavernous inner sanctum, with its high beams, low lights and numerous boxing and racing pictures. It's a great place to unwind, grab a drink and make a new friend.

CAMPBELL APARTMENT *Bar*
☎ 212-953-0409; 15 Vanderbilt Ave at 43rd St; ⏰ 3pm-1am Mon-Sat, to 11pm Sun; ⊖ S, 4, 5, 6, 7 to Grand Central-42nd St

Take the lift beside the Oyster Bar, or the stairs to the West Balcony, and head out the doors to the left to reach this sublime cocktail spot. This used to be the apartment of a landed railroad magnate and has the velvet, mahogany and murals to prove it. Cigars are welcome,

ARENA
It's slim pickings for dance halls and clubs in Midtown East, but nearby **Arena** (☎ 212-278-0988; www.arena nyc.net; 135 E 41st St near Lexington Ave; ⏰ Thu-Sat night; ⊖ 4,5,6 to Grand Central-42nd St) is shaking things up. A former theater, Arena's been reclaimed for club nights and the occasional transvestite gathering by promoters around town. Music is house, electronica and funk and the crowd eclectic and offbeat. The huge space is dominated by two large screens on either side and small tables in the middle of the spacious club.

but sneakers and jeans are not. The Apartment is a great way to enjoy the grandeur of the train station, martini in hand.

MORRELL WINE BAR & CAFÉ *Bar, Café*
☎ 212-262-7700; 1 Rockefeller Plaza, W 48th St btwn Fifth & Sixth Aves; ⏰ 11:30am-11pm Mon-Sat, noon-6pm Sun; ⊖ B, D, F, V to 47th-50th Sts-Rockefeller Center

This mega haven for grape geeks was one of the pioneers of the wine-bar craze that swept through NYC. There are over 2000 bottles of wine to choose from, and there are a whopping 150 wines available by the glass. The airy, split-level room, right across from the famous skating rink at Rockefeller Center, is as lovely as the vino.

SUBWAY INN *Pub*
☎ 212-223-8929; 143 E 60th St btwn Lexington & Third Aves; ⏰ 11am-4am Mon-Sat, noon-2am Sun; ⊖ 4, 5, 6 to 59th St

This is a classic watering hole, with cheap drinks and loads of authenticity, right down to the barmen's white shirts and their thin black ties. It should truly be landmarked, as the entire space – from the vintage neon sign outside to the well-worn red booths and old geezers huddled inside – is reminiscent of bygone days. The dive, which of-

Bryant Park, a welcome splash of green amid concrete and glass

fers, among other things, plenty of cheapo shots, is an amusing place to recover from a shopping spree at posh Bloomingdale's (p155), just around the corner.

⭐ PLAY
🔲 BRYANT PARK
Outdoor Venue

☎ 212-768-4242; www.bryantpark.org; Sixth Ave btwn W 40th & W 42nd Sts; 🕙 7am-11pm Mon-Fri, to 8pm Sat & Sun in summer, 7am-7pm Jan-Apr & Sep-Dec;

🔘 F, V, B, D to 42nd St-Bryant Park, 7 to Fifth Ave; ♿

Fashion Week, free films, Latin dancing, concerts and Broadway shows (plus ice-skating in winter): there's always something going on at this grassy haven behind the New York Public Library. With free wi-fi and a cute coffee bar, it's everyone's favorite satellite office. Come early for free films in summer – blankets suggested.

>MIDTOWN WEST

Teeming Midtown is full of energy and glaring neon lights, thanks mostly to the frenetic splendors of Times Sq and New York's jaunty Broadway district. It's also filled to the brim with savory food carts, catering to the office crowd rushing along Sixth Ave, and the often-overlooked Diamond District, a four-block frenzy of gold and jewel trading.

Shoppers looking for electronic bargains will find a bonanza of discount stores along Seventh and Eighth Aves, and don't be surprised if you hear samba music and Portuguese as you browse: Midtown also encompasses Little Brazil, an enclave of tasty restaurants and tropical-themed bars. The southern stretch of Midtown contains the famed Garment District, home to designers' offices, and wholesale and retail shops. The northern tip of this area is Columbus Circle, the gateway to both the Upper West Side and Central Park, backed by the gleaming Time Warner Center.

MIDTOWN WEST

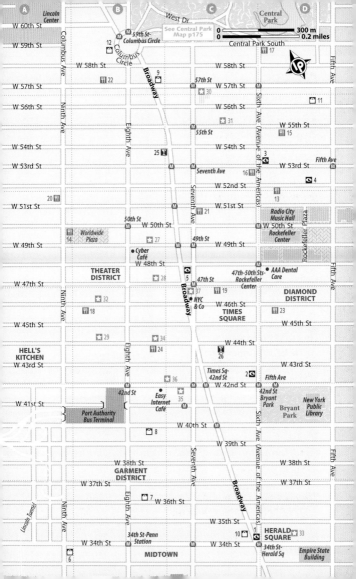

⊙ SEE

⊙ HERALD SQUARE

cnr Broadway, Sixth Ave & 34th St; ⊕ B, D, F, N, Q, R, V, W to 34th St-Herald Sq
Prepare for crowds as you enter the convergence of Broadway, Sixth Ave and 34th St. It's a shopping mecca anchored by a New York landmark of sorts: Macy's department store (p166). The busy square has a small, leafy park offering refuge to foot-sore bargain seekers. South of Macy's on Sixth Ave you'll find an uninspiring string of chain stores, but hidden among them is discount gem Daffy's, stuffed with designer labels that have been (steeply) marked down.

⊙ INTERNATIONAL CENTER OF PHOTOGRAPHY

☎ 212-857-0000; www.icp.org; 1133 Sixth Ave at W 43rd St; adult/child under 12 $12/free, voluntary contribution 5-8pm Friday; 🕑 10am-6pm Tue-Thu, Sat & Sun, to 8pm Fri; ⊕ B, D, F, V to 42nd St-Bryant Park
It's a museum that doubles as a school, offering classes on all things photography related, while continuously rotating its 60,000 photos, a massive permanent collection spanning from daguerreotypes to modern prints. You'll see some Henri Cartier-Bresson, Man Ray, Matthew Brady, Robert Capa and lots of Weegee, who documented New York's nightlife and crime in the 1930s.

⊙ PALEY CENTER FOR MEDIA

☎ 212-621-6800/6600; www.mtr.org; 25 W 52nd St; adult $10, senior & student $8, child under 14 free; 🕑 noon-6pm Tue & Wed, Fri-Sun, to 8pm Thu; ⊕ E, V to Fifth Ave-53rd St, N, R, W to 49th St, 1 to 50th St, B, D, F, V to 47th-50th Sts-Rockefeller Center; ♿
Formerly the Museum of Television and Radio, the Paley Center

THE MOMA
Japanese architect Yoshio Taniguchi made the most of glass, steel and aluminum when he redid the **Museum of Modern Art** (MoMA; ☎ 212-708-9400; www.moma.org; 11 W 53rd St btwn Fifth & Sixth Aves; adult/student $20/16, 4-8pm Fri free; 🕑 10:30am-5:30pm Sat-Mon & Wed-Thu, to 8pm Fri; ⊕ E, V to Fifth Ave-53rd St, B, D, F to 47th-50th Sts-Rockefeller Center) in 2004. The sumptuous space is its own universe, filled with 100,000 pieces. Most of the big hitters — Matisse, Picasso, Cézanne, Rothko, Pollock — are housed in the central five-story atrium, where peaceful, airy galleries contain works from the departments of Painting and Sculpture, Architecture and Design, Drawings, Prints and Illustrated Books, and Film and Media. The museum's atrium/sculpture garden — returned to its original, larger vision of the early '50s by Philip Johnson — is a joy to sit in.

Herald Square, a mecca for shopping – and yellow vehicles

for Media is dedicated to the small screen and classic radio moments. There are more than 100,000 tapes at your disposal in the archives – pull out that favorite *Star Trek* episode without shame and watch it one more time. There are also retrospective screenings and frequent exhibitions on the rise of modern mass media.

◻ SHOP
◻ B & H PHOTO-VIDEO
Cameras & Accessories
☎ 212-502-6200; www.bhphotovideo .com; 420 Ninth Ave; ◷ 9am-7pm Mon-Thu, 9am-1pm Fri, 10am-5pm Sun; ◉ A, C, E to 34th St-Penn Station

A trip here is an experience unto itself – it's big, buzzy and bristling with every kind of camera, video or DVD equipment you could desire.

◻ CLOTHINGLINE/SSS SAMPLE SALES
Fashion & Accessories
☎ 212-947-8748; www.clothingline .com; 2nd fl, 261 W 36th St; ◷ 10am-6pm Mon & Wed, to 7pm Tue & Thu, check website for Sat & Sun; ◉ 1, 2, 3 to 34th St-Penn Station
Line up early to get your hands on designer goods marked down by as much as 75 percent. Sales happen only on the weekends, and you can find names like Helmut Lang, Rag & Bone, Ben Sherman

and others. Check the website to see what's on the block while you're in town.

🏠 **DRAMA BOOKSHOP** *Books*
☎ 212-944-0595; www.dramabook shop.com; 250 W 40th St; ⏱ 10am-8pm Mon-Sat, noon-6pm Sun; 🚇 A, C, E to 42nd St-Port Authority Bus Terminal
Broadway fans will find treasures in print at this expansive bookstore, which has taken its theater (plays and musicals) seriously since 1917. Staffers are good at recommending worthy selections. Check out the website for regular events, such as talks with playwrights.

🏠 **MACY'S** *Department Store*
☎ 212-695-4400; www.macys.com; 151 W 34th St at Broadway; ⏱ 10am-8:30pm Mon-Sat, 11am-7pm Sun; 🚇 B, D, F, N, Q, R, V, W to 34th St-Herald Sq
Mind your fingers on the old wooden elevators, a highlight of a Macy's trip. The store's goods, mainly linens, clothing, furniture, kitchenware, shoes and more, are affordable and basic. You can lose yourself for hours here, the world's largest department store.

🏠 **OMO NORMA KAMALI**
Fashion & Accessories
☎ 212-957-9797; www.normakamali collection.com; 11 W 56th St at Sixth Ave; ⏱ 10am-7pm Mon-Sat, noon-6pm Sun; 🚇 N, Q, R, W to 57th St

You won't want to leave the glistening, white-walled, four-story temple that is Norma Kamali's flagship shop. Her one-of-a kind dresses, coats and swimwear hang off dangling mannequins. When you see something you like, a clerk will find it in your size. It's not for bargain hunters, but fashion seekers.

🏠 **TIME WARNER CENTER** *Mall*
☎ 212-484-8000; www.timewarner .com; 1 Time Warner Center; ⏱ 10am-9pm; 🚇 A, B, C, D, 1 to 59th St-Columbus Circle; ♿
Shop till you drop in Manhattan's glossy urban mall, built to look like a glass-covered mountain and home to more than 40 stores, an organic market, a couple of clubs and theaters, as well as tony residences and $500-a-meal restaurants.

🍴 EAT

🍴 **ANTHOS** *Greek* $$$
☎ 212-582-6900; www.anthosnyc.com; 36 W 52nd St near Fifth Ave; ⏱ lunch & dinner; 🚇 B, D, F, V to 47th-50th Sts-Rockefeller Center, E, V to Fifth Ave-53rd St
Flower-filled Anthos has eye-catching chocolate-brown chairs offset by creamy white linens and walls – a pleasing decor that will fade into the background once you start to eat. Crispy turbot with fried oyster and olives, roasted

Time Warner Center is a multiuse urban shopping temple

cod with whipped feta and Tuscan kale, and braised baby goat with manouri cheese will whisk you away to Crete – as will the extensive white wine list. Lunch offers a $28 prix fixe, and for $95 you can sample the chef's tasting menu.

BANN *Korean* $$
☎ 212-582-4446; www.bannrestaurant
.com; 350 W 50th St btwn Eighth & Ninth
Aves; ✆ lunch & dinner; ◉ C, E to
50th St
You'll have to hunt for the entrance to discreet Bann (tucked inside Worldwide Plaza). A fusion of modern and traditional Korean, Bann lets you do your own barbecue or experiment with some of its offbeat pairings, such as *dak nalke*

jorim (spicy chili-glazed chicken wings with fried plantain) or *cham chi hwe* (ahi tuna tartare served with thinly sliced green apple). The crisp elegance makes it a favorite for business lunches, but the low lights and intimate black tables with granite tops give it a romantic glow at night.

BENOIT *Bistro* $$
☎ 646-943-7373; http://benoitny.com;
60 W 55th St near Sixth Ave; ✆ breakfast, lunch & dinner Mon-Sat, brunch,
lunch & dinner Sun; ◉ F to 57th St
Alain Ducasse's New York eatery Benoit is full of bright blond wood, red banquettes, glinting sconces and a more laid-back black-and-white bar. You'll be transported

THE PLATTER CLUB

Known to its many fans as the gyro spot, the chicken and rice plate, or – most famously – the Platter Club, the family-run food cart **Best Halal** (www .53rdandsixth.com; cnr W 53rd St & Sixth Ave; dishes $3-5; ☽ dinner; ⊕ B, D, F, V to 47th-50th Sts-Rockefeller Center, E, V to Fifth Ave-53rd St) has long lines stretching down the block every night, well into the wee hours. There's a different cart there during the day but Best Halal moves in at 7pm, and until 4am dishes up succulent rice and chicken, topped with the secret white sauce that many believe is the ingredient that makes this food worth waiting for.

to Paris by fresh-baked croissants, garlicky escargots, tender duck l'orange, cassoulet and roasted chicken for two. Ducasse fans will also want to check out his more upscale **Adour** (Map p151; ☎ 212-710-2277; 2 E 55th St at Fifth Ave) in the St Regis Hotel; it's got a knockout wine list.

🍴 BLT MARKET
American $$$

☎ 212-521-6125; www.bltmarket.com; 1430 Sixth Ave near W 58th St; ☽ breakfast, lunch & dinner; ⊕ F, N, Q, R, W to 57th St; ⛨

It's in the Ritz-Carlton on Central Park, but aside from that, you might as well be back on the farm. All the food at BLT Market mimics the decor: clean, fresh and changing with the seasons. On a recent visit, chef

Laurent Tourondel's organic menu featured seasonal squash and black cod, smoked trout with a cilantro and avocado puree and roasted Hudson Valley duck.

🍴 BRAZIL BRAZIL GRILLE
Brazilian $$

☎ 212-957-4300; www.brazilbrazil restaurant.com; 330 W 46th St btwn Eighth & Ninth Aves; ☽ lunch & dinner; ⊕ A, C, E, 1, 2, 3 to Times Sq-42nd St; ⛨ ⛨

Most of W 46th St is informally known as 'Little Brazil,' a stretch of businesses, shops and restaurants that cater to the expat Brazilian community. This restaurant, with its relaxed vibe, hefty (and affordable) drinks, live weekend music, and delicious *frango a passarinho* (chicken in white wine, garlic and olive oil), *lula frita* (calamari) and *camarao alhoe* (garlic shrimp) is a favorite. Another nearby standout is **Via Brasil** (☎ 212-997-1158; 34 W 46th St near Sixth Ave; ☽ 11am-10pm; ⊕ N, R, W, 1, 2, 3 to Times Sq-42nd St); its long room has waving palm trees and super-friendly waiters. The menu's got authentic *feijoada* (beans and meat), *moquecas* (fish stew) and more.

🍴 EMPANADA MAMA
South American $

☎ 212-698-9008; 763 Ninth Ave at W 51st St; ☽ lunch & dinner; ⊕ C, E, 1 to 50th St, N, R, W to 49th St; ⛨ Ⓥ ⛨

With its cheery red entrance, long green banquettes down a narrow, brick wall, succulent empanadas and great prices, what's not to love about Empanada Mama? The service, unfortunately: it's a little slow and diffident, but these addictive, meat-stuffed pastry treats are too addictive to walk away from. You can get wheat, corn and oven-baked empanadas filled with tasty beef or chicken (veggie options too), or *arepas* (stuffed corn patties), or a big plate of *arroz con pollo* (chicken with rice), or shredded beef, or many other South American favorites.

INSIEME Italian $$$
☎ 212-582-1310; 777 Seventh Ave near W 51st; ☺ breakfast, lunch & dinner; ◉ 1 to 50th St

The name means 'together' in Italian, and that's a clue about the menu: one side contains traditional Italian dishes and the other lists innovative and modern twists from the chef. Pick between the two while you sit in the square, small-tabled room that looks out on Seventh Ave. Enjoy the bustle along with some buckwheat pasta with ricotta cheese, lamb carpaccio, tender veal or fried classics like calamari.

LE BIARRITZ
French $$
☎ 212-245-9467; www.lebiarritz.com; 325 W 57th St near Eighth Ave; ☺ lunch & dinner; ◉ A, B, C, D, 1, 9 to 59th St-Columbus Circle; ♿ ♂

A local favorite, shabby-chic Le Biarritz dishes up traditional fare from Provence, the owner's birthplace. Perfect for pre- or post-theater dining, Biarritz has a generous prix-fixe dinner for $34, or you can choose a la carte: cassoulet, roasted lamb Provençal, margret duck breast, rabbit civet in mustard sauce, beef bourguignonne and grilled chicken paillard with artichokes and black olives feature on the menu.

VIRGIL'S REAL BARBECUE
American BBQ $$
☎ 212-921-9494; 152 W 44th St btwn Broadway & Eighth Ave; ☺ lunch & dinner; ◉ N, R, S, W, 1, 2, 3, 7 to Times Sq-42nd St

Rather than specializing in one specific style of BBQ (styles vary

---

DIAMOND DISTRICT
This four-block section of jewelry stores between Fifth and Sixth Aves from W 46th St to W 48th St is a bewildering experience for visitors, but it's where you can find a big bargain on gold and other precious metals. Check out the basics at www.diamonddistrict.org. Staffed mostly by Orthodox Jews, it stands to reason that **Diamond Dairy** (☎ 212-719-2694; mezzanine level, 4 W 47th St; meals $10; ☺ breakfast & lunch; ◉ B, D, F, V to 47th-50th Sts-Rockefeller Center) is one of the city's best kosher restaurants. It's hidden behind a bunch of stalls selling gold.

in sauce type and meat base throughout the US), Virgil's celebrates them all. Menu items cover the entire BBQ map, with Oklahoma State Fair corndogs, pulled Carolina pork and smoked Maryland ham sandwiches, and platters of sliced Texas beef brisket and Georgia chicken-fried steak. Meats are smoked with a combo of hickory, oak and fruitwoods, keepin' it all real.

🍸 DRINK

🍸 DIVINE BAR WEST *Bar*
☎ 212-265-9463; 236 W 54th St near Broadway; ⏱ 4:30pm-1am; 🚇 F, N, Q, R, W to 57th St, B, D, E to Seventh Ave, C, E to 50th St, A, B, C, D, 1 to 59th St-Columbus Circle

If you worked in Midtown, you'd need a place to blow off some steam too – that's what Divine Bar West offers the buttoned-down business crowd that enjoys its brightly colored chrome bar stools and zebra-patterned seats. It offers a long wine list, extensive beer choices and lots of mixed drinks that you can imbibe over a shared platter of tapas or cheese.

🍸 JIMMY'S CORNER *Bar*
☎ 212-221-9510; 140 W 44th St near Broadway; ⏱ 11:30am-4am; 🚇 N, Q, R, S, W, 1, 2, 3, 7 to Times Sq-42nd St, B, D, F, V to 42nd St-Bryant Park

Dive bar or sports bar? The debate rages on. Either way, Jimmy's Corner – long and slender – is bursting with old-time regulars and tons of boxing history, including pictures of owner Jimmy with Ali. A few tables are hidden way in the back, but the most fun is had when you snag a coveted seat at the bar. Mixed drinks abound – including the house special, Jimmy's Hurricane – but the safest bet is to stick to beer.

🍸 MOBAR *Bar*
☎ 212-805-8826; Mandarin Oriental, 80 Columbus Circle at W 60th St; ⏱ 4pm-midnight; 🚇 A, B, C, D, 1 to 59th St-Columbus Circle

Head up to the 35th floor of Columbus Circle and you'll discover MOBar, a sleek and sensual rendezvous for a romantic drink. Slip into one of the leather banquettes – which have suitably high backs for a privacy-loving clientele – and let one of MOBar's kimono-clad servers bring you a relaxing cocktail. The bright-red walls give off a rosy glow that only intensifies as the sun goes down and the Japanese-style lanterns take over. Despite being on the 35th floor, external views aren't that great, but there's enough to look at inside to keep you happy.

⭐ PLAY

⭐ AMBASSADOR THEATER
Theater

☎ ticket inquiries 800-927-2770, ext 4148; www.ambassadortheater.com; 219 W 49th St; ⏱ hours vary; ⊕ C, E to 50th St; ♿ ⛲

Classically horseshoe-shaped, the Ambassador's one of the most intimate large-sized venues on Broadway. If you're in town while *Chicago* is still playing, you'll feel every kick and hear every note Roxie Hart hits, even if you're in the cheap seats in the back.

⭐ BILTMORE THEATER *Theater*

☎ 212-399-3000; www.biltmoretheater .net; 261 W 47th St; ⏱ hours vary; ⊕ C, E, 1 to 50th St; ♿ ⛲

Pockmarked in the 1980s by arson and vandalism, the once-grand Biltmore seemed destined for the wrecking ball, despite its landmarked interior. A face-lift and fresh infusion of cash revived it in the 1990s, and now it's one of the premiere theaters on Broadway. Home to the Manhattan Theater Club, it covers American and European works.

⭐ BIRDLAND *Jazz Music*

☎ 212-581-3080; www.birdlandjazz .com; 315 W 44th St; admission $10-40; ⏱ club from 7pm, shows around 8:30pm & 11pm; ⊕ A, C, E to 42nd St-Port Authority Bus Terminal

Named for Charlie Parker, or 'Bird,' this jazz club has been turning out big-name acts since 1949 when Thelonious Monk, Miles Davis, Stan Getz and others made music and cut records in front of a live audience. Today you're likely to catch big names from European festivals, like Montreux, North Sea Jazz and other up-and-coming local talent. Regular performers include the Chico O'Farrill Afro-Cuban Jazz Big Band, Barry Harris and David Berger's Sultans of Swing.

⭐ CARNEGIE HALL *Live Music*

☎ 212-247-7800; www.carnegiehall.org; W 57th St & Seventh Ave; ⏱ hours vary; ⊕ N, R to 57th St

One of the world's most celebrated music halls, Carnegie's not the biggest, nor the grandest, but definitely one of the most acoustically blessed venues you'll find. Its soaring space still leaves you feeling intimately acquainted with the performers, who can range from jazz greats to opera stars to folk singers like Cesaria Evora.

⭐ CITY CENTER *Dance*

☎ 212-581-1212; www.citycenter.org; 131 W 55th St; ⊕ N, Q, R, W to 57th St; ⏱ hours vary; ♿ ⛲

This red-domed wonder almost went the way of the wrecking ball in 1943, but was saved by preservationists, only to face extinction again when its major ballet

Carnegie Hall (p171) has hosted jazz, folk and opera – and it can host you too

companies departed for Lincoln Center. Today, this overlooked treasure hosts the Paul Taylor Dance Company, Alvin Ailey and American Ballet Theater, as well as the New York Flamenco Festival in February and other dance performances.

⭐ **DON'T TELL MAMA** *Cabaret*
☎ 212-757-0788; www.donttellmamanyc.com; 343 W 46th St; 2 drink minimum; ⏰ 4pm to 1am; ⊕ N, R, 1, 2, 3 to Times Sq-42nd St
Piano bar and cabaret venue extraordinaire, Don't Tell Mama is an unpretentious little spot that's been around for more than 25 years and has the talent to prove

it. Its regular roster of performers aren't big names, but true lovers of cabaret who give each show their all and don't mind a little singing help from the audience sometimes. If you want your cabaret a bit more sinister and sexy, head to **The Box** (Map pp64-5; ☎ 212-982-9301; www.theboxnyc.com; 189 Chrystie St; ⊕ F, V to Second Ave). It's risqué and ribald and could get shut down at any moment, but its (very) late night shows might tickle your fancy.

⭐ **LITTLE KOREA** *Bars, Karaoke*
Broadway & Fifth Ave & btwn W 31st & W 36th Sts; ⏰ 24hr; ⊕ B, D, F, N, Q, R, V, W to 34th St-Herald Sq

Herald Sq is a bit on the tasteless side when it comes to finding foodie treats; luckily, you can head for quality refueling at nearby Little Korea, a small enclave of Korean-owned restaurants, shops, salons and spas. It's full of kitschy fun and its late-night hours means it attracts lots of club goers and party animals seeking Korean BBQ while they drink and sing karaoke into the wee hours.

⭐ **MAJESTIC THEATER**
Theater
☎ 212-239-6200; www.majestic-theater .net; 247 W 44th St; ⏲ hours vary; 🚇 any train to 42nd St
A fabled performance house that has seen the likes of Angela Lansbury, Julie Andrews and several Barrymores on its stage, the Majestic is still (still!) selling out every night for *Phantom of the Opera,* 20 years after Andrew Lloyd Webber's creation debuted.

⭐ **NEW AMSTERDAM THEATER** *Theater*
☎ 212-282-2900; www.newamsterdam theater.net; 214 W 42nd St; ⏲ hours vary; 🚇 any train to 42nd St; ♿ 👶
If your kids are into theater, watch their eyes pop as they pass through the art deco entrance, into the art nouveau interior of carved and painted plaster, stone, wood, murals and tiles – all of which evoke early-20th-century theater-going – on their way to see *Mary Poppins,* the musical.

⭐ **NEW VICTORY THEATER**
Arts, Theater
☎ 646-223-3020; www.newvictory.org; 209 W 42nd St; 🚇 any train to Times Sq-42nd St; ⏲ hours vary; ♿ 👶
Budding thespians and dancers flock to the upbeat energy of this kid-focused theater. New Victory puts on comedy, dance, music, puppetry and drama shows for the 12-and-under set, and a range of offerings for teenagers.

>CENTRAL PARK

A vast and majestic swath of 843 flowery, tree-filled acres, Central Park (www.centralparknyc.org) is the city's universal backyard, shared equally by billionaires and paupers and everyone in between.

Its glassy lakes, meandering woodlands and lush green lawns offer an unbelievably wide range of physical activities: jogging, skateboarding, cycling, Frisbee-playing, volleyball and more. But cultural fun isn't overlooked either: Shakespeare in the Park, free summer concerts and weekend tango dancing are all part of the Central Park experience.

While sections of Central Park swarm with people, there are also large chunks of land, particularly in the northern section, left untouched. Less populated spots above 72nd St include the Harlem Meer (110th St), the North Meadow Recreation Area (just above 97th St on the west side) and the Ramble (mid-park from 73rd to 79th Sts), a bird-watcher's paradise. Even in winter New Yorkers flock to the park – skiing and snowshoeing if there's snow, and turning out every New Year's Eve for a fast-paced midnight run.

The best subway options are A, B, C, D, E or 1 to 59th St-Columbus Circle, N, R or W to Fifth Ave-59th St or 4, 5 or 6 to 59th St-Lexington Ave.

CENTRAL PARK

◉ SEE
Arsenal **1** C6
Bowling Lawns **2** B5
Central Park Wildlife
   Center **3** C6
Great Lawn **4** B4
Jacqueline Kennedy
   Onassis Reservoir **5** C3
Seneca Village **6** B4
Strawberry Fields **7** B5

Tisch Children's Zoo ......(see 3)
Wollman Skating
   Rink **8** C6

⒕ EAT
Central Park Boathouse ...**9** C5
Conservatory Pond
   Kiosk **10** C5
Harlem Meer Kiosk **11** C1
Tavern on the Green **12** B5

★ PLAY
Belvedere Castle **13** B4
Bike Hire ....(see 9)
Boat Hire ....(see 9)
North Meadow
   Recreation Center **14** B2
Rock Climbing Center ...(see 14)
Safari Playground **15** B3

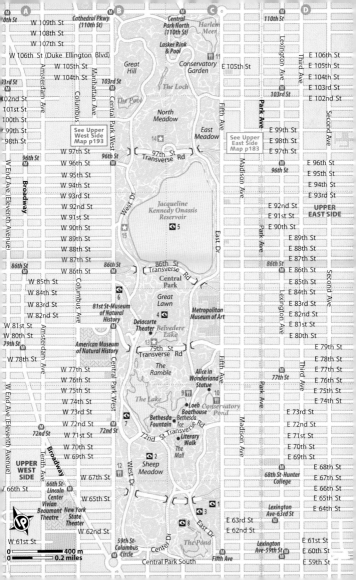

SEE

ARSENAL

E 64th St; admission free; ☉ **9am-5pm Mon-Fri**

Before there was a Central Park there was an armory: the Arsenal, built between 1847 and 1851 to house munitions. The landmarked structure looks like a medieval castle and these days is used by the Central Park Wildlife Center. The reason to visit here is not to see the building, though, but to view Olmsted's original blueprint for the park, treasured here under glass in a 3rd-floor conference room.

BOWLING LAWNS

north of Sheep Meadow at 69th St

There are two 15,000-sq-ft bowling lawns – one for croquet and one for lawn bowling, where members of the 80-year-old New York Lawn Bowling Club still mix it up with tournaments from May to October.

CENTRAL PARK WILDLIFE CENTER

☎ **212-861-6030; www.centralparknyc .org; E 64th St at Fifth Ave; adult/child under 3/child $8/free/3;** ☉ **10am-5pm**

Time your arrival if you can for the feeding hours: 11:30am, 2pm and 4pm. That's when the center's penguins, polar bears, rowdy tamarin monkeys and other

creatures go crazy – especially the sea lions, who love to chow down. The Tisch Children's Zoo, between 65th and 66th Sts, is perfect for smaller children.

GREAT LAWN

btwn 72nd & 86th Sts

This massive emerald carpet was created in 1931 by filling in a former reservoir. Not far from the actual lawn are several other big sites: the Delacorte Theater, home to the annual Shakespeare in the Park festival, and its lush Shakespeare Garden; the panoramic Belvedere Castle; the leafy Ramble, the epicenter of both birding and gay-male cruising; and the Loeb Boathouse, where you can rent rowboats for a romantic float in the middle of this urban paradise.

JACQUELINE KENNEDY ONASSIS RESERVOIR

For decades the former first lady who lived across Fifth Ave started her day with a brisk walk around this 1.58-mile reservoir. No longer in use as a drinking source, it's become one big reflecting pool, showcasing New York's blue skies and dramatic skyline. The most beautiful time to be here is at sunset, when you can watch the sky turn from brilliant shades of pink and orange to cobalt blue, just as the city's lights slowly flicker on.

Stephen Malone and Paddy
Hansom driver

How did you get this job? I inherited it. My dad was a blacksmith from Ireland and when he came over here in the 1960s he started driving a horse and carriage through Central Park. **Have you heard a lot of marriage proposals?** Thousands, one nearly every day. And I've never heard a 'No' answer. My carriage must be lucky. **Have you had any 'only in New York' moments?** Every day. But one stands out. I picked up a couple a few years ago, older folks from New Hampshire. They're celebrating their wedding anniversary and chatting away. And the woman says, 'We got engaged in a cab just like this. The driver was a nice man from Ireland named Paddy.' I couldn't believe it. I said, 'Yeah, that was my Dad.' **How about your horse, Paddy. Any special New York moments?** Oh sure. The doormen at the Ritz Carlton Hotel bring carrots on a silver platter around noon every day. Plus Paddy's a film actor. He's been in both of the *Eloise* movies, and a movie with the Olsen twins.

NEIGHBORHOODS

CENTRAL PARK

STATUARY IN THE PARK

Peeking out of unexpected corners are numerous statues and works of art in Central Park that are worth taking a moment to admire.

> **Maine Monument** (at the Merchant's Gate at Columbus Circle), a tribute to the sailors killed in the mysterious explosion in Havana Harbor in 1898 that sparked the Spanish American War. Ironically, a statue of Cuban independence seeker **José Martí** is just a little further east.

> At Scholar's Gate (Fifth Ave at 60th St), there is a small plaza dedicated to **Doris Chanin Freedman**, the founder of the Public Art Fund, where you can see a new sculpture every six months or so.

> **Angel of the Waters** is an instantly recognizable statue atop Bethesda Fountain, but don't overlook the **Falconer Statue**, tucked away on a rise overlooking the 72nd St Transverse nearby.

⊙ SENECA VILLAGE
btwn 81st & 89th Sts
Marked by a simple plaque, Seneca Village was home to Manhattan's first prominent community of African American property owners (c 1840).

⊙ STRAWBERRY FIELDS
Standing just across from the famous Dakota building – where *Rosemary's Baby* was filmed in 1967, and where John Lennon was fatefully shot in 1980 – is this poignant, tear-shaped garden, a memorial to the slain star. It's the most visited spot in Central Park, and is maintained with some help from a $1-million grant from Lennon's widow Yoko Ono, who still resides at the Dakota. The peaceful spot contains a grove of stately elms and a tiled mosaic that's

often strewn with rose petals from visitors. It says, simply, 'Imagine.'

⊙ WOLLMAN SKATING RINK
☎ 212-439-6900; btwn 62nd & 63rd Sts; admission free, skate hire $8; ☽ Nov-Mar
Far less visited than the rink at Rockefeller Center, Wollman's is something to behold during the holiday season, when it's got lights dangling from everywhere. Strap on some rented skates and take a few spins.

🍴 EAT

🍴 CENTRAL PARK BOATHOUSE
Seafood, American Traditional $$$
☎ 212-517-2233; E 72nd St at Park Dr N; ☽ noon-4pm Mon-Fri, 9:30am-4pm Sat & Sun Nov 4-Apr 14, noon-4pm &

> Literary Walk, between Bethesda Fountain and the 65th St Transverse, is lined with statues, including the requisite **Christopher Columbus** and literati such as **Robert Burns** and **Shakespeare**.
> Near Conservatory Pond, kids crawl over the giant toadstools of the **Alice in Wonderland** statue. Replete with Alice of flowing hair and dress, a dapper Mad Hatter and mischievous Cheshire Cat, this is a Central Park treasure and a favorite of kids of all ages. Nearby is the **Hans Christian Andersen** statue, where Saturday story hour (11am June to September) is an entertaining draw.
> **Cleopatra's Needle**, located on the hillock above 82nd St and East Dr, is an obelisk from Egypt, donated in 1877 to the US as thanks for helping build the Suez Canal.
> Near Harlem Meer is a soaring **Duke Ellington** statue, depicting the man and his piano.
> At E 67th St is **Balto** the dog, a replica of an Alaskan sled dog who helped deliver a life-giving serum to a snowbound village suffering a diphtheria outbreak in 1925, an event that captured the world's imagination as people followed his trek by radio.

5:30-9:30pm Mon-Fri, 9:30am-4pm & 6-9:30pm Sat & Sun Apr 15-Nov 3; V
Beautifully located on the Park's biggest lake, the Central Park Boathouse offers everything in the way of ambience and setting, but very little in the way of cutting-edge cuisine. It's got a café, an outdoor bar and a more formal dining room, all serving up adequate shrimp, calamari and seafood dishes (burgers too).

KIOSKS
Sandwiches, Snacks $
E 76th St near Conservatory Pond & E 108th St near Harlem Meer; 11am-8pm Jun-Sep; V
When the weather gets warm the Parks Department opens up these small snack shacks. They both sit right on the edge of small ponds, so you can grab a pretzel on a nice

day and then watch the ducks swim your way (hoping you'll share) while you eat.

TAVERN ON THE GREEN
American Traditional $$$
☎ 212-873-3200; Central Park West at W 67th St; lunch & dinner; 1 to 66th St-Lincoln Center, B, C to 72nd St
Inside this iconic restaurant, the rooms seem to go on forever, with window views into the park and a series of interlocking gardens to dine in. The standard American fare is a bit stodgy, but this is about the ambience, after all.

★ PLAY
Several of Central Park's most celebrated arts events happen in the summer: Shakespeare in the Park (www.publictheater.org) and

Summerstage (www.summerstage .org) are the two big ones. If you miss those, there are plenty of year-round activities to enjoy.

⭐ BELVEDERE CASTLE
Bird-Watching

mid-park at 79th St; admission free; ⏱ 10am-5pm Tue-Sun

The castle has a Discovery Room that covers two floors and has an information panel on the trees in the park. More exciting, however, is the display of common birds to be found in the nearby Ramble, and the bird-watching kits you can borrow for free – kids too.

⭐ BIKING CENTRAL PARK
Cycling

☎ 212-517-2233; www.centralpark.com /pages/sports/bicycle-riding.html; E 72nd

TANGO IN CENTRAL PARK

It's not quite the docks of Buenos Aires, but pretty darn close. Every Saturday night at 6pm from June to September is tango time in Central Park. Aficionados, neophytes and dabblers gather at the Shakespeare statue near Literary Walk for a little cheek-to-cheek dancing. Even if you aren't one to tango, take a look. You can also swing by a sister event, Tango Porteño every Sunday night at South St Seaport (p46). For info and details go to http://spiceevents.net /tango_cp_sssp.html.

St at Park Dr N; adult 1st hr $9, then per hr $5, child 1st hr $6, then per hour $3, incl helmets

There are several places that rent bikes in Central Park, but an easy location to grab one is the Boat-house (p178). Bikes aren't allowed on the small pathways inside the park, but there's a wide road that's easy to follow when circum-navigating the park. Around the reservoir is a dirt track, and around the tennis courts to the north are some family-friendly tracks off the main road. Remember that bike traffic goes counter-clockwise around the park, and you must obey traffic lights.

⭐ BOATING IN CENTRAL PARK
Boating

☎ 212-517-2233; www.thecentralpark boathouse.com; E 72nd St at Park Dr N; 1st hr $10, then per quarter hr $2.50, $30 deposit, 4 per boat

Set out for a romantic row across Central Park's Boathouse Lake, a tranquil (and fairly shallow) body of water that's home to lots of carp and sun-loving turtles. You'll get to experience the park from a unique point of view.

⭐ NORTH MEADOW
RECREATION CENTER *Sports*

☎ 212-348-4867; www.nyccentral parknyc.org; mid-park at 97th St; equipment free; ⏱ 9am-6pm Mon-Fri, 10am-4:30pm Sat & Sun

Runners and riders share Central Park's wide open spaces

Trade your ID for a sack full of fun games – baseballs, gloves, bats, Frisbees, basketballs, hula hoops and more. Staff at the NMRC happily lend out their field kits for a day free of charge, but call ahead during busy summer months.

ROCK CLIMBING CENTRE
Rock Climbing

☎ 212-348-4867; www.nyccentral parknyc.org

New York's urban rock-climbing community flocks to Worthless Boulder (a 10ft-tall rock at the park's north end) near Harlem Meer. Some scaling skills of your own can be harnessed at the supervised **Climbing Wall** (North Meadow Recreation Area; adult/child $7/5; ⚊ Tue & Thu evening, Sun), just north of 97th St. Kids can climb on Sundays.

SAFARI PLAYGROUND
Playground

W 91st St; admission free; ⚊ 7:30am-dusk

For kids, there's Safari Playground, a jungle-themed play area featuring 13 hippo sculptures, a tree house and a kiddie jogging path.

>UPPER EAST SIDE

Old money and Irish bars make for strange neighbors on the Upper East Side's leafy, shady blocks, stretching from the lower edge of Central Park to around 96th St.

Its two central avenues – Park and Madison – are generally known as New York's 'Gold Coast,' thanks to the miles of luxury boutiques and jaw-dropping brownstones that line them. As the neighborhood moves further east, along Lexington Ave and all the way to the East River, it gets progressively more working class, although it's now a world away from the immigrant (and gang-filled) enclave it was four decades ago. The crumbly and ornate buildings show traces of those darker days, but most Upper East Siders are preppy college kids, young families and single 30-somethings.

The neighborhood's cultural interests and night life focus on its two greatest assets: Central Park and fantastic museums, most notably the Metropolitan. Those looking for wild drinking and dancing will do better downtown, but for an evening of adult drinking, dining and discussion, the Upper East Side does just fine.

UPPER EAST SIDE

◉ SEE
Frick Collection..............**1** A5
Gagosian......................**2** B3
Gracie Mansion...........**3** D1
Metropolitan Museum
 of Art **4** A2
Neue Galerie................**5** A2
Solomon R Guggenheim
 Museum...................**6** A1
Temple Emanu-El.........**7** A5
Whitney Museum of
 American Art............**8** B4

🛍 SHOP
Barneys.........................**9** B6
BIS Designer Resale......**10** B2
Donna Karan................**11** B5
Ralph Lauren................**12** B4
Zitomers **13** B4

🍴 EAT
Andre's Patisserie.......**14** C2
Beyoglu......................**15** C3
Cafe Sabarsky.............**16** A2
La Goulue **17** B6

Pie by the Pound.........**18** C3
Sfoglia **19** B1

▼ DRINK
Auction House.............**20** C1
Bemelmans Bar...........**21** B3
Stir..............................**22** D4

✦ PLAY
92nd Street Y...............**23** B1
Dangerfield's...............**24** D6

A
Jacqueline
Kennedy Onassis
Reservoir

B
19
23 ★
E 92nd St
E 91st St
E 90th St
E 89th St

Fifth Ave
Madison Ave

C
20 🍴

D
VP

0 ————————— 400 m
0 ————————— 0.2 miles

3 ⊙

6 ⊙
16 🍴
5 ⊙

E 88th St
E 87th St

E 86th St
86th St Ⓜ
E 85th St
14 🍴 E 84th St

Park Ave
Third Ave

Second Ave

First Ave

York Ave

10 🏠
E 83rd St
E 82nd St

⊙ 4
Metropolitan
Museum of Art

Lexington Ave

E 83rd St

E 81st St
15 🍴
E 80th St
18 🍴

79th St Transverse
Rd
E 80th St

Central
Park

E 79th St
E 78th St

See Central Park
Map p175

Lenox Hill
Hospital
⊙ 2
🍴 21
🏠 13
⊙ 8

77th St Ⓜ
E 77th St
E 76th St
E 75th St

UPPER
EAST
SIDE

First Ave

E 76th St

Lake
Conservatory
Pond

Madison Ave
Third Ave

E 74th St
22 🍴
E 73rd St

72nd St Transverse Rd

🏠 12
E 72nd St
E 71st St

Second Ave

1 ⊙
E 70th St

York Ave

E 69th St

11 🏠
E 68th St
68th St-
Hunter
College Ⓜ
E 67th St

Lexington Ave
Park Ave

Fifth Ave

East Dr

E 66th St

Rockefeller
University

7 ⊙
17 🍴
65th St
Transverse Rd
E 65th St

First Ave

E 65th St
E 64th St
E 63rd St

Lexington Ave Ⓜ
9 🏠

Madison Ave

See Midtown East
Map p151

MIDTOWN

Third Ave

E 62nd St
24 ★
E 61st St
E 60th St

Eighth Ave

The Pond
Fifth Ave
59th St Ⓜ

Queensboro Bridge

SEE

FRICK COLLECTION

☎ 212-288-0700; www.frick.org; 1 E 70th St at Fifth Ave; admission $12; ⏱ 10am-6pm Tue-Thu & Sat, 10am-9pm Fri, 1-6pm Sun; Ⓜ 6 to 68th St-Hunter College

Along spectacular Fifth Ave, in what was once known as 'millionaires row,' the private collection of former steel magnate Henry Clay Frick waits to be discovered. His taste in art was as exquisite as his decorating sense; the collection and the home are gorgeous. Look for Jean-Antoine Houdon's stunning figure *Diana the Huntress*, works by Titian and Vermeer, and portraits by Gilbert Stuart, El Greco, Goya and John Constable.

GRACIE MANSION

☎ 212-570-4773; East End Ave at E 88th St; admission $7; ⏱ appt only Tue-Thu; Ⓜ 4, 5, 6 to 86th St

This stately mansion is (in theory) the residence of the Mayor of New York – though few of them actually live here – and is worth visiting just for the views. Surrounded by Carl Schurz Park and the East River esplanade, Gracie Mansion is a throwback to American elegance c 1930 and earlier. History buffs should book a tour, but do it at least two months in advance of your trip; the waiting list is long and walk-ins aren't accepted.

The Frick Collection – exquisite art in an elegant setting

There's enough art for days of wandering at the Met

☺ METROPOLITAN MUSEUM OF ART

☎ 212-535-7710; www.metmuseum
.org; Fifth Ave at E 82nd St; admission by
suggested donation; ⏲ 9:30am-5:30pm
Tue-Thu & Sun, to 9pm Fri & Sat; ☺ 4, 5,
6 to 86th St

What can you say about this
gorgeous behemoth? Its size,
and the depth and breadth of its
collection, simply overwhelms.
More than five million come a year
for special exhibits, or just to see
the cavernous Great Hall entrance,
the Temple of Dendur, the Tiffany
windows in the American Wing,
the collection of African, Oceanian
and other works, as well as the
famed European Collection on the
2nd floor – it's a city within a city,
really, and it's easier to get lost
here than in Central Park outside.
Avoid rainy Sundays in summer
if you don't like crowds. But, during horrible winter weather, you
might find the 17-acre museum
deserted at night – a real NYC
experience. The rooftop garden
becomes a wine bar on weekend
evenings in the summer.

☺ NEUE GALERIE

☎ 212-628-6200; www.neuegalerie.org;
1048 Fifth Ave at E 86th St; admission $15,
child under 12 not admitted; ⏲ 11am-
6pm Sat-Mon & Thu, to 9pm Fri; ☺ 4, 5,
6 to 86th St

Gustav Klimt, Paul Klee and Egon
Schiele are just some of the

NEIGHBORHOODS

UPPER EAST SIDE

marquee names hanging on the walls of the Neue Galerie, which opened in 2000 to showcase Austrian and German art. It also boasts a lovely street-level eatery, Cafe Sabarsky (p188), serving Viennese meals, pastries and drinks.

◉ SOLOMON R GUGGENHEIM MUSEUM
☎ 212-423-3500; www.guggenheim .org; 1071 Fifth Ave at E 89th St; adult $18, senior & student $15, child under 12 free; ⊙ 10am-5:45pm Sat-Wed, to 7:45pm Fri; ◉ 4, 5, 6 to 86th St; ♿
Excellent exhibits from around the world come frequently to the Guggenheim, which is slightly

less overwhelming than some other Manhattan museums. Its curving walls bring you in a spiral downward, showcasing Piet Mondrians, Wassily Kandinskys and more.

◉ TEMPLE EMANU-EL
☎ 212-744-1400; www.emanuelnyc .org; 1 E 65th St; ⊙ 9am-7pm; ◉ 6 to 68th St-Hunter College; ♿
A premiere house of worship, Temple Emanu-el was once part of the Lower East Side Jewish community; as their lot improved, so did the temple's location. It houses a renowned collection of Judaica, and tells the story of its transformation into a ritzy Upper East Side house of worship with murals on the walls.

◉ WHITNEY MUSEUM OF AMERICAN ART
☎ 212-570-3676; www.whitney.org; 945 Madison Ave at E 75th St; adult $15, senior & student $10, child under 12 free; suggested donation 6-9pm Fri; ⊙ 11am-6pm Wed-Thu, Sat & Sun, 1-9pm Fri; ◉ 6 to 77th St; ♿
Focused pretty much exclusively on American works, the Whit-ney pays ample homage to the Rothkos, the Pollocks and the Hoppers in its collection, but also makes room for newcomers and new mediums. To give you a taste of what you're likely to find,

Art isn't just confined to galleries

some recent exhibits included a retrospective of William Eggleston photos (with a nod to his color-saturated influence on modern filmmakers like Gus Van Sant) and a look at the Paris years of sculptor Alexander Calder.

SHOP

BARNEYS *Department Store*
☎ 212-826-8900; www.barneys.com; 660 Madison Ave; ☽ 10am-8pm Mon-Fri, 10am-7pm Sat, 11am-6pm Sun; ◉ N, R, W to Fifth Ave-59th St

No true shopper could skip a visit to this revered institution, which stretches its youthful apparel, sophisticated looks, designer duds and cosmetics and accessories over four floors. The best department store in town carries the best of today's designers – Marc Jacobs, Miu Miu, Prada and more. Bargains (comparatively speaking) are on the 7th and 8th floors; or try the Barneys Co-Ops on the Upper West Side, in Soho and in Chelsea (p133).

BIS DESIGNER RESALE
Fashion & Accessories, Footwear
☎ 212-396-2760; www.bisbiz.com; 1134 Madison Ave; ☽ 10am-6pm Mon-Wed, Fri & Sat, 10am-7pm Thu, noon-7pm Sun; ◉ 4, 5, 6 to 86th St

Dying for a pair of gorgeous Christian Louboutin shoes at a (semi) affordable price? Here's your best shot at finding some: BIS Designer

Resale, the city's top luxury thrift store. Vintage Hermes scarves and bags, Chanel rings, bracelets and all sorts of clothes (ask clerks what they might have in brand names you like; they sometimes have extra goods in the back) fill the small store, but vintage in this case doesn't mean cheap. Prices are 50 to 74 percent of originals.

DONNA KARAN
Fashion & Accessories
☎ 866-240-4700; www.donnakaran .com; 819 Madison Ave at E 68th St; ☽ 10am-6pm Mon-Sat, noon-6pm Sun; ◉ 6 to 68th St-Hunter College

Head to the top floor if you're looking for markdowns, but oth-

PHARMACIST TO THE STARS

When your clientele consists mainly of fussy Upper East Siders, you know you'd better stock the very best of everything. That's why Zitomers (☎ 212-737-2016; www.zitomers.com; 969 Madison Ave at E 76th St; ☽ 9am-8pm Mon-Fri, 9am-7pm Sat, 10am-6pm Sun; ◉ 6 to 77th St), the preferred neighborhood pharmacy to the Upper East Side, carries all things European — including products that aren't exactly (ahem) FDA approved. We're not talking illicit drugs — just high-powered sunscreens and skin-care creams that usually are only available across the pond. This three-story drugstore is sure to have a cure for whatever ails you.

erwise be prepared to pay handsomely for Donna's *tres chic* city-slicker looks. Men won't find many options, but women can dress themselves for life in this three-story store, which has hair pieces, sunglasses, bags, shoes, belts and jewelry to match the wrap jersey dresses and sharp pantsuits that this designer is known for.

🛍 RALPH LAUREN
Fashion & Accessories

☎ 866-606-2100; www.ralphlauren.com; 867 Madison Ave at E 71st St; ☽ 10am-6pm Mon-Sat, noon-6pm Sun; ⊕ 6 to 68th St-Hunter College

You'll feel like you've walked into a country estate when you enter this shop, housed in the former Rhinelander Mansion (a French Renaissance Revival wonder built in 1898). Women and men can deck themselves out in casual wear – jeans, white tops, etc – and more formal wear, with gossamer gowns for the ladies and sleek suits for men.

🍴 EAT

🍽 ANDRE'S PATISSERIE
European/Hungarian Bakery $

☎ 212-327-1105; 1631 Second Ave; ☽ 10am-9pm; ⊕ 4, 5, 6 to 86th St; V ☺

This narrow little café/bakery is the perfect antidote to a cold day.

You'll be thoroughly defrosted once you sample the peppery goulashes, homemade stews, warm crepes and the other Old Country favorites that sprinkle the menu. Andre's also has an abundant selection of strudels, chocolate, cinnamon and cabbage kugelhopf, Bavarian chocolates, decadent cakes and more.

🍽 BEYOGLU
Turkish, Middle Eastern $$

☎ 212-650-0850; 1431 Third Ave; ☽ lunch & dinner; ⊕ 4, 5, 6 to 86th St; ♿ V

Best in the summer when you can sit outside, Beyoglu's fresh Turkish cuisine is light and enticing, from the feta-laden salads to the grilled fish and ample meze.

🍽 CAFE SABARSKY
Austrian $$

☎ 212-288-0665; www.wallse.com; 1048 Fifth Ave at E 86th St; ☽ breakfast, lunch & dinner; ⊕ 4, 5, 6 to 86th St; V ☺

It can get a little tight in this popular Neue Galerie café on the weekends, but the food and opulent ambience make it worth the fight for a table. Authentic Austrian food – trout-filled crepes, goulash, sausage and strudel – are served on heavy platters and silver cups brought from Vienna.

☷ LA GOULUE
French Bistro $$$

☎ 212-988-8169; www.lagoulue
restaurant.com; 746 Madison Ave btwn
E 64th & E 65th Sts; ⏱ noon-11:30pm
Mon-Sat, 11:30am-11:30pm Sun; ⊕ 6 to
68th St-Hunter College, N, R, W to Fifth
Ave-59th St; ♿

There may be bistros with better
French food in Manhattan, but
none more inviting in the heart
of ritzy Madison Ave. La Goulue
attracts legions of loyal fans who
enjoy the outdoor wicker seats,
big shady yellow awning and
thrown-wide French doors as
much as the steak au poivre, coq
au vin, crispy duck and haricots
verts. The menu's a bit staid, but
who cares what's on the plate
when fellow patrons include the
likes of Demi Moore and Ashton
Kutcher, Jude Law, Kim Cattrall,
Rod Stewart and Bruce Spring-
steen? If it's good enough for The
Boss, it's good enough for us.

☷ PIE BY THE POUND
Pizzeria $

☎ 212-517-5017; www.piebythepound
.com; 1542 Second Ave near E 80th St;
⏱ 11am-11pm; ⊕ 6 to 77th St; Ⓥ ♿

You don't really have to eat a
pound of pizza here, although
there's no doubt some people are
tempted to. The name refers to the
way staffers dole out the goods.
Instead of the traditional slice,

pies here are square and long,
and servers lop off as much or as
little as you want, weigh it, and
there you have your pie. Pie by
the Pound has tons of veggie op-
tions, lots of variations on cheese,
and great sausage, pancetta and
salami meat pies.

☷ SFOGLIA *Italian* $$$

☎ 212-831-1402; http://sfoglia
restaurant.com; 1402 Lexington Ave at
E 92nd St; ⏱ lunch & dinner Mon-Sat,
closed 2-5:30pm; ⊕ 6 to 96th St; ♿

A darling of the critics since it
opened a few years back, Sfoglia
brought its winning combo of
fresh seafood and homemade
Italian from Nantucket to New
York, and its tiny but attractive
Upper East Side space is packed
every day. Innovative pairings like
wild mussels with tomato, garlic,
salami and fennel pollen; spinach
and ricotta balls cooked in brown
butter with preserved lemon; or
breaded pork chops with pickled
carrots and mustard will have you
swooning.

☷ DRINK
☷ AUCTION HOUSE *Bar*

☎ 212-427-4458; 300 E 89th St;
⏱ 7:30pm-4am; ⊕ 4, 5, 6 to 86th St

Dark maroon doors lead into a
sexy, candlelit hangout that's
perfect for a relaxing drink.
Victorian-style couches and fat,

THE DIRTY ECO-TINI

Several high-end hotels in Midtown East and the Upper East Side have started making 'green' drinks. Martinis are made with organic vodka and olives, and proceeds from the drinks go to the Trust for Public Land, a nonprofit group that works to preserve city playgrounds and parks. Two hotels that make a dirty martini with a green footprint are **70 Park Ave** (70 Park Ave; 🕑 11am-1am; 🚇 N, R, 4, 5, 6 to Grand Central-42nd St) and the **Muse** (130 W 46th St; 🕑 2pm-midnight; 🚇 B, D, F, V to 47th-50th Sts-Rockefeller Center).

overstuffed easy chairs are strewn about the wood-floored rooms. Those looking to mix can gather round the various fireplaces and admire the scene reflected in the gilt-edged mirrors propped up on the walls. The bar's well-crafted martinis taste pretty darn good from the depths of a comfortable chair.

🍸 BEMELMANS BAR *Bar*
☎ 212-744-1600; www.thecarlyle.com; Carlyle Hotel, 35 E 76th St; after 9:30pm Sun-Fri $20, after 9:30pm Sat $25; 🕑 noon-2am Mon-Sat, to 12:30am Sun; 🚇 6 to 77th St

The only surviving commissioned mural from Ludwig Bemelmans still on display to the public infuses this namesake café with the artist's legendary wit. Bemel-

mans' plush red interior is a perfect place to canoodle, making it a favorite for in-love couples and those wishing to conduct an affair of the heart with discretion. Suave and sophisticated piano jazz is the musical mainstay. Also in Carlyle Hotel is the fantastic Carlyle's, a great cabaret lounge and bar.

🍸 STIR *DJ Bar*
☎ 212-744-7190; http://stirnyc.com; 1363 First Ave near E 73rd St; 🕑 5pm-1am Mon-Wed, 5pm-2am Thu, 5pm-4am Fri, 8pm-4am Sat, 8pm-1am Sun; 🚇 6 to 77th St

A bland entryway turns into a jazzy little bar, with sleek leather banquettes against the wall and fuzzy, brightly colored ottomans to sit on around the room. A DJ spins tunes ranging from '80s alternative to hip hop and punk on weekends, and a varied local crowd lines up to sample the staple drink: flavored martinis. At happy hour (late afternoon) prices drop as low as two bucks a pop.

⭐ PLAY

🎭 92ND STREET Y *Arts*
☎ 212-415-5500; www.92y.org; 1395 Lexington Ave at E 92nd St; 🕑 hours vary; 🚇 6 to 96th St

The Y is a bastion of literary greatness (as well as a venue that caters for music and dance), with its Unterburg Poetry Center hosting frequent readings, plus a Biographers and Brunch lecture series on Sundays, featuring top-shelf authors. Recent appearances have included Paul Auster, Margaret Atwood, Joan Didion and Michael Chabon. Almost all the big-name readings sell out, so if there's a particular author you want to hear, reserve well in advance.

⭐ **DANGERFIELD'S**
Comedy Club
☎ 212-593-1650; www.dangerfields
.com; 1118 First Ave at E 61st St;
⏲ shows at approx 8:30pm & 10pm;
🚇 6 to 59th St

New York's oldest and (some claim) funniest comedy club, Dangerfield's is something of an institution. Crowds still pack in for the no-food-or-drink-minimum shows (a rarity in New York, where most clubs make you consume as you laugh), and it features only top-tier talent – no amateur nights allowed. Gone are the days when comedic stars would regularly pop in for a cameo, but on the odd occasion an old friend like Jerry Seinfeld, Chris Rock or Jay Leno might pop in.

>UPPER WEST SIDE

Sedate but still charming, the Upper West Side retains its aura of unconventional happiness in the face of increasing gentrification. Its cheery mix of aging liberals, wealthy young families, wide-eyed students and gainfully employed actors and musicians has helped protect the Upper West Side from the ravages of development; stretches of chain stores abound, but plenty of old-school options, such as Zabar's and Barney Greengrass, remain.

Strong on the arts, it houses Lincoln Center, where you can see the Metropolitan Opera House, Jazz at Lincoln Center, the world-famous Juilliard School of Music and, in summer, outdoor performances and free dance nights (mostly salsa, tango and swing, with lessons thrown in).

Nearby Columbia University translates into a college-town feeling on its upper reaches – the bars are plentiful and cheap. It's flanked by two fabulous green spaces that stretch north alongside the neighborhood: Central Park on its east edge and Riverside Park to the west. The plentiful parkland contributes to its friendly, bohemian vibe.

UPPER WEST SIDE

◉ SEE
American Museum of
　Natural History...........**1** C3
Children's Museum of
　Manhattan **2** B2
Dakota Building **3** C4
Lincoln Center **4** C5
New-York Historical
　Society.....................**5** C3
Riverside Park **6** B2

⬜ SHOP
Maxilla & Mandible........**7** C3
Off Broadway Boutiques...**8** C4
West **9** C4
Zabar's.........................**10** B3

⽥ EAT
Barney Greengrass.......**11** C2
Cafe con Leche **12** B1
Josie's Restaurant **13** B4
Kefi **14** B3
Pio Pio **15** B1
Roppongi.....................**16** C3

▼ DRINK
Maritime Café at Pier 1...**17** B4
Prohibition **18** C2
West 79th Street Boat
　Basin Café..................**19** B3

▦ PLAY
Cleopatra's Needle **20** B1
Iridium.........................**21** C5
Jazz at Lincoln Center ...**22** C5
Leonard Nimoy
　Thalia.........................**23** B1
Symphony Space........(see **23**)

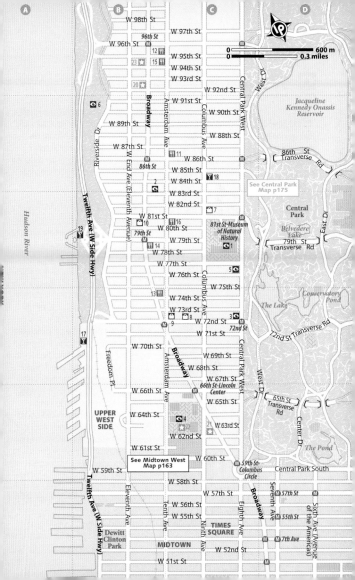

👁 SEE

📷 AMERICAN MUSEUM OF NATURAL HISTORY

☎ 212-769-5000; www.amnh.org; Central Park West at W 79th St; suggested donation adult $14, senior & student $10.50, child $8, last hour free; 🕙 10am-5:45pm, Rose Center to 8:45pm Fri; 🚇 B, C to 81st St-Museum of Natural History, 1 to 79th St
From the outside, it's hard to tell just how massive this museum really is. Its exhibits go on for days through three huge halls, plus there's the Rose Center for Earth and Space (free tapas, jazz and drinks on Friday nights), Imax theaters, a planetarium, and oh, did we mention the special kid's section where all exhibits are touchy-feely and interactive? Even experts can't help but be dazzled by the more than 30 million bits and bobs in here.

📷 CHILDREN'S MUSEUM OF MANHATTAN

☎ 212-721-1234; www.cmom.org; 212 W 83rd St btwn Amsterdam Ave & Broadway; admission $9, child under 1 free; 🕙 10am-5pm Wed-Sun; 🚇 1 to 86th St, B, C to 81st St-Museum of Natural History
As much for mommy and daddy as the little ones, this museum doesn't talk down to kids. It's got a discovery center, a postmodern media center, the top-of-the-line Inventor Center where the world's future Bill Gates can prod, poke and disassemble whatever he wants. During summer months, kids can splash around with outdoor waterwheels and boats for lessons on buoyancy and currents. The museum also runs craft workshops on the weekends and sponsors special exhibitions.

📷 DAKOTA BUILDING

1 W 72nd St at Central Park West; 🚇 B, C to 72nd St; ♿
A turreted, gabled building described in 1884 as so far uptown

Explore the American Museum of Natural History

it was in 'the Dakotas,' this sand-colored gem quickly became the epitome of cool, housing Boris Karloff, Rudolph Nureyev, Lauren Bacall and, most famously, John Lennon, who was fatally shot at its gated entrance.

LINCOLN CENTER

☎ 212-875-5900; www.newyorkphil harmonic.org; Lincoln Center Plaza, Broadway at W 64th St-Lincoln Center; performance hours vary, tours btwn 10:30am-4:30pm; ⊕ 1 to 66th St; ♿ ⚹

Sprawling Lincoln Center is a miniature city in its own right: Avery Fisher Hall, home to the New York Philharmonic, currently undergoing a redesign, sits next to Alice Tully Hall, the locus of the Chamber Music Society. The New York State Theater plays host to the **New York City Ballet** (www.nycballet .com) and the **New York City Opera** (www.nycopera.com). Walter Reade Theater hosts the New York Film Festival and shows quality films daily. There are the Newhouse and Beaumont theaters, Juilliard School and, last but not least, the Metropolitan Opera House, with its sweeping, grand, red-carpeted staircase. Daily tours of the Lincoln Center and theaters are available (tickets adult $15, student & senior $12, child $8; call ☎ 212-875-5350 for tour information).

NEW-YORK HISTORICAL SOCIETY

☎ 212-873-3400; www.nyhistory.org; 2 W 77th St at Central Park West; adult/child under 12 $10/free; 10am-6pm Tue-Sun; ⊕ 1 to 79th St, B, C to 81st St-Museum of Natural History

Founded in 1804 to preserve the city's historical and cultural artifacts, this gem is often overlooked by visitors tramping to the nearby American Museum of Natural History. A pity, since its collection of more than 60,000 objects is as quirky and fascinating as NYC itself. Only here can you see 17th-century cowbells and baby rattles and the mounted wooden leg of Gouverneur Morris. The Henry Luce III Center for the Study of American Culture, which opened in 2000, is a 21,000-sq-ft showcase of more than 40,000 objects from the museum's permanent collection, and features items such as fine portraits, Tiffany lamps and model ships. The place always hosts unique special exhibits, too, with recent examples including 'Here is New York: Remembering 9/11' and 'Audubon's Aviary: Portraits of Endangered Species.'

RIVERSIDE PARK

www.riversideparkfund.org; Riverside Dr from W 68th to W 155th Sts; 6am-1am; ⊕ 1, 2, 3 to any stop btwn 66th & 157th Sts; ♿

Another classic beauty designed by Central Park creators Olmsted and Vaux, this waterside spot, running north on the Upper West Side and banked by the Hudson River, is lusciously leafy and tranquil. Plenty of bike paths and playgrounds make it a family favorite.

SHOP

MAXILLA & MANDIBLE
Novelty Store

☎ 212-724-6173; www.maxillaand mandible.com; 451 Columbus Ave near W 82nd St; ☾ 11am-7pm Mon-Sat; ◉ B, C to 81st St-Museum of Natural History

'The World's First and Only Osteological Store' has been around since 1983, ideally situated about a block from the Museum of Natural History. Fans of bones, fossils and beetle-studded jewelry will be entranced by the varied goodies on display at this specialty shop. Most people come in to gawk at the dangling skeletons and rows of neatly arranged bones, but few can resist picking up a few novelty items like lucite bracelets filled with brightly colored shield bugs from Thailand. They come in rings and necklaces, too.

OFF BROADWAY BOUTIQUES *Thrift Store*

☎ 212-724-6713; www.boutiqueoff broadway.com; 139 W 72nd St near Amsterdam Ave; ☾ 10:30am-8pm Mon-

Fri, 10:30am-7pm Sat, 1-7pm Sun; ◉ 1, 2, 3 to 72nd St

Dressing divas since 1970, Off Broadway's clothes are sparkling, vivid and far, far too garish for almost everyone's taste – and yet somehow this thrift shop has stayed in business for nearly 40 years. Maybe it's the odd gem or two tucked into the back section, called Re-Runs, that keeps people flocking in: hidden in the bins are vintage finds by Yves St Laurent, Dior and others. The owner also scours the globe for emerging designers and features their clothes in the front of the shop. There are real bargains to be had, but you'll have to search for them.

WEST *Fashion & Accessories*

☎ 212-787-8595; http://west147nyc .blogspot.com; 147 W 72nd St; ☾ 10am-7:30pm Mon-Sat, 11am-7pm Sun; ◉ B, C, 1, 2, 3 to 72nd St

Pick up your politically correct, organic T-shirts here – and pair them with some pumped up footwear too. This newcomer lights up staid W 72nd St with its brightly colored sneakers by Nike, Brand Jordan, Adidas and Clarks high-top casuals. T-shirts and jackets (by Canada Goose and Arc'teryx) carry whimsical and off-beat logos and messages like 'Not Black, Not White. Grey,' along with the always classic 'Give Peace a Chance.'

ZABAR'S *Food & Drink*

☎ 212-787-2000; www.zabars.com; 2245 Broadway; ⏰ 8:30am-7:30pm Mon-Fri, 8am-8pm Sat, 9am-6pm Sun; ⊖ 1 to 79th St

An unofficial Upper West Side landmark, Zabar's still has that special 'only in New York' vibe that makes you feel like you're in an original Woody Allen movie. People bustle and bump around the gourmet foods discussing their lives, politics and the freshness of the gefilte fish as if they were the only ones in the room.

EAT

BARNEY GREENGRASS
Kosher Deli $$

☎ 212-724-2707; www.barneygreen grass.com; 541 Amsterdam Ave at W 86th St; ⏰ breakfast & lunch; ⊖ 1 to 86th St; ♿ ⛲

The self-proclaimed king of sturgeon, Barney Greengrass serves up the same heaping dishes of eggs and salty lox, bialys and fishy caviar, and melt-in-your-mouth chocolate babkas that first made it famous when it opened a century ago. Pop in to fuel up in the morning or for a quick lunch; there are rickety tables set amid the crowded produce aisles. Besides salmon and whiting, kippered eggs and other Jewish delicacies, you can of course get a perfect New York bagel.

CAFE CON LECHE
Cuban, Puerto Rican $$

☎ 212-678-7000; 726 Amsterdam Ave near W 96th St; ⏰ lunch & dinner; ⊖ B, C, 1, 2, 3 to 96th St; ♿ ⛲

A cozy hideaway on the Upper West Side, not far from the northern reaches of Central Park

SOMETHING FISHY WITH YOUR FISH?

Your server swears the salmon in tonight's special has just been caught off the Alaskan coast and is 100 percent pesticide free. Don't believe him? Get more information on the spot by texting 30644 from your cell (mobile) phone. Type FISH and then the type you are considering eating: SALMON, in this example. You'll get an immediate reply from the Blue Ocean Institute, a nonprofit marine conservation group. Blue Ocean will send you details on any significant environmental concerns about the fish you may be eating for dinner – and red flags are given to species that are overfished or known to contain high levels of PCBs, mercury or pesticides. Blue Ocean will also text you an alternative fish choice – one that's greener for the planet and healthier for you. And sushi lovers can get in on the action too – just download Blue Ocean's latest guide to ecofriendly sushi choices at www.blueocean.org and you can go crazy with the sashimi without worrying about eating dangerously depleted species.

SHAKE SHACK EXPANDS

The impossibly popular burger and hot dog stand known as the Shake Shack is reportedly coming to the Upper West Side, courtesy of celebrity chef Danny Meyer's growing empire. The organic burger stand made famous in Madison Sq Park (p142) is scheduled to open in 2009 at a new location at 366 Columbus Ave at W 77th St, a welcome addition to the Upper West Side.

and St John the Divine Cathedral, Cafe con Leche's breezy yellow doors lead into a cheery dining room that's short on luxury but long on friendly service. Great Cuban coffee and heaping plates of *arroz con pollo* (chicken and rice), *ropa vieja* (shredded beef) and *mofongo* (a Puerto Rican specialty) keep it busy late into the evening.

JOSIE'S RESTAURANT
Health Food $$

☎ 212-769-1212; 300 Amsterdam Ave; dinner Mon-Fri, lunch & dinner Sat & Sun; ⊕ 1, 2, 3 to 72nd St; ♿ Ⓥ ⚤

Organic fare (with its provenance listed on the menu) that satisfies vegans, vegetarians and meat eaters alike has kept Josie's around for more than a decade. Its clean, simple ambience is reflected in the food – steak, salads, gorgeous veggie dishes, but nothing too processed or tortured.

KEFI *Greek* $$

☎ 212-873-0200; 222 W 79th St btwn Broadway & Amsterdam Ave; dinner; ⊕ 1 to 79th St; ⚤

Seafood and feta aficionados will go crazy for Kefi's rustic Greek fare done at comparatively low-budget prices. The low-ceilinged, street-level dining room, tricked out with bright blue Greek charms to ward off the evil eye, gets noisy and crowded some nights, but you can still enjoy the grilled-to-perfection shrimp, *branzino*, striped bass and calamari. For traditionalists, Kefi offers plenty of meze, feta, tzatziki and moussaka to dig into. Cash only and no reservations.

PIO PIO *Peruvian* $$

☎ 212-665-3000; 702 Amsterdam Ave at W 94th St; lunch & dinner; ⊕ 1, 2, 3 to 96th St; ♿ ⚤

Swallow hard before you order the two-person Matador Combo, which is really enough food to feed you and a bull. It comes with an entire rotisserie chicken – the specialty of the house – plus rice and beans, *tostones* (deep-fried plantains), a salad and a massive plate of fries. Those without cast-iron stomachs might prefer to just order pieces of rotisserie chicken from the menu. Pio Pio is famous for its well-marinated and crispy golden birds.

🍴 ROPPONGI *Japanese* $$
☎ 212-362-8182; 434 Amsterdam Ave; ⏱ lunch & dinner; ⊕ 1 to 79th St, B, C to 81st St-Museum of Natural History; 🚹 🅅 🛆

Melt-in-your-mouth, five-flavor sashimi, perfectly round rice and delicately cooked noodles, salmon with green-olive moromi miso, and sushi rolls accompanied by mango salsa and orange compote are regular fixtures at this Upper West Side standout, which has the friendliest waiters ever. On a nice night you can sit outside and watch the scenesters roll up to insanely popular Haru across the street; it's twice the price of Roppongi and about half the fun.

🍸 DRINK
🍸 MARITIME CAFÉ AT PIER 1 *Café*
☎ 917-612-4330; W 70th St at the Hudson River; ⏱ noon-midnight; ⊕ 1, 2, 3 to 72nd St

Here is an ingenious use of the Riverside Park esplanade – an outdoor café with grilled grub, fruity cocktails and lounge chairs set up on the grass for those who reserve in advance. It's the same front-row view of the Hudson River sunset you'll get from the neighboring West 79th Street Boat Basin Café, but with much better lounge chair service. Summertime

brings frequent live music, as well as movies, shown al fresco at the end of the connecting pier.

🍸 PROHIBITION *Bar*
☎ 212-579-3100; 503 Columbus Ave near W 84th St; ⏱ 5pm-3am; ⊕ B, C, 1 to 86th St

There's not much that's prohibited at Prohibition – in fact, the bar is nicely set up to accommodate a lot of drinking. There's a live band almost every night up front, but decibel levels are low enough that your ears won't bleed. Those who want to talk can head into the back, which is band-free, and for those who prefer sports, there's a billiard table. Sexy red walls and inventive drinks (lavender martinis and rum mojitos) add a little flair, and the bite-sized burgers are a perfect bar snack.

🍸 WEST 79TH STREET BOAT BASIN CAFÉ *Riverside Café*
☎ 212-496-5542; www.boatbasincafe .com; W 79th St at Henry Hudson Parkway; ⏱ lunch & dinner Apr-Oct, weather permitting; ⊕ 1 to 79th St; 🛆

Sunsets on the Hudson – it's not quite the same as sundown in the Caribbean, but its pretty darn good, all the same. This café, located on the far west side of Manhattan, offers a great location from which to watch the action, and suck back a cold one while you do it. Come the hot weather, the West 79th

Street Boat Basin Café is everyone's favorite evening hangout.

⭐ PLAY

⭐ CLEOPATRA'S NEEDLE *Club*
☎ 212-769-6969; www.cleopatrasneedle ny.com; 2485 Broadway btwn W 92nd & W 93rd Sts; 🕙 4pm-late; 🚇 1, 2, 3 to 96th St

Come early and you'll probably make the daily happy hour, when martinis are half price. Cleopatra's Needle (named after the statue in Central Park) is small and narrow, just like its namesake. Grab a small table or sit at the bar to enjoy Mediterranean-style food. There's no cover, but a $10 minimum. If you come early, be prepared to stay late: Cleopatra's famous for all-night jam sessions that hit their peak around 4am.

⭐ IRIDIUM *Jazz Music*
☎ 212-582-2121; www.iridiumjazzclub .com; 1650 Broadway; cover $25-40; 🕙 6:30pm-late; 🚇 A, B, C, D, 1 to 59th St-Columbus Circle

Consistently pulling in the biggest names in town, Iridium is pricey and a bit fussy, but it's clear why when you get inside: service, sight lines and acoustics are done to perfection, allowing you to slip away on a swell of glossy jazz.

Music lovers should beat a (rhythmic) path to Jazz at Lincoln Center

Reserve early, especially when the Mingus Big Band is in town.

⭐ JAZZ AT LINCOLN CENTER
Jazz Music

☎ 212-258-9595; www.jazzatlincoln center.org; Time Warner Center, Broadway at W 60th St; ⏱ hours vary; 🚇 A, B, C, D, 1 to 59th St-Columbus Circle

There are three venues that make up Jazz at Lincoln Center: Rose Theater, Allen Room and Dizzy's Club Coca-Cola. The first two are pretty fancy, but it's the last one you're likely to visit because it's got nightly shows year round. Ignore the obnoxious name and focus on the musical talent – it's world class, just like the excellent Central Park views.

⭐ LEONARD NIMOY THALIA
Cinema

☎ 212-236-5849; www.symphony space.org; 2537 Broadway; tickets $7-10; ⏱ daily; 🚇 1, 2, 3 to 96th St; 🚹 🚻

Name any obscure French or Japanese or Mexican film and you can bet it's been shown here. This secret little cinema can be counted on to show the most eclectic and esoteric films from around the world and through the ages. It's a film buff's fantasy come true.

⭐ SYMPHONY SPACE
Live Music

☎ 212-864-1414; www.symphonyspace .com; 2537 Broadway; ⏱ hours vary; 🚇 1, 2, 3 to 96th St; 🚹 🚻

Home to National Public Radio's renowned literary readings, Symphony Space is a gem supported by community contributions. It often has three-day series that are dedicated to just one musician, and has an affinity for world music. In the basement is UnWINed, a tapas and vino bar that never charges a cover to listen to its free nightly live band.

>HARLEM

Hip and happening Harlem has held on to its rough edges amid an influx of money and development, and still remains one of Manhattan's most community-oriented neighborhoods. With development surging along the commercial 125th St strip, Harlem's changing one storefront at a time, but not without constant involvement from local leaders determined to keep this Afro-centric nabe's special energy alive.

Settepani's, the iconic Lenox Lounge jazz club, the Malcolm Shabazz Market and other well-known parts of Harlem are along Lenox Ave, the main drag. The west side, by Columbia University, has Riverside Church, the Cathedral of St John the Divine, and Smoke, a funky jazz club. Historic Harlem is along and above the 125th St shopping center, where the Apollo, Studio Museum and the Schomburg Center are located. The east side has El Museo del Barrio, a grassroots museum featuring Puerto Rican, Dominican and Caribbean artists.

HARLEM

🅒 SEE

🅢 SHOP

🍴 EAT

🆈 DRINK

⭐ PLAY

◉ SEE

◉ ABYSSINIAN BAPTIST CHURCH

☎ 212-862-7474; www.abyssinian.org; 132 Odell Pl (W 138th St) btwn Adam Clayton Powell Jr Blvd & Lenox Ave; ⓨ services 9am & 11am Sun; ◉ 2, 3 to 135th St

Founded by an Ethiopian businessman, the Abyssinian Baptist Church began as a downtown institution but moved north to Harlem in 1923, mirroring the migration of the city's black population. Its charismatic pastor, Calvin O Butts III, is an important community activist whose support is sought by politicians of all parties. The church has a superb choir and the building is a beauty. If you plan on visiting with a group of 10 or more, the congregation requests that you call in advance to see if space is available.

◉ APOLLO THEATER

☎ 212-531-5337; 5253 W 125th St at Frederick Douglass Blvd; tours weekdays $16, Sat & Sun $18; ⓨ tours 11am, 1pm & 3pm Mon, Tue, Thu, Fri, 11am Wed, 11am & 1pm Sat & Sun; ◉ A, B, C, D to 125th St

This has been Harlem's leading space for political rallies and concerts since 1914. Virtually every major black artist of note in the 1930s and '40s performed here, in-

Songs, architecture, history or prayer, there are many reasons to visit Abyssinian Baptist Church

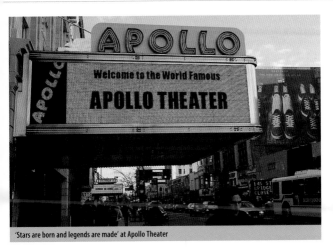
'Stars are born and legends are made' at Apollo Theater

cluding Duke Ellington and Charlie Parker. After a desultory spell as a movie theater and several years of darkness, the Apollo was bought in 1983 and revived as a live venue. Now the Apollo interior is more beautiful than ever: gold sconces and balconies, and plush red seats. Its famous weekly Amateur Night, 'where stars are born and legends are made,' still takes place on Wednesdays, with a wild and ruthless crowd that's as fun to watch as the performers.

🏛 CATHEDRAL OF ST JOHN THE DIVINE
☎ 212-316-7540; www.stjohndivine .org; 1047 Amsterdam Ave at W 112th St;

🕙 7am-6pm Mon-Sat, to 7pm Sun; 🚇 1 to 110th St; ♿

A beloved spiritual and artistic center in Manhattan, the cathedral's massive nave is a mix of Romanesque and Gothic Revival styles blended harmoniously together. Started in 1892, the cathedral's still not done – the finishing touches on the towers should be in place by 2050, if workers stay on schedule.

🏛 EL MUSEO DEL BARRIO
☎ 212-831-7272; www.elmuseo.org; 1230 Fifth Ave at E 104th St; suggested donation adult $6, senior & student $4, child under 12 free, seniors free on Thu; 🕙 11am-5pm Wed-Sun; 🚇 2, 3 to Central Park North-110th St; ♿

Growing out of the Nuyorican and Civil Rights Movement in East Harlem, El Museo remains the only major museum in the city dedicated to Puerto Rican and Latin work, with a permanent collection of pre-Colombian and Taino artifacts, and revolving modern-art exhibits. At press time it was undergoing a long overdue face-lift, and planning to reopen in the 2009 fall.

GENERAL US GRANT NATIONAL MEMORIAL

☎ 212-666-1640; www.nps.gov/gegr; Riverside Dr at W 122nd St; ⏰ 9am-5pm; ⓜ 1 to 125th St

Popularly known as Grant's Tomb, this landmark holds the remains of Civil War hero and president Ulysses S Grant and those of his wife, Julia. Completed in 1897 (12 years after his death) the granite structure cost $600,000 and is the largest mausoleum in the country.

MUSEUM OF THE CITY OF NEW YORK

☎ 212-534-1672; www.mcny.org; 1220 Fifth Ave at E 103rd St; admission by suggested donation; ⏰ 10am-5pm Tue-Sun; ⓜ 2, 3 to Central Park North-110th St; ♿

This collection spans the past, present and future of the five boroughs in lithographs, photo-graphs, cartoons, clothes and more. Exhibits cover all facets of city life, from hard-core skaters in Brooklyn to famous city interior designers.

RIVERSIDE CHURCH

☎ 212-870-6700; www.theriverside churchny.org; 490 Riverside Dr at W 120th St; ⏰ 7am-10pm via Claremont Ave entrance, visitors center 10am-7pm Wed; ⓜ 1 to 116th St; ♿

Famous for combining its spiritual beliefs with progressive politics, Riverside Church has had Martin Luther King Jr, Fidel Castro and Nelson Mandela holding forth from its pulpit.

SCHOMBURG CENTER FOR RESEARCH IN BLACK CULTURE

☎ 212-491-2200; www.nypl.org/research /sc/sc.html; 515 Lenox Ave; ⏰ noon-8pm Tue & Wed, noon-6pm Thu & Fri, 10am-6pm Sat; ⓜ 2, 3 to 135th St

The nation's largest collection of documents, rare books, record-ings and photographs relating to the African American experience resides at this center near W 135th St. Arthur Schomburg, born in Puerto Rico, started gathering works on black history during the early 20th century while becoming active in the movements for civil rights and Puerto Rican independ-ence. His impressive collection was purchased by the Carnegie

David Green
Contractor

What's your favorite part of New York? Harlem, definitely, because of the people. There's a real community here. **What's a tourist trap that's worth the trip?** Sylvia's (p210) – it's the real thing, even when those big buses pull up and unload tourists. It's a great place to eat. **Where do you take visitors when they come to Harlem?** If it's summer, I take them up to 145th St on the weekends to check out the basketball tournaments. Nike, Adidas, all the big sponsors are there, and the kids can play. Down on 116th St too, there are some courts where the action is pretty hot. We'd do some shopping on 125th St, see what the African sellers have going on, then walk along 116th St around Seventh Ave. That's where you'll find the best African and Jamaican restaurants in Harlem. **Did you play in the basketball tournaments?** Oh yeah, back in the day, but I can't do it now. You have to have some tricks to keep up with those kids.

Foundation and eventually expanded and stored in this branch of the New York Public Library.

🖼 STUDIO MUSEUM IN HARLEM

☎ 212-864-4500; www.studiomuseum.org; 144 W 125th St at Adam Clayton Powell Jr Blvd; admission by suggested donation; ⏱ noon-6pm Wed-Fri & Sun, 10am-6pm Sat; 🚇 3 to 125th St, 2, 4, 5, 6 to 125th St; ♿

An eclectic mix of work by African American and Caribbean artists hangs on the walls of the Studio Museum. Exhibits range from abstract expressionism to political cartoons, and they go a long way toward debunking the myth that no great African American artists emerged in the first half of the 20th century.

🛍 SHOP

🛒 B OYAMA HOMME
Fashion & Accessories

☎ 212-234-5128; www.boyamahomme.com; 2330 Adam Clayton Powell Blvd Jr at W 136th St; ⏱ 2-8pm Mon, 11am-8pm Tue-Fri, 10:30am-6pm Sat; 🚇 C to 135th St

Bernard Oyama is the 'Haberdasher of Harlem,' and one look at his wing-tipped shoes, two-tone suits and sleek fedoras and you'll get an urge to shoot your cuffs, too. His boutique sells tailor-cut suits, an

assortment of shirts, and items like ties, pocket squares, gloves, cuff links and suspenders.

🛒 HARLEM'S HEAVEN HAT BOUTIQUE *Hats*

☎ 212-491-7706; www.harlemsheaven.com; 2538 Adam Clayton Powell Jr Blvd at W 147th St; ⏱ noon-6pm Tue-Sat; 🚇 3 to Harlem-148th St

Evetta Petty's been designing custom hats from her Harlem location for more than 15 years – and if you've been looking for just the right hat for Easter Sunday, or a day at the races, Evetta's got many, many options for you. There are also some fantastic retro creations, glittering and fancy fedoras, some men's hats and a great treasure trove of vintage brooches, sunglasses and earrings.

🛒 LIBERTY HOUSE
Arts & Crafts, Fashion & Accessories

☎ 212-932-1950; 2878A Broadway near W 112th St; ⏱ 10am-6:45pm Mon-Sat, noon-5:45pm Sun; 🚇 1 to Cathedral Parkway-110th St

A 1960s grassroots cooperative designed to promote the work of American artisans and farmers, Liberty House retains its ecofriendly mission even in today's global economy. Women and children can pick up organic, natural-fiber clothes (no sweatshop labor here, thank you very much!) and its imported goods are bought directly from artists and artisan collectives who use only recycled or non-endangered woods and materials.

SOH-STRAIGHT OUT OF HARLEM *Arts & Crafts*

☎ 212-234-5944; http://straightout harlem.com; 704 St Nicholas Ave btwn W 145th & W 146th Sts; ⏲ 11am-6pm Wed, Fri & Sat, 11am-8pm Thu, 10am-4pm Sun; ⊕ A, B, C, D to 145th St

An eclectic mix and match of local artists' fanciful creations and useful household items, Straight Out of Harlem functions as a boutique shop and art gallery/event space. You can pick up whimsical 'urban cherubs' (aka city angels) while you are here, grab a great Appalachian quilt, or a wall print from celebrated graffiti artist Manny Vega, who's responsible for the four-story mural at 104th St and Lexington Ave.

EAT

AFRICA KINE *Senegalese, Moroccan* $

☎ 212-666-9400; www.africakine.com; 2nd fl, 256 W 116th St; ⏲ lunch & dinner; ⊕ B, C to 116th St; ♿

One of the first African restaurants to open up along the stretch of W 116th St now known as Little Senegal, Kine's succulent lamb and fish dishes, with big bowls of brown rice, garlicky veggies and sometimes couscous, bring in a big lunchtime crowd. Kine doesn't look like much from the outside, but it's a real treat for Africa aficionados. For hard-core Senegalese fans, check out nearby Le Baobab (☎ 212-864-4700; 120 W 116th St near Lenox Ave; ⏲ lunch & dinner; ⊕ B, C to 116th St). It's a small hole in the wall with minimal decor, mostly doing takeout for taxi drivers, but the food is authentic and flavorful. House specialty *poulet yassa* (spicy lemon chicken with rice) sells out fast; call ahead if you want it for dinner.

COMMUNITY FOOD AND JUICE *American Comfort* $$

☎ 212-665-2800; www.community restaurant.com; 2893 Broadway near W 113th St; ⏲ breakfast, lunch & dinner; ⊕ 1 to 116th St-Columbia University; V ♿

At long last, a green restaurant in northern Manhattan. The energy-saving kitchen equipment, recycled wood tables, filtered water (not bottled) speak to the owners' green ethos, but the real show stopper is the food and wine: organic, biodynamic, locally grown and bought at peak freshness, rotating with the changing seasons. Weekend brunches, with light blueberry pancakes,

SOUL FOOD

The reigning queens of Harlem soul food are alive and well:

Amy Ruth's (☎ 212-280-8779; www .amyruthsharlem.com; 113 W 116th St near Lenox Ave; 🕑 lunch & dinner; 🚇 2, 3 to 116th St) Delicious collard greens, mac 'n' cheese, fried chicken and biscuits.

Sylvia's (☎ 212-996-0660; www .sylviassoulfood.com; 328 Lenox Ave; 🕑 lunch & dinner; 🚇 2, 3 to 125th St) All the same fixins as Amy Ruth's, plus chicken-n-waffles, Southern gravy and more.

veggie scramble and warm faro porridge, are insanely popular. Mains include warm lentil salad, 'bowl of beets' (with pistachio nuts, goat cheese and balsamic vinegar), country fried chicken or a grass-fed-beef burger.

🍴 EL PASO TAQUERIA
Mexican $

☎ 212-860-9753; www.elpasotaqueria .com; 237 E 116th St; 🕑 lunch & dinner; 🚇 6 to 116th St; 🚻 Ⓥ ⚭
There are three of these fantastic Mexican joints around town, all of them in upper Manhattan. The prettiest one, covered in blue and green *azulejos* (tiles), is the branch in **East Harlem** (🕑 212-831-9831; 1642 Lexington Ave at 104th St). The **original El Paso Taqueria** (🕑 212-996-1739; 64 East 97th St) is a few blocks south. The

newest one, at 116th St in Harlem, offers the same authentic Mexican food as its sibling locations: fresh *flautas* (long, thin stuffed tortillas), bangin' burritos and a variety of chicken, pork and beef mole dishes that are *muy, muy, muy bueno*.

🍴 MELBA'S
American Comfort, Southern Soul $

☎ 212-864-7777; http://melbas restaurant.com; 300 W 114th St at Frederick Douglass Blvd; 🕑 dinner Tue-Sat, lunch & dinner Sun; 🚇 B, C to 116th St; 🚻 ⚭
Pack in for the Sunday brunch and pile your plate high with sweet-potato pancakes, Melba's French toast, eggnog waffles and Southern fried chicken (yes, they go together), or grab some lighter fare: turkey sausage, veggie frittata and grits. Lunch and dinner can be classic soul – mac 'n' cheese, collard greens, braised ribs, smothered chicken – or healthy comfort food in the form of large salads with generous toppings.

🍴 RAO'S RESTAURANT
Italian $$$

☎ 212-722-6709; www.raos.com; 455 E 114th St; 🕑 dinner Mon-Fri, reservations required; 🚇 6 to 116th St; 🚻
So you want to go to Rao's. Who doesn't? Getting a reservation is

like trying to find a shamrock – you just gotta be lucky. Serving clams, baked ziti and classic lasagna without pause since 1896, Rao's is an institution, a standard-bearer, a disappearing slice of New York. If you can't get a table, stop for a drink at the bar; it's worth the trip.

🍴 SETTEPANI'S
American, Italian $

☎ 917-492-4806; www.settepani.com; 196 Lenox Ave; 🕙 lunch & dinner; 🚇 2, 3 to 116th St; 🚫 Ⓥ ♿

Pretty Settepani's is a glorious sight on a warm day – its rust-colored awning flutters in breezes that flow up and down broad Lenox Ave, and people of many

different backgrounds enjoy fresh salads, sandwiches, quiches and desserts. It's one of several bright coffee hangouts springing up in Harlem. The service is sometimes a little slow, but people are rarely in a rush to leave anyway.

🍴 SOCIETY *Coffee Shop* $

☎ 212-222-3323; www.cupofnyc.com; 2104 Frederick Douglass Blvd at W 114th St; 🕙 7am-10pm Mon-Thu, 7am-midnight Fri, 9am-midnight Sat, 9am-9pm Sun; 🚇 2, 3 to 116th St; 🚫

A sleek, brick-walled, wooden-table-filled coffee shop that's a popular Harlem hangout, especially among young students who make liberal use of its free

Drop in to Settepani's for coffee, quiche and dessert

wi-fi. The weekend brunches are a madhouse; at quieter times you can sit for hours sipping your latte or glass of wine and nibble on all sorts of cakes and snacks while soaking in the relaxed, comforting ambience.

⛄ DRINK

⛄ DEN *Bar*
☎ 212-234-3045; www.thedenharlem .com; 2150 Fifth Ave near E 132nd St; ✦ 6pm-2am Mon-Fri, 8pm-4am Sat, 11am-5am Sun; ⊕ 2, 3 to 135th St
This is a very sexy place, visited by some very sexy people who like to laugh, drink and eat, as well as share the stage on Kill Karaoke night (Tuesday). Part art gallery (the work of local painters is shown on the walls), part gin joint (sip your Uncle Tom Collins with your tongue in cheek) and part soul restaurant (with pulled pork and sushi on the menu), the Den is also gorgeous to look at. It's located on the 1st floor of a restored brownstone, where you'll feel right at home. Wednesday, Friday and Saturday nights you'll get live hip-hop and blues.

⛄ REVIVAL *Bar*
☎ 212-222-8338; www.harlemrevival .com; 2367 Frederick Douglass Blvd at W 127th St; ✦ lunch Tue-Fri, dinner daily, brunch Sat & Sun, daily happy hour 5-7pm; ⊕ A, C, E to 125th St

Swing by for happy hour, when drinks are two for one, and try the Frangelico-flavored Harlem Hazelnut specialty cocktail, or the chocolate martini that's named for Frederick Douglass – they're delicious! Revival is a sleek, upscale restaurant and a pleasant place to have a drink at any time of night.

☆ PLAY

☆ LENOX LOUNGE
Jazz Music, Lounge
☎ 212-427-0253; www.lenoxlounge .com; 288 Lenox Ave btwn W 124th & W 125th Sts; ✦ noon-4am; ⊕ 2, 3 to 125th St
The classic art deco Lounge, which frequently hosts big names, is an old favorite of local jazz cats, though it's a beautiful and historic house for anyone who wants a nice place to imbibe. Don't miss the luxe Zebra Room in the back.

☆ MOBAY UPTOWN *Live Music*
☎ 212-876-9300; www.mobay restaurant.com/harlem/home.htm; 17 W 125th St; ✦ 11am-11pm Mon-Wed, to 12:30am Thu-Sat, to 10pm Sun; ⊕ A, C, E, 2, 3 to 125th St
An extension of MoBay's in Brooklyn, this Caribbean eatery (with Jamaican, Haitian and vegetarian dishes) likes to add a little jazz to its cooking. It has jazz

nights every Tuesday to Sunday from 8pm until midnight in the lounge (where you can order nibbles) and gospel brunches every Sunday from 11am to 5pm, and then a live band comes in for the evening.

⭐ PERK'S *Club*
☎ 212-666-8500; 553 Manhattan Ave at W 123rd St; 🕐 4pm-4am Mon-Sat; 🚇 2, 3 to 125th St

On the weekends, Perk's is packed with hip-swinging dancers who take over the floor and move to the fusion sounds produced by the DJ. On weeknights this sedate-looking club pulls in the best local jazz artists to play live sets. You can't go wrong either way.

⭐ SMOKE *Club*
☎ 212-864-6662; 2751 Broadway near W 106th St; 🕐 5pm-4am; 🚇 1 to W 103rd St

Smoke has defied the odds of its no-man's-land location (not deep in Harlem but north of the Upper West Side) and flourished as an intimate and welcoming club. Its long dark drapes and fluffy sofas give it a homey feel, and the low covers appeal to the local student population.

>BROOKLYN

New York City's most densely populated borough is a sprawling amalgamation of brownstones, skyscrapers, cobblestone streets and narrow highways, with an eclectic mix of hipster yuppies, working-class Latino and Caribbean families, and a surging influx of Eastern European immigrants.

It's mesmerizing, overwhelming and ripe for exploration. Start with the warren of reclaimed factories in Dumbo, then explore the old brownstones of Carroll Gardens, Red Hook or Cobble Hill, also renowned for fabulous restaurants. Park Slope is a laid-back, gay-friendly neighborhood mirroring Manhattan's upscale lifestyle. For a singular experience, head to Coney Island and check out the freak shows and 1926 roller coaster.

Closest to Manhattan – in price and lifestyle – is hip Williamsburg, a former industrial area now embraced by recent grads and 30-somethings. The incoming wave of condos has yet to eclipse the old-school Polish community who lived and worked here for generations, so for now it's still possible to bar-hop along Bedford Ave while peering into myriad offbeat and avant-garde stores and art galleries.

BROOKLYN

◉ SEE

111 Front Street Galleries	1	G4
Brooklyn Museum of Art	2	E3
Coney Island Boardwalk	3	A6
Dumbo Arts Center	4	G4
New York Transit Museum	5	F5
Pierogi 2000	6	G2
Prospect Park	7	E3

⌂ SHOP

3R Living	8	E6
Asha Veza	9	F6

Barking Brown	10	G6
Cloth	11	F6
Ghostown	12	G2
Jacques Torres Chocolate	13	G4
Sahadi's	14	F5

🍴 EAT

Grimaldi's	15	G4
Habana Outpost	16	F6
Nathan's Famous Hot Dogs	17	A5
Red Bamboo	18	G6
River Cafe	19	G4
Totonno's	20	A5

🍸 DRINK

68 Jay St	21	G4
Henry Street Ale House	22	G4
Last Exit	23	F4
Union Hall	24	E6

★ PLAY

Barbes	25	D6
Brooklyn Masonic Temple	26	G6
Gutter	27	G2
Rebar at Retreat	28	G4
St Ann's Warehouse	29	G4

Please see over for map

◉ SEE
◉ 111 FRONT STREET GALLERIES

www.frontstreetgalleries.com; 111 Front St near Washington St; ☼ hours vary; ⊕ A, C to High St

Local artists exhibit their latest works in this orange-colored mega-gallery – a restored factory that actually houses about 11 galleries and ateliers. There's also a dash of international flair from visiting artists-in-residence; Dumbo runs several such programs a year.

◉ BROOKLYN MUSEUM OF ART

☎ 718-638-5000; www.brooklynmuseum .org; 200 Eastern Parkway; suggested donation $8; ☼ 10am-5pm Mon-Fri, 11am-6pm Sat & Sun; ⊕ 2, 3 to Eastern Parkway

Perched on the edge of Prospect Park, this 560,000-sq-ft beaux arts museum is full of dazzling diversity. Its permanent collections include ancient Egyptian and Assyrian masterpieces, plus an entire floor dedicated to the sculptures of Rodin. Innovative rotating exhibits range from studies of the feminist experience to explorations of Jesper Just's *Romantic Delusions*. On 'First Fridays' (the first Friday night of every month), the museum throws a dance party, and locals show up to boogie down.

Stroll the historic boardwalk (p219) at Coney Island

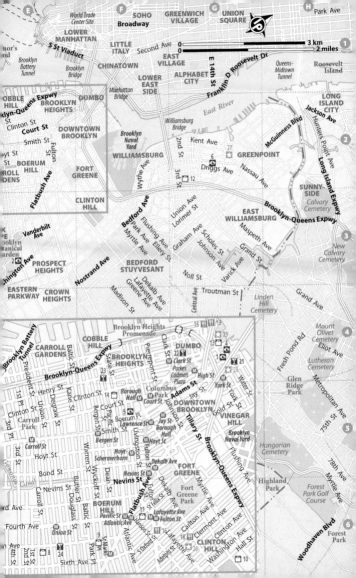

What does a Wiccan do? Working as a Wiccan means I study witchcraft and I try to help people achieve their goals or desires, sometimes with spells, or rituals. **Are there many Wiccans in New York?** There are quite a few, most in the Bronx. There's a big Botanica here – it was an old grocery store that we turned into a sort of witchcraft store. Also, I think the cultural mix of the Bronx is a factor. **What kind of spells do you usually cast for people who need your services?** There are two spells people always want: the 'I-want-to-meet-my-soulmate' spell and the 'I want-to-win-the-lotto' spell. In New York people are always looking for love or money. Or both. **Did you grow up in New York? What's one place you think people shouldn't miss?** I d grow up here – it's a great city still, although it's getting to be a place that only the rich can afford. But there are still some great pockets to hang out in Ground Zero shouldn't be missed, because it's a very emotional and power ful place to visit.

CONEY ISLAND BOARDWALK

www.coneyisland.com; 1000 Surf Ave;
D, F, N, Q to Coney Island-Stillwell Ave
Change is on the horizon for
Coney Island. As of press time, a
major developer was preparing to
start the first phase of a sweeping
overhaul of the boardwalk area,
but just exactly when it will begin
(and how much of the historic
area will be included) was still being worked out with the city. Until
then, the kitschy and somewhat
dissolute charm of Coney Island
remains intact, along with the
stunning Atlantic views and surrounding Russian community.

DUMBO ARTS CENTER

☎ 718-694-0831; www.dumboartscenter
.org; 30 Washington St; noon-6pm
Thu-Mon; A, C to High St
Stop by this Dumbo nerve center
and learn all about the artist
community – who works where
and is planning what exhibit. This
center plans the annual Dumbo
art festival and is home to a great
local gallery.

NEW YORK TRANSIT MUSEUM

☎ 718-694-1600; www.mta.info/mta
/museum; Boerum Pl at Schermerhorn St;
admission $5, some tours $15; 10am-
4pm Tue-Fri, noon-5pm Sat & Sun; 2,
3, 4, 5 to Borough Hall, M, R to Court St

Occupying an old subway station
built in 1936 (and out of service
since 1946), this museum takes on
100-plus years of getting around
the Big Apple. Kids love the models of old subway cars, bus drivers'
seats and the chronological
display of turnstiles from the late
19th century. Best is the downstairs area, on the platform, where
everyone can climb aboard 13
original subway and elevated-train
cars, dating from the 1904 wicker-
seat, army-green-and-crimson
Brooklyn Union Elevated Car.

PIEROGI 2000

☎ 718-599-2144; 177 N 9th St btwn
Bedford & Driggs Aves; noon-6pm
Thu-Mon; L to Bedford Ave
A gallery that's grown in reputa-
tion and scope since its start in
2000, Pierogi 2000 handles about
1000 artists from Williamsburg and
elsewhere, displaying most of their
works in the front room. People can
flip through drawings and other
artist renderings in the back room
if they wish. The back room is also a
community center/meeting space
for cultural gatherings.

PROSPECT PARK

www.prospectpark.org; Grand Army Plaza;
5am-1am; 2, 3 to Grand Army
Plaza, F to 15th St-Prospect Park;
Although not quite as famous
as the iconic Central Park, this
lush green oasis is considered an

equal masterpiece from designers Olmsted and Vaux. Its 585 acres contain the gorgeous Brooklyn Botanical Gardens, numerous lakes, bike paths, meadows and running routes. The soaring arched entrance at Grand Army Plaza, not far from the Brooklyn Museum of Art and next to the Brooklyn Public Library, is one of the borough's most celebrated sights.

🛍 SHOP

🛍 3R LIVING *Homewares*
☎ 718-832-0951; 276L Fifth Ave, near Garfield Pl; 🕙 11am-7pm Sun-Wed, to 8pm Thu-Sat; 🚇 M, R to Union St
A design-conscious ecostore that still manages to emphasize the three Rs – Reduce, Reuse and Recycle. This shop is full of nifty home ideas and solutions, and all use 'green' products imported under fair-trade agreements. The in-store recycling center has separate bins for old batteries, crayons, laser-printer cartridges, CDs and cell phones.

🛍 ASHA VEZA
Fashion & Accessories
☎ 718-783-2742; www.ashaveza.com; 69 Fifth Ave, Park Slope; 🕙 noon-7pm Wed-Fri, 11am-7pm Sat, noon-6pm Sun; 🚇 F, M, R to Fourth Ave-9th St
Graceful designs from global dressmakers, including fashion-forward lines from new talent in Eastern Eu-

rope and Southeast Asia. The store owner tries to buy directly from designers wherever they are in the world and avoids big brands.

🛍 BARKING BROWN
Fashion & Accessories, Homewares
☎ 718-638-3757; www.barkingbrown .com; 468 Myrtle Ave in Fort Greene; 🕙 10am-10pm Mon-Sat; 🚇 G to Clinton-Washington Ave
One-of-a-kind designs for men and women, including hats, jewelry, handbags and pants, tops and jackets. There are also home furnishings.

🛍 CLOTH *Fashion & Accessories*
☎ 718-403-0223; www.clothclothing .com; 138 Fort Greene Pl; 🕙 noon-7:30 Tue-Sun; 🚇 B, Q, 2, 3, 4, 5 to Atlantic Ave
Modern clothes for 20- and 30-somethings at bargain prices, located in a quaint store not far from the Brooklyn Academy of Music.

🛍 GHOSTOWN
Fashion & Accessories
☎ 718-387-0990; 335 Grand St near Havemeyer St; 🕙 noon-8pm; 🚇 J, M, Z to Marcy Ave, G, L to Metropolitan Ave-Lorimer St
A used and gently worn clothing store that also doubles as a club on certain nights of the week, Ghostown carries men's and women's streetwear from local designers and brands. The parties

Art you can eat at Jacques Torres Chocolate

come and go; check in with the owners while you're in town.

🍫 JACQUES TORRES CHOCOLATE *Food & Drink*
☎ 718-875-9772; www.mrchocolate
.com; 66 Water St, Dumbo; ⏰ 9am-7pm
Mon-Sat; ⊕ A, C to High St
Serious chocolatier JT runs this small European-style store with a three-table café, filled with the most velvety and innovative chocolates ever crafted. Take a few to the nearby Empire Fulton Ferry State Park for a snack and a view between the Brooklyn and Manhattan Bridges. The shop also does a brisk internet business, and makes its delicacies available at Chocolate Bar (p121) in the Meatpacking District.

🍫 SAHADI'S *Food & Drink*
☎ 718-624-4550; 187 Atlantic Ave near
Clinton St; ⏰ 9am-7pm Mon-Sat; ⊕ 2,
3, 4, 5 to Borough Hall
Kalamata olives, fresh hummus, sweet figs and dates, and briny pickles – all sorts of Middle Eastern treats are sold at this specialty store, run by a Middle Eastern family.

🍴 EAT
🍴 GRIMALDI'S *Pizza* $
☎ 718-858-4300; www.grimaldis
brooklyn.com; 19 Old Fulton St; ⏰ lunch
& dinner; ⊕ A, C to High St; ♿ Ⓥ ♿
Legendary pizza with perfect crust and spicy sauces, topped with bubbling cheeses of all types. If the 'no reservations' policy

creates long lines, everybody stops complaining once the pizza's dished up.

ⵏ HABANA OUTPOST *Latin* $

☎ 718-858-9500; www.habanaoutpost .com; 757 Fulton St; 🕐 noon-midnight Wed-Mon; ⓒ C to Lafayette Ave; 🚳 Ⓥ 🚼

A solar-powered and self-styled 'eco-eatery,' Habana's a smallish café with a big courtyard and delicious Latin fare. Side dishes of plantains, yellow rice, and grilled corn go perfectly with burritos, quesadillas and enchiladas. Goes without saying that the food is organic.

ⵏ NATHAN'S FAMOUS HOT DOGS *Hot Dogs* $

☎ 718-946-2202; 1310 Surf Ave; 🕐 breakfast, lunch & dinner till late; ⓒ D, F to Coney Island-Stillwell Ave

If you eat 'em, this is the place for an all-beef dog with sauerkraut and mustard. A frightening time to visit is July 4, when Nathan's holds a hot dog–eating contest (the record stands at Takeru Kobayashi's 50 and a half).

ⵏ RED BAMBOO *Vegan* $$

☎ 718-643-4267; www.redbamboobrook lyn.com; 271 Adelphi St; 🕐 lunch daily, dinner Wed-Sun; ⓒ C to Lafayette Ave

River Cafe, a floating wonder with great food and beautiful views

The best 'vegetarian Caribbean soul food' you're likely to taste ever in your life. Red Bamboo is serious about elevating vegan dishes; it's got fresh soups, spicy tofu, tons of leafy greens and even some dishes with its eponymous ingredient.

▥ RIVER CAFE
American $$$
☎ 718-522-5200; www.rivercafe.com; 1 Water St; 🕑 lunch & dinner daily, brunch Sat & Sun; ◉ A,C to High St; Ⓥ ♿

It takes a beating from purists who sniff the words 'tourist trap,' but they've probably never actually been to this floating wonder with beautiful views from under Manhattan Bridge. The seared mahimahi with almond crust and scallop ceviche are just two of many innovative dishes the kitchen produces, and River Cafe's brunches are legendary for their Bloody Marys and perfect eggs.

▥ TOTONNO'S *Pizza* $
☎ 718-372-8606; 1524 Neptune Ave near W 16th St; 🕑 noon-8pm Wed-Sun; ◉ D, F, N, Q to Coney Island-Stillwell Ave; ♿

Open daily as long as there's fresh dough – when it goes, the shop closes for the day. It's part of the only-do-it-when-it's-fresh ethos that's run this place for decades.

The crust tastes better and the sauce sweeter, making the experience worth a Coney Island trip.

▾ DRINK

▾ 68 JAY STREET *Bar*
☎ 718-260-8207; 68 Jay St; 🕑 2pm-3am; ◉ A, C to High St

Paint-spattered but still elegant, with rounded arches and a big columned doorway, 68 Jay Street is a rarity among bars – it turns the music down to a comfortable level for discussion among patrons. Consequently, you hear a lot of art-world buzz as the regulars – all members of said world – dish the dirt over drinks.

▾ HENRY STREET ALE HOUSE *Pub*
☎ 718-522-4801; 62 Henry St near Orange St; 🕑 4pm-4am; ◉ A, C to High St, 2, 3 to Clark St

Steps from the subway, this near-perfect pub serves up gourmet cheese, fresh apple slices and other fragrant snacks with its 16 varieties of beer.

▾ LAST EXIT *Bar*
☎ 718-222-9198; http://lastexitbar .com; 136 Atlantic Ave near Henry St; 🕑 4pm-4am; ◉ 2, 3, 4, 5 to Borough Hall, M, R to Court St, F, G to Bergen St

Sometimes the laid-back bartenders put on a pub quiz, other times a DJ shows up to spin. Most of the time it's locals unwinding over beers, happy to talk to strangers and let the night slip away.

▼ UNION HALL *Bar*

☎ 718-638-4400; 702 Union St btwn Fifth & Sixth Aves, Park Slope; ⏲ 4pm-4am Mon-Fri, noon-4am Sat & Sun; ◉ M, R to Union St, 2, 3 to Bergen St, F to Seventh Ave

Up front, leather settees and armchairs sit next to the masculine full-wall bookshelves and the fireplace makes the Hall feel like an old-world gentleman's club during gentler times. Things get busy-rowdy later on, with a clanking bocce court in back and an

indie-rock stage in the basement. If you're thinking of clanking the bocce ball, prepare to wait an hour or two. Good snacks.

☆ PLAY

☆ BARBES *Live Music, Arts*

☎ 718-965-9177; www.barbesbrooklyn .com; 376 9th St at Sixth Ave; no cover charge for bar, suggested $10 donation for live music; ⏲ 5pm-2am Mon-Thu, noon-4am Fri-Sat, noon-2am Sun; ◉ F to Seventh Ave

This bar and performance space, owned by two French musicians and longtime Brooklyn residents, is named after the North African enclave of Paris. It hosts music,

Patrons leave St Ann's Warehouse, a performance space with a spicy history

readings and film screenings in
the back room, and plays eclectic
music, ranging from Lebanese
diva Asmahan to Mexican *bandas,*
Venezuelan *joropos* and Romanian
brass bands.

⭐ GUTTER *Bowling*
☎ 718-387-3585; 200 N 14th St btwn
Berry & Wythe Sts; 🕙 4pm-4am
Mon-Thu, noon-4am Fri-Sun; Ⓛ L to
Bedford St
An unselfconscious and un-hip
bar (designed to look so un-hip, in
fact, that it had to be on purpose),
this refurbished old warehouse
is now a bar/bowling alley, with
eight working lanes to play on.
Beer comes in pitchers, you've got
to put on bowling shoes, and the
loser buys (house rules).

⭐ REBAR AT RETREAT
Live Music
☎ 718-797-2322; www.rebarnyc.com;
147 Front St; 🕙 11:30am-2am Sun-Tue,
to 4am Wed-Sat; Ⓕ F to Jay St
Beautifully decorated and full of
art, Rebar has 15 beers on tap,
an organic-wine list, live music
and a cozy, sexy vibe thanks to its
delicate hanging lights and warm
wooden glow.

⭐ ST ANN'S WAREHOUSE *Arts*
☎ 718-254-8779; 38 Water St btwn
Main & Dock Sts; 🕙 hours vary; Ⓐ A, C
to High St
This avant-garde performance
company took over an old spice
mill and turned it into an exciting venue for the arts. Now the
cavernous space regularly hosts
innovative theater and attracts the
Brooklyn literati crowd.

>SNAPSHOTS

In a city with endless possibilities, it can be hard to find the neighborhood offering the best options for what interests you. Here's a breakdown to make it easy.

Live music, free concert, great setting — Dumbo (p22)

ACCOMMODATIONS

There's no shortage of great hotels in New York City, just a lack of space for more rooms! You'll get lots of bang for your buck in terms of service at most locations, but truly spacious accommodations are pretty much a rarity unless you're willing to dig out the pocketbook.

For relaxing, family-friendly, old-fashioned hotels, great for visitors wanting to visit museums and cultural highlights, try the Upper West and East Sides. Boutique-hotel lovers can pick and choose from among the classic, super-stylish hotels around Union Sq, Bryant Park and Times Sq, or the slightly edgier downtown hotels. Business travelers and Broadway aficionados tend to stick to Midtown. You can find bargains in older hotels in Chelsea and among the B&Bs of Greenwich Village and the East Village.

Accommodations in New York fall into five broad categories. Book yourself into a B&B and you'll likely end up in an old brownstone or converted loftlike flat. Rooms tend to be bright and spacious, but bathrooms are usually shared, as are all common spaces. B&Bs can save you money as long as you don't mind early morning chatter over a communal breakfast table.

Boutique hotels tend to have mini rooms tricked out like glam jewel boxes. Colors are seductive, as are amenities – expect brand names likes Bulgari and high-end linens, plus a celebrity-filled basement or rooftop bar.

Classic hotels, like the Waldorf Astoria, are a throwback to the days of Coco Chanel and W Somerset Maugham, when travelers came with trunks and entourages and booked suites to stay for months. You'll find big ballrooms, grand and sweeping staircases, gilt-covered wall hangings and dangling chandeliers – and usually smallish rooms with deep carpeting and lots of knick-knacks to distract from the hotel's somewhat faded glory.

Manhattan also has a few 'travelers' hotels. These are European-style locales with mini-kitchenettes in rooms, beds plus pull-out sofas (to pack in a third or fourth guest) and lots of floral-print bedspreads. Some rooms will have private baths and others will share toilets with the whole floor.

Hostels are dormlike rooms with bunk beds stacked one over the other. Decor is minimal to nonexistent in the dorms, but often the hostels have backyard gardens, quaint surroundings and a cheery clientele.

Good resources to use include Lonely Planet's Hotels & Hostels (www .hotels.lonelyplanet.com), Just New York Hotels (www.justnewyorkhotels .com), New York Deals on Hotels (www.newyork.dealsonhotels.com), New York City Hotels Today (www.newyorkcityhotelstoday.com) and NYC Hotels (www.nyc-hotels.net). Hotels sometimes offer special internet-only deals too. Priceline (www.priceline.com), Hotwire (www.hotwire.com), Orbitz (www.orbitz.com), Hotels.com (www.hotels.com), Hoteldiscounts .com (www.hoteldiscounts.com) and Travelzoo (www.travelzoo.com) all claim prices that are up to 70 percent less than standard rates.

BEST NEWCOMERS
> Gild Hall (www.wallstreetdistrict.com)
> 6 Columbus (www.6columbus.com)
> LondonNYC (www.thelondonnyc.com)
> The Standard (www.standard hotels.com)
> Greenwich Hotel (www.greenwichny hotel.com)

BEST BOUTIQUES
> W Union Sq (www.starwoodhotels.com)
> Mercer (www.mercerhotel.com)
> 60 Thompson (www.60thompson.com)
> Gansevoort (www.hotel gansevoort.com)
> Casablanca Hotel (www.casablanca hotel.com)

Above Sitting outside the Mercer, one of the city's best boutique hotels

SPORTS & ACTIVITIES

Baseball aficionados will know that New York's two most successful sporting franchises are in the middle of a major transition: the Yankees and the Mets, the city's two premiere teams, are in new homes.

The House that Ruth Built, as the old Yankee Stadium in the Bronx was called, was on its way out as of research time, to be replaced in 2009 with a brand-new facility across the street. Likewise, the Mets' Shea Stadium in Queens was phased out in 2008, and the team will be playing in the ramped-up CitiField Stadium by 2010. Despite cries from hardcore fans, both old stadiums are scheduled to be razed, and the land slated for use as public parks. How this will affect New York's World Series–dominating Yankees is anybody's guess; one can only hope it improves the luck of the perennially second-placed Mets.

The New York Knicks, who haven't brought glory to their hometown in a loooong time, still play in Madison Sq Garden, also home to the far more successful women's pro-team, the New York Liberty. As of press time, the New Jersey Nets basketball team was still slated to move to Brooklyn, but the new stadium under development to house them there was behind schedule. The New York Rangers play ice hockey at Madison Sq Garden from October to April.

NY Giants football tickets sell out years in advance, but tickets to New York Jets football games are easier to come by. Both teams will make a move to a new stadium in New Jersey, which they'll share sometime in the next five years. But to finance their ritzy new digs, the Jets and the Giants have adopted a controversial new pricing plan for their seats. As of 2008, season ticket holders had to bid on lifetime rights to their seats – with one big fan ponying up $200,000 apiece for the right to sit in the same two 50-yard-line seats at every home game. That's in addition to buying tickets to the actual games, which cost $700 a pop for front row. But all is not lost for the average fan. You can still snag a seat without robbing a bank, but it's unlikely you'll get a primo view. One-time ticket buyers are routed to the nosebleed section, but it won't cost you over $100.

The US Open is the year's final Grand Slam tennis event (spanning the Labor Day weekend) and is held at Flushing Meadows. Reserved tickets are only required for Arthur Ashe Stadium, which is sold out months ahead. Day-session ground passes are sold on the morning of each day's play: get in line before 9am.

Most sporting events can be booked through **Ticketmaster** (☎ 212-307-7171).

ARCHITECTURE

New York is still a city of varied scale, although increasingly it is turning tall and vertical. You can see its colonial past in a few quaint structures – short, squat rows of Federalist-style houses – in Lower Manhattan, and Colonnade Row (p91) along Astor Pl is a great example of pre-1900s architecture. Sadly, fires wiped out most of New York's early housing stock; later, developers switched to less flammable materials.

The city's love of art deco is visible in the Chrysler Building, Grand Central Terminal's interior, and the Empire State Building. Inside Rockefeller Center you'll find the GE Building, another art deco construction that's lauded for the frieze over the main entrance depicting Wisdom.

The Time Warner Center, a mixed-use building at Columbus Circle, was the first major skyscraper built in the city after September 11. Its striking, black-glass exterior and sloping facade are considered an architectural feat and it's one of the city's toniest addresses.

By far the most common facade in the city, however, is beaux arts, used on the New York Public Library and the thousands of huge, solid apartment buildings that sprang up pre- and post-WWII. They line the large avenues running up both the Upper East and West Sides, done in an off-white stone, with great flourishes carved around windowsills and under the eaves.

ICONIC BUILDINGS
> Empire State Building (p152)
> Colonnade Row (p91)
> Dakota Building (p194)
> Time Warner Center (p166)
> Chrysler Building (pictured left; p152)

HISTORIC & RELIGIOUS BUILDINGS
> Cathedral of St John the Divine (p205)
> Federal Hall (p44)
> St Paul's Chapel (p46)
> St Patrick's Cathedral (p154)
> St Patrick's Old Cathedral (p80)

BARGAIN & SOUVENIR SEEKING

What could be better than a good bargain? That's why the weekend market was invented. New Yorkers love to amble around the city's parks and squares, eyeing other people's cast-offs and hand-me-downs.

Chinatown and Times Sq are famous for T-shirts. Shops around here are generally open from 10am to 8pm daily, with stores owned by Orthodox Jews closing Fridays and reopening Sunday mornings.

For real finds, dig through Chelsea's Antique Garage Flea Market, the affiliated Hell's Kitchen Flea Market, the Chelsea Outdoor Market or the 17th Street Market: all of them are open weekends and full of gently used hand-me-downs (see p132 for more information).

Tribeca, Soho and Lower Manhattan are great for window-shopping and browsing. Mainstream department-store offshoots like Soho Bloomingdale's abound, but you'll also find quirkier options around Nolita, the Lower East Side, and Greenwich and East Villages.

Don't forget to check for sample sales while you're here; www .dailycandy.com has a page devoted to nothing else. Other good sources to check include www.lazarshopping.com, www.nysale.com and *New York Magazine*'s rundown at http://nymag.com/shopping.

WHERE TO FIND BARGAINS
> Orchard Street Bargain District (p68)
> Century 21 (p48)
> Chinatown (p56)
> Barney's Co-Op (p133)
> Bis Designer Resale (p187)

BEST DEPARTMENT STORES
> Takashimaya (p156)
> Macy's (p166)
> Barney's (p187)
> Filene's Basement (p144)
> Pearl River Mart (pictured above; p57)

BARS

There's no shortage of cool places to wet your whistle while in New York. Whether you're a whiskey freak or a brandy snob, or just a plain old beer drinker, you can find a bar to make you feel at home.

Experimental types should try some of the legendary cocktails: they're constantly evolving into something new. You can get the classics – a martini, a sidecar and, of course, the Manhattan – but you can also find drinks with a twist. Pomegranate, sake, passionfruit and honey are the latest 'must-mix' ingredients; there's always a race on to create the next big winner.

Old-school Irish pubs can be found all over the city, usually with the doors thrown wide and a soccer or football game on. Microbreweries exist at Chelsea Piers and Union Sq and in Brooklyn. Chelsea is where to go for the *dernier cri* in chic drinks, but there's sure to be a secret bar somewhere on the Lower East Side thumbing its nose at that crowd and serving up the anti-cocktail.

For those who don't care what's in or what's out, the laid-back pubs in Greenwich Village that value conversation over trends are the best bet.

Many bars, particularly those downtown, have late-afternoon happy hours, when drinks are half their regular price, and some clubs repeat the fun after midnight, all the better to draw in the club-hopping crowd.

QUIET DRINK SPOTS
> Little Branch (p113)
> Whiskey Ward (p73)
> Park (p137)
> Campbell Apartment (p160)
> Bill's Gay Nineties (p159)

BEER & WINE BARS
> Jimmy's Corner (p170)
> DBA (p100)
> Morrell Wine Bar & Café (p160)
> Chelsea Brewing Company (p137)
> Bar Veloce (p137)

CLUBBING & NIGHTLIFE

Despite a strong challenge from the Meatpacking District, clubbing in New York is still all about the wild, wild west – west Chelsea, that is.

New York's clubs tend to open and shut doors with alarming frequency, as cops periodically crack down on underage drinking and notorious drug dealing. But, for the most part, Chelsea is still the magnet, since owners can switch locations fairly easily just by moving a few blocks north or south if they have to.

Smaller, slightly more intimate clubs are the norm in the Meatpacking District, where recent hotspots include 1Oak. Kiss & Fly is a Euro-dancehall kind of vibe, breezy and fun, where nobody takes the scene too seriously.

The Lower East Side is also vying for attention with The Box, a bizarre, late-night supper/cabaret club.

To get on top of the options that are out there, grab the Sunday and Friday editions of the *New York Times,* and the weekly editions of *New York Magazine, Time Out New York* and the *New Yorker*. The *Village Voice* has good information on dance clubs and a weekly column (Fly Life) that runs down where the best DJs are playing. Also try **Clubfone** (☎ 212-777-2582; www.clubfone.com).

BIG CLUBS
> Cain (p138)
> Eagle NYC (p138)
> Home (p138)
> Level V (p125)
> Marquee (p139)

DANCE SPOTS
> Cielo (pictured above; p124)
> 718 Sessions at Club Deep (p148)
> Pink Elephant (p139)
> 1Oak (p138)
> Kiss & Fly (p124)

COMEDY & CABARET

Life is a cabaret, old chum, except in New York City, where an old Prohibition-era law actually makes it illegal to have more than three people dancing in a club unless the owner has applied for a (very hard to get) special license.

For some reason that arcane legislation is still on the books, but no worries: everyone ignores it. Cabaret is alive and well, from the classic shows put on at Café Carlyle to the raucous burlesque-like performances at The Box, and the laugh-till-it-hurts cabaret/comedy that has kept the Duplex in business for 40 years. These plucky establishments, like Don't Tell Mama, manage to hang in there even as popular taste has moved away from the ribald, Broadway-esque performance style.

Comedy clubs are also enjoying a bit of a comeback, although they're nowhere near as popular as they were in the 1980s, when Jerry Seinfeld, Chris Rock and the Belushi brothers were on the circuit. Dangerfield's and Comic Strip Live still fill the room with their nightly shows on the Upper East Side. Caroline's, Gotham Comedy Cellar and Laugh Factory New York dominate the Midtown action. Clubs usually have two showings nightly; your ticket price gets you in for a full set (usually three or four comics), but there's often a two-drink minimum on top of that for table service. Most clubs now also serve food so you can nosh while you laugh.

BEST COMEDY & CABARET
> Duplex (p115)
> The Box (p172)
> Don't Tell Mama (p172)
> Comedy Cellar (p114)
> Dangerfield's (p191)

BEST LOUNGE ACTS
> Bemelmans Bar (p190)
> Lenox Lounge (p212)
> Bar Next Door (p112)
> Revival (p212)
> Divine Bar West (p170)

FASHION & COUTURE

There are two – possibly three – places in New York where devotees of fashion and haute couture tend to congregate: the Upper East Side and the Meatpacking District. Occasionally a few forward-thinking fashionistas will venture downtown to the less stylized boutiques of Tribeca.

The 'Gold Coast' along Madison Ave is a 40-block stretch of big-name designers: Armani, Kors, Ferragamo, Bulgari, Prada and much more. The few thrift shops that populate this area, as you can imagine, have waiting lists to inspect the merchandise: these stores get last year's cast-offs from the well-heeled, and the working-class girls line up waiting to buy.

In the Meatpacking District, the aura is a little less rarified, but the focus is still on high-end fashion. Edgier, more youthful names like Malandrino (p120), Miele (p120) and McQueen (p117) are all the rage.

Downtown in Tribeca is where almost-but-not-quite-discovered young models like to browse; the flashy boutiques are more willing to take a chance on the latest European and Asian imports.

Don't forget to sign up for a list of the day's sample sales at www.daily candy.com and www.nymag.com/shopping before you go.

BEST SHOPPING SPOTS
> Fifth Ave (p156)
> Madison Ave (p155)
> Chinatown (p56)
> Gansevoort St (p117)
> Orchard Street Bargain District (p68)

TOP SHOPS
> Donna Karan (p187)
> Issey Miyake (p48)
> Carlos Miele (p120)
> Te Casan (p85)
> John Varvatos (p84)

FOOD SHOPPING

Green, leafy things are sprouting all over New York, thanks to the new local and organic food craze that's taken hold in the city. If you're in town during the warmer months, seek out the network of green markets that populate Manhattan. The main one is in Union Sq – it sometimes doubles as a craft market – and you'll often spot five-star chefs there early in the morning, planning the day's menu.

If outdoor markets are too rustic for you, there are plenty of big chains and revered mom-and-pop type bodegas to be found. Check out the many Whole Foods stores around the city for the best in fair-trade and organic eats. Trader Joe's, another high-end gourmet organic shop, just opened two doors down from Whole Foods in Union Sq. If you're looking for old-school New York, it's Zabar's on the Upper East Side, Balducci's on the West Side, or the quaint market inside Grand Central Terminal. Chelsea Market on the West Side is great if you get hungry while shopping; it also houses a slew of delectable restaurants.

BEST FOOD STORES
> Balducci's (p120)
> Chelsea Market (p133)
> Trader Joe's (p96)
> Whole Foods at Filene's
  Basement (p144)
> Zabar's (pictured above; p197)

BEST SPECIALTY SHOPS
> Murray's Cheese (p109)
> Barney Greengrass (p197)
> Union Sq Greenmarket (p142)
> Grand Central Market (p152)
> Canal St stalls in Chinatown (p56)

FOOD

New York's constant influx of world-class chefs means plenty of first-rate cooking for those who lust after a truly inimitable dining experience. Classic diners, brasseries and intimate bistros stud the entire city, and original restaurants with ties to foreign lands are practically ubiquitous.

It's not a question of whether you want Chinese tonight, but do you want Szechuan or Mandarin? French Thai or traditional? Big, bean-filled burritos from Northern Mexico or spicy, sauce-laden concoctions with mole and chilis from the Oaxaca region? Every budget and preference can be accommodated in New York City.

Some places are so hot you can only book online (ahem… Momofuku; p98). New Yorkers are addicted to **Open Table** (www.opentable.com), which lets you read reviews, follow the 'buzz,' and book and instantly confirm reservations at hundreds of eateries.

To help you navigate your way through New York's rich foodie pickings, grab a copy of *Time Out New York,* which reviews 100 restaurants in every issue, or a Zagat guide at any newsstand. The *Village Voice* also has a database of cheap eats on its website (www.villagevoice.com). With so much to choose from, you definitely won't go hungry.

HARD TO GET RESERVATIONS
> Momofuku (p98)
> Il Buco (p87)
> Sfoglia (p189)
> Bond St (p86)
> Rao's Restaurant (p210)

COUPLE SPOTS
> Benoit (p167)
> BLT Market (p168)
> Roppongi (p199)
> Schiller's Liquor Bar (p72)
> Insieme (p169)

BEST BELOW 14TH ST
> Mediterranean: Turks and Frogs Tribeca (p87)
> Seafood: Pearl Oyster (p112)
> Steak: STK (p123)
> Veggie: Tuck Shop (p99)
> Italian: Lavagna (p99)

BEST ABOVE 14TH ST
> Prix fixe: Le Biarritz (p169)
> Sushi: Aburiya Kinnosuke (p157)
> Latin: Sofrito (p159)
> Organic: Community Food and Juice (p209)
> Fusion: L'Atelier (p158)

Top left You can't visit NYC without sampling diner fare **Above** Schiller's Liquor Bar – warm decor, cold beer

GAY & LESBIAN NEW YORK

Gay Pride is a month-long celebration in June of the city's longstanding and diverse queer communities, and an apt description of New York's gay and lesbian lifestyle: unabashedly out and empowered in a city noted for its overachievers. For more details on Gay Pride, check out www.heritageofpride.org.

New York doesn't differentiate much between heterosexual and homosexual – at least, not when it comes to dancing, drinking and eating. Chelsea, Greenwich Village, Jackson Heights and Park Slope are famously gay-friendly communities, but there's hardly any establishment in town where gays and lesbians wouldn't feel welcome. The one rule to remember is that the age of consent in New York for sex (of any kind) is 17.

The magazines *HX* and *Next* are available at restaurants and bars, or pick up *LGNY* and *NY Blade* from street-corner boxes and the lifestyle magazine *Metrosource* at shops and the LGBT Community Center. *Time Out New York* features a good events section. Useful counseling, referral and information centers include the **Gay & Lesbian Hotline** (☎ 212-989-0999; glnh@glnh.org) and the **LGBT Community Center** (☎ 212-620-7310; www.gaycenter.org; 208 W 13th St at Seventh Ave; ⏰ 9am-11pm).

Above Statues of two gay couples by George Segal in Sheridan Square (p105)

LITERARY NEW YORK CITY

Here's a funny tidbit: most of New York's most celebrated living authors reside in Brooklyn. How's that for a switch? Actually, it's not all that new. Isaac Bashevis Singer, Truman Capote, Norman Mailer, William Styron all lived there. Today, Brooklyn hosts a new generation of writers, including Jonathan Safran Foer, Jonathan Lethem, and Colson Whitehead.

But perhaps no other place has the celebrated history of Greenwich Village. Edna St Vincent Millay, EE Cummings, James Baldwin, William S Burroughs, Mark Twain, Edith Wharton, Henry James and other great writers have lived in that neighborhood. In contrast, the East Village favors nonfiction: the roiling socialist speeches of Emma Goldman and pro-birth-control advocate Margaret Sanger were handed out on seditious pamphlets.

The Oak Room in the Algonquin Hotel is also hallowed ground (Dorothy Parker drank here), and Harlem resounds with the energy of Ralph Ellison, Zora Neale Thurston, Langston Hughes and others.

The 92nd Street Y (p190) stages the most interesting author events north of 14th St. Bluestockings (p68), a LES bookstore, is your best bet for face-to-face time with an author. And KGB Bar (pictured below; p101) has a weekly reading series. For the inside scoop, visit www.clubfreetime.com.

CLASSIC NEW YORK READS
> *Just Above My Head*, James Baldwin
> *The Mambo Kings Sing Songs of Love*, Oscar Hijuelos
> *Motherless Brooklyn*, Jonathan Lethem
> *Lush Life*, Richard Price
> *Rise and Shine*, Anna Quindlen

NEW YORK IN HISTORY
> *Low Life*, Luc Sante
> *Bonfire of the Vanities*, Tom Wolfe
> *The Tenement Saga*, Sanford Sternlicht
> *The Gangs of New York*, Herbert Asbury
> *Gay New York: Gender and Urban Culture*, George Chauncey

LIVE MUSIC

Catching a live band in New York is easy – just head towards the sound of music. In the summer and spring, New Yorkers take the party outside. Listen to bluesy jazz on the lawn in Battery Park (p44), salsa and swing at South Street Seaport (p46) and Lincoln Center (p195), all kinds of bands at Central Park Summerstage, and somewhat unplanned but free (and very popular) breakout performances at McCarren Park Pool in Williamsburg (www.freewilliamsburg.com).

To stay on top of what's happening year-round, check out www.whatsupnyc.com, which posts tips about spontaneous performances in the city that aren't promoted anywhere but passed around by word of mouth (like the surprise early morning show once put on by His Purpleness, Prince, in Brooklyn's Prospect Park).

There are still plenty of old jazz haunts in the West Village and Harlem, and some laid-back dive bars paying homage to punk and grunge on the Lower East Side and in Hell's Kitchen. Lincoln Center has set the standard for high-quality performances for decades now and continues to showcase artists from all genres. Symphony Space (p201) on the Upper West Side is known for live world music from under-appreciated performers.

BEST BARS FOR ROCK
> Pianos (p75)
> Arlene's Grocery (p74)
> Bowery Ballroom (p74)
> Prohibition (p199)
> Living Room (p74)

BEST BARS FOR ECLECTIC SOUNDS
> Irving Plaza (p148)
> Mercury Lounge (p75)
> 55 Bar (p114)
> Smoke (p213)
> Le Poisson Rouge (p114)

MUSEUMS & GALLERIES

Art is everywhere in New York City, from huge institutions like the Metropolitan (p14), the MoMA (p15) and the Guggenheim (p186) to avant-garde ateliers in Chelsea, Dumbo and the Lower East Side. And now there's a newcomer: the New Museum of Contemporary Art (p67).

Chelsea, from about 21st to 26th Sts on 10th and 11th Aves, is one long strip of salons, shops, art dealers and galleries. Midtown Manhattan has also become an art-world offshoot. The Lower East Side is the new place to showcase up-and-coming artists; Dumbo is where they work and live.

New York Magazine's free online reviews (www.nymetro.com), *Time Out New York*'s comprehensive listings (www.timeoutny.com) and the *Gallery Guide* in major galleries are indispensable in sorting through your options. The *New York Times*' weekend edition and the venerable *Village Voice* (www.villagevoice.com) are your backup sources, and www.westchelseaarts.com provides an exhaustive database of current galleries. The city's **Department of Cultural Affairs** (www.nyc.gov/html/dcla) maintains an event calendar and allows you to search for galleries and attractions by art type and borough. If you're pressed for time, head out on a comprehensive tour through Chelsea and Soho by calling **New York Gallery tours** (☎ 212-946-1548; www.nygallerytours.com).

FIVE MUST-SEE SPOTS	**EAST-SIDE STANDOUTS**
> White Box (p132)	> Gallery OneTwentyEight (p63)
> White Columns (p117)	> Participant Inc (pictured above; p68)
> New Museum of Contemporary Art (p67)	> Lower East Side Tenement Museum (p66)
> Greene Naftali (p130)	> ABC No Rio (p67)
> Gagosian (p130)	> Nuyorican Poets Café (p102)

V

SNAPSHOTS

NYC FOR KIDS

New York is a blast for kids. They have their own museums, restaurants and theaters, and even a few after-hours hangouts they can call their own.

The American Museum of Natural History is a real kid-friendly stand-out, as is the Children's Museum. Young children are generally welcome in upscale dining rooms as long as it's on the early side, but there are plenty of quirky diners and bistros that cater to kids.

Parents might find moving about the city a bit stressful at first: squeezing strollers in and out of ill-configured subway stops isn't easy. Don't panic if someone grabs your stroller from behind as you're hauling it up the subway steps: New York etiquette mandates that weighted-down parents get a helping hand. The too-skinny-turnstiles at subway exits and entrances are another problem; catch the attention of the station clerk to get buzzed through the larger gates to the side. A few Manhattan museums don't allow strollers on certain days but will give you baby carriers to make up for it.

To make the cultural capital your personal playground, pick up a *Time Out New York Kids,* published four times a year and available at newsstands. It has tons of fabulous information and listings. **GoCity Kids** (www.gocitykids.com) is a useful online reference, as is **New York Kids** (www.newyorkkids.net).

FUN PLACES FOR KIDS
> American Museum of Natural History (p194)
> Children's Museum of Manhattan (pictured above; p194)
> Safari Playground (p181)
> Central Park Wildlife Center (p176)
> South Street Seaport (p46)

FAMILY FRIENDLY EATS
> S'Mac (p99)
> Tuck Shop (p99)
> Cafe Con Leche (p197)
> Pio Pio (p198)
> Pie by the Pound (p189)

NYC FOR LOVERS

It's not all bottom lines and boardroom deals in hard-nosed New York: there's room for love too. Where else can you get the romantic thrill of rowing across the lake in Central Park (p180), canoodling on the roof of the Empire State Building (p13) or dining at the Top of the Rock (p17)? Nowhere – so you better take advantage while you're here.

There's no need to be shy about your affection. New Yorkers are quite accustomed to seeing couples – same-sex or otherwise – walking arm-in-arm, holding hands, trading smooches and even snuggling closely while enjoying an outdoor concert at night. Just don't block the sidewalk when you're moving in tandem – that might net you some annoyed stares.

Famously romantic NYC experiences include a ride around Central Park in a horse-and-buggy (p177), a kiss in the middle of blaring Times Sq (p16), dressing to the nines for a concert at Lincoln Center (195), hand-holding across the table at a dark and secluded jazz club, and sharing a drink at a sexy rooftop bar.

BARS FOR CANOODLING
> Happy Ending (p73)
> Underbar (p148)
> Gold Bar (p60)
> Auction House (p189)
> Park (p137)

CLASSIC DATE BARS
> Bemelmans Bar (p190)
> Rise (p51)
> Den (p212)
> MoBar (p170)
> Campbell Apartment (p160)

PARKS & GREEN SPACES

Not all parks have to be used for exercise: New Yorkers have perfected the art of turning their green spaces into multi-use common areas. Consider these summer activities: Monday night outdoor films in Bryant Park, Shakespeare in the Park in Central Park, Central Park's Summerstage concerts, Battery Park's Hudson River Park concerts and its River to River Festival, and the Lincoln Center Dance Nights (OK, that one will definitely get your heart rate going). And don't forget the city's two roving outdoor tango parties: Saturday nights in Central Park and Sunday at the South Street Seaport.

It just goes to show there's plenty of ways to enjoy New York's more than 28,000 acres of greenery. While you're here, you are welcome to make use of any of the city's 614 baseball fields, 550 tennis courts, numerous basketball courts, golf and track courses, as well as its indoor and outdoor swimming pools: just go to www.nycgovparks.org for locations and details.

BEST PARKS
> Central Park (p174)
> Riverside Park (pictured above; p195)
> Prospect Park (p219)
> Governor's Island (p47)
> Battery Park (p44)

BEST PARK ACTIVITIES
> Biking in the Hudson River Park (p105)
> Walking the Jacqueline Kennedy Onassis Reservoir in Central Park (p176)
> Boating in Prospect Park (p219)
> Picnicking in Battery Park (p44)
> Dancing under the stars at Lincoln Center (p195)

SPAS

Picture this heavenly scenario: a few hours of shopping, light tea and then a blissful spa treatment that leaves you glowing and refreshed. Divine, right?

Well, that's now the standard at several high-end New York department stores: Takashimaya, Saks Fifth Ave and Bloomingdales all want you to go for the trifecta of pampering while you're in their stores.

But let's say you're only in town for a short visit. No problem: go to **Juvenex** (☎ 646-733-1330; www.juvenexspa.com; 5th fl, 25 W 32nd St btwn Fifth & Sixth Aves), an Asian-themed 24-hour spa in Little Korea. Its primary clientele are the dancers and performers from Broadway shows (hence the flexible hours) and it's also got special treatments for couples that involve hot tubs and rose petals (book those treatments in advance).

A visit to the spa means different things: a simple and straightforward after-work-out massage, a mani-pedi (manicure and pedicure), a waxing (bikini, Brazilian or otherwise), any number of different facials and topical skin treatments, or a combination of minimally invasive procedures to erase fine lines, peel away surface layers of old skin, zap broken capillaries, and so on and so on. Most spas have also picked up on the organic craze and are offering biodegradable wraps, chemical-free creams and soaps, and scenting your steam room with fresh, citrusy smells that won't irritate sensitive sinus tissues.

And spas are not just for women: several cater exclusively to men, and even unisex places offer male facials and 'handshake upkeep' treatments.

THEATER

Though some longtime favorites recently ended their runs, the big Broadway show is still king in New York.

There are 38 Broadway theaters that put on the lavish, million-dollar spectacles that enthrall crowds. Upkeep on these grande old dames (the theaters, not the stars) is steep, hence the hefty price of many Broadway tickets: sometimes $100 or more. However, there are ways to get half-price tickets. Run by the Theatre Development Fund (www.tdf.org), New York has three discount TKTS booths that sell steeply discounted seats to same-day Broadway shows. The main booth is in Times Sq, with another at South Street Seaport, and a third in Brooklyn (see the website for details). Most evening curtain calls are at 8pm, with Wednesday and weekend matinees starting at 2pm.

Besides the heavy hitters on Broadway, there's experimental theater on the Lower East Side, world-class ballet at Lincoln Center, or a low-key, nonprofit production of Chekhov, Stoppard or Miller in downtown revival theaters.

To keep track of it all, start with the Sunday and Friday editions of the *New York Times,* as well as the weekly editions of *New York Magazine, Time Out New York* and the *New Yorker.* The *Village Voice* has good information on alternative and off-off-Broadway productions. The **Department of Cultural Affairs** (☎ 212-643-7770) has a hotline that lists events and concerts at cultural institutions, while **NYC On Stage** (☎ 212-768-1818), a 24-hour information line, publicizes music, theater and dance events. Other good sources include **All That Chat** (www.talkinbroadway.com/allthatchat/), **NYC Theater** (www.nyc.com/theater) and the **Broadway Line** (☎ 888-276-2392).

CELEBRATED THEATERS	POPULAR SHOWS
> Joseph Papp Public Theater (p102)	> Wicked (www.wickedthemusical.com)
> Biltmore Theater (p171)	> Chicago (www.chicagothe musical.com)
> New Amsterdam Theater (p173)	> Chorus Line (www.achorusline.com)
> Newhouse at Lincoln Center (p195)	> The Lion King (www.thelionking.org)
> Harry de Jur Playhouse at Abrons Art Center (p74)	> Ave Q (www.avenueq.com)

VISTAS & VIEWPOINTS

Doesn't matter whether you're 100 stories above street level, or three levels below in the subway stations, there's always something to see. There are a thousand ways to observe the city as it goes by in a flash: from the swaying top of the Empire State Building (p13), from the back of a zippy pedicab, even as you clip-clop along in a hansom cab.

The views from the top seem to be the most sought after, but Manhattan can be entrancing from alternative angles. Take a trek to the NY Transit Museum (p219) and take its tour through a defunct section of the subway system to see how the city looks from the bottom up.

More scenic options can be found in Central Park, especially at its gorgeous central fountain located at Bethesda Terrace, near the Ramble. (The adjacent Bow Bridge is a popular place to pop the question, by the way.)

Harlem Meer is a scenic pond with honking geese and weeping willows, and Battery Park (p44) offers gorgeous views of New York Harbor. For the best sunset, take the Staten Island Ferry (p46): time the return trip right and you'll catch the glowing sun as it dips behind Manhattan's skyscrapers.

WHERE TO FIND GREAT VIEWS
> Plunge (p124)
> Crossing the Brooklyn Bridge (pictured above; p22)
> Taking a water taxi (p262)
> Biking the Hudson River Park (p105)
> Ferry to Governor's Island (p47)

PICTURE-PERFECT NEW YORK STATUES
> Jose Marti (Columbus Circle)
> George Washington (Federal Hall)
> Duke Ellington (Harlem)
> Giovanni da Verrazano (Battery Park)
> Eleanor Roosevelt (Riverside Park)

FREE NYC

It's a bit counterintuitive, but there are a few things that don't cost an arm and a leg in this town – the trick is finding them. For that, New Yorkers have a few tools: www.lifebooker.com, www.freenyc.net, www.clubfree time.com and www.freeinnyc.net. These four websites can provide you with free events for a month of Sundays, and then some. LifeBooker is actually a booking service that hooks you up with last-minute, half-price spa services, hair cuts, manicures and pedicures at salons; the theory being that it's better to have someone pay half-price and fill an empty chair than get nothing. Clubfreetime lists all kinds of cultural, social and intellectual events in up-to-the-moment postings; Freenyc and Freeinnyc do much the same, and add in things like free yoga in the park and free gallery events.

Don't forget that most museums (with the exception of the Metro-politan, which is always suggested donation) have at least one evening a week where they drop their entry fee and take suggested donations. Also consider buying a CityPass (www.citypass.net), which can get you steeply discounted admission into seven major attractions.

TOP FREEBIES

> Staten Island Ferry (pictured above; p46)
> Museum of Modern Art on Friday evenings (p164)
> Shakespeare in the Park (p176)
> River to River Festival (p51)
> Summerstage (p179)

BEST HAPPY HOURS

> Cleopatra's Needle (p200)
> DBA (p100)
> Whiskey Ward (p73)
> Henry Street Ale House (p223)
> Stir (p190)

>BACKGROUND

Grand Central Terminal (p152) functions like clockwork

BACKGROUND

HISTORY

Long before Giovanni da Verrazano sailed by Staten Island in 1524, or Henry Hudson came looking for land to claim for the Dutch East India Company in 1609, great numbers of Algonquin-speaking people had made the Manhattan area their home.

The Lenape Native Americans fished New York Bay for oysters and striped bass, and laid down well-worn trading routes across the hilly island (Manhattan means 'island of hills' in one native dialect); those same routes later became Broadway, Amsterdam Ave and other large city thoroughfares. Legend says that Dutch trader Peter Minuit bought the island from the Lenape for trinkets worth about $24, but historians say it's unlikely the Lenape agreed to anything of the sort, since it was a culture that didn't adhere to the idea of private property. In any case, the Dutch assumed control of the island and by 1630 the colony numbered 270, with a number of Belgians (Walloons), French Huguenots and English mixed in.

Peter Stuyvesant arrived to impose order on the unruly colony of New Amsterdam in 1647, but his intolerant religious views led to unrest. Few resisted the bloodless coup by the British in 1664, and the colony was renamed New York. It became a British stronghold and remained stead-fastly loyal to George III through much of the Revolutionary War in the 1770s. George Washington's ragtag army of farm boys was almost wiped out by Britain's General Cornwallis and his troops in what is currently Brooklyn Heights – only a daring, all-night march north saved them.

Post-Revolutionary times were good for most New Yorkers, even though the founding fathers disliked the bustling seaport city. The capital moved further south, to Washington DC, but the masses didn't go with it, and by 1830 the population had expanded to 250,000, mostly composed of immigrants working in dangerous factories and living in tenements on the Lower East Side. At the same time, corrupt politicians bilked millions from public works projects and industrial barons amassed tax-free for-tunes. A lack of space forced building sprawl upward rather than outward; skyscrapers peppered the horizon and the city continued to expand its network of subways and elevated trains. In 1898 the five independent districts of Staten Island, Queens, the Bronx and Brooklyn merged with Manhattan into the five 'boroughs' of New York City. With wave after wave of immi-grants arriving, the population reached three million in 1900.

AFRICAN BURIAL GROUND

Africans have been in New York City since the 17th-century Dutch era. Brought over as slaves, they built many of the colonial attractions of Lower Manhattan. Their contributions were largely forgotten as slavery disappeared from the north, but the African Burial Ground (www .africanburialground.gov) – the final resting place of some 400 slaves taken mostly from Ghana that was discovered accidentally in 1991 – is a poignant reminder of their suffering. The site is at Duane and Elk Sts, adjacent to 290 Broadway, and a permanent exhibition is on display at the Schomburg Center for Research in Black Culture (p206) in Harlem.

Speakeasies, flappers, gangsters, the 19th Amendment (which gave women the right to vote) and a Harlem Renaissance brought incredible vitality to New York in the years before and after WWI. Margaret Sanger preached about birth control in Washington Sq Park, Wall St made golden boys out of hayseeds, and F Scott Fitzgerald chronicled it all in *The Great Gatsby*. When the stock market crashed on Black Tuesday (October 29, 1929), the apparently limitless future of New York was smashed overnight. Hard times followed, and even though Manhattan was the nation's premier city after WWII, economically things continued to stagnate. Only a massive federal loan program rescued the city from bankruptcy in the 1970s.

LIFE AS A NEW YORK RESIDENT

New York City is the original 'melting pot,' the term used by the nation's leaders to encourage mixing between old settlers and new arrivals at the turn of the 20th century. Popular theory held that incoming immigrants would assimilate to the dominant culture (which was primarily Anglo-Saxon at the time) and create a unified population free of ethnic and class divisions. Instead, the opposite happened: Italians coming into New York City didn't settle in the Irish enclave of Greenwich Village or the Eastern European Jewish communities of the Lower East Side. They established their own beachhead, which became known as Little Italy, and proudly spoke their language and practiced their traditions. Dominicans of the 1950s and 1960s settled in what became Spanish Harlem, and Puerto Ricans still own most of the Bronx. Along the way other nationalities arrived and rubbed shoulders and traded quips, and if the perfect homogeneity the city planners envisioned never materialized, well, nobody misses it because a vibrant hybrid culture of multi-culti influences has taken its place. No matter what their ethnic roots, your average New Yorker today knows a smattering of Spanish or another foreign language (or is perfectly bilingual), has a good sense of the Chinese lunar calendar (how else to know when the Chinese New Year is coming with its fabulous dragon parade?) and can order a bagel with a *schmear* (dab of cream cheese) without batting an eye.

Which is not to say that all New Yorkers live together in perfect harmony – in a city of about nine million, there are bound to be a few problems. Politicians are expected to resolve most of these conflicts and if they don't, they can kiss that second term goodbye. When it comes to the city's overall well-being, New Yorkers have no problem banding together in amazing displays of solidarity.

New Yorkers do everything double-time, and exchanging one-liners while on the fly is a highly prized skill. You'll hear such exchanges every-where ('How you doin', 'Hey, what's happening', 'You got the time, buddy?'), so don't hold back if someone sends a well-meaning inquiry your way. Politeness – please, thank you, etc – is also important, and displays of class status, such as slighting the taxi driver or doorman, do not go over well in democratic Manhattan. There are a few things that raise local ire: do not exit the subway stairs and stop to pull out your map, thereby blocking those behind you. Move to the corner and then look. Don't go into an eatery dur-ing the busy lunch hour rush and keep everyone waiting while you decide. Hang back until you are ready to order. A jacket and tie are expected at upscale restaurants, but otherwise feel free to wear what you wish.

GOVERNMENT & POLITICS

New York City has five borough presidents, a city-wide comptroller, a public advocate and a 51-member city council to balance mayoral power. Buoyed by the November 4, 2008, election of Democrat Barack Obama to the presidency, Democrats in New York made significant gains in upstate territories and State Legislature races. For the first time in generations, New York State has a Democratic majority in its legislature, and a Democratic governor. Only New York City – traditionally the bluest region of the whole state – is unlikely to put a Democrat in power in 2009. But that's only because its billionaire mayor Mike Bloomberg, an Independent, has announced he will run for a third term in office. Bloomberg successfully repealed a law prohibiting third terms for local officials, with the backing of the City Council. With the city's economic fortunes on the wane in late 2008, Bloomberg instituted a round of cost-saving measures, scaling back city services and agencies. Housing remains a hot issue, with a grassroots push to improve housing options for the low-income and working-class families who have been priced out of Manhattan and practically all of the surrounding boroughs. America's ongoing debate on immigration reform has also fired up pockets of resistance in New York City, home to some of the largest émigré communities in the country. Local politicians pressured to take a stand have come out in favor of amnesty programs that would grant legal status to long-time undocumented residents.

ECONOMY

At press time, the US was grappling with its first major recession in more than a decade, and New York hadn't escaped the downturn. Workers' salaries haven't kept pace with inflation, and most of the middle and upper-middle class have been priced out of the city. For a while New York looked immune to the economic woes, thanks largely to the influx of foreign cash from bargain-seeking tourists. But all that changed in late 2008, when a series of Wall St and bank meltdowns (Bear Stearns laid off most of its staff, Lehman Bros crashed completely) rocked the foundation of the city's finances and set off a global economic crisis. With Wall St in turmoil, the city lost its largest source of tax revenue almost overnight, abruptly putting an end to what formerly seemed to be an invincible run of good fortune.

Still, hopes are high among New Yorkers that the nation's new president will turn the country's situation around. Many New Yorkers are also reassured by the thought of a third term of Mayor Bloomberg's strict fiscal policies – although it looks like the incumbent mayor will face a strong challenge from US Congressman Anthony Weiner from Queens. Whoever becomes mayor in 2009 will need to ruthlessly tighten the belt on city spending. New Yorkers, already looking at likely subway-fare hikes and increased costs on water and heating bills, won't react kindly to any increases in property or state income taxes. Already the question hovering on most people's lips is: 'how can I afford to live here?' With Democrats in charge of the nation and now New York State, residents are looking to that party for answers after almost a decade of Republican rule.

ENVIRONMENT

New Yorkers are increasingly worried and affected by the environment, and have taken proactive steps to try and make a difference. Many restaurants have stopped serving bottled water and now offer their own filtered and recycled *agua fresca* in place of plastic or glass bottles.

Mayor Bloomberg won kudos from most city residents for his proposal to bring congestion pricing to the city; his idea got shot down by state lawmakers, but various versions to limit traffic jams are still on the table. More New Yorkers are turning to bicycles to navigate the city; it's a novel way to get around, and with subway fares increasing and quality of service decreasing, many prefer to pedal. It's still not as smooth riding around New York as it is in Paris or Copenhagen: bicyclists have to be on the defensive, supremely careful and obey all traffic laws.

City residents are also worried about development encroaching on the Croton Watershed, a pristine and delicate wetland system that cleans much of the rainwater that flows into the city and into New Yorkers' taps. Environmentalists have held off the worst of the development, but it's a battle that will intensify in coming years. The dangers of too much building can be seen in the Gateway National Park in Jamaica Bay, Queens. The once massive wetland system has been reduced to just a few miles of shoreline, and Army Corp of Engineer scientists predict the marshland – dying of unknown reasons – will be gone entirely in 25 years. The city has recently taken steps to limit building on the marshy edges, but many fear it's too little too late.

FURTHER READING
NYC IN LITERATURE

Bonfire of the Vanities (Tom Wolfe; 1987) Delve into the status-obsessed '80s with this gripping novel of an uptown investment banker's entanglement with the world of the black South Bronx.

Go Tell It on the Mountain (James Baldwin; 1953) A day in the life of 14-year-old John Grimes, bringing readers into Harlem during the Depression.

The Invention of Everything Else (Samantha Hunt; 2008) The Brooklyn author goes back to the 1940s, creating historical fiction out of the adventures of scientist Nikola Tesla, who lived in the Hotel New Yorker.

Jazz (Toni Morrison; 1992) Pulitzer Prize–winner Morrison explores the Harlem Jazz Age through the tales of three tragic, intersecting lives.

Lush Life (Richard Price; 2008) Screenwriter and novelist Price tackles the gentrification of the Lower East Side and the lives of three friends who witness a shocking murder.

Motherless Brooklyn (Jonathan Lethem; 1999) This oddly compelling tale – of grown-up orphan Lionel Essrog, a detective with Tourette's syndrome who is investigating the death of his boss – explores crevices and histories of north Brooklyn 'hoods that newcomers never knew existed.

Push (Sapphire; 1996) A wrenching modern-age story about an abused young Harlem woman, 16-year-old Precious Jones.

Small Town (Lawrence Block; 2002) A chilling thriller about one man's response to losing his wife in the September 11 attacks: by becoming a serial killer on a vengeance spree.

MUSIC UNDER NEW YORK
Every year the MTA invites the best talents in New York City to play in the subway system. Violinists, barbershop quartets, Chinese dulcimer players, Haitian folk singers, cellists, jazz ensembles, salsa bands, opera singers and hip-hop dancers are just a small sampling of the kinds of shows you could be in for. Artists have to audition before becoming part of the official lineup. For a list of participating locations, visit www.mta.info/mta/aft/muny.

The Story of Junk (Linda Yablonsky; 1997) Years after her grim existence as a heroin junkie living in the down-and-out, pre-gentrified artists' Lower East Side, Yablonsky recalls all the shocking, seedy details.

FILMS & TV
American Gangster (2007) A Harlem-based drug drama, this one deals with heroin importation and an alliance with the Mafia, as well as the tale of one very honest policeman. It's based on a true story.
Fatal Attraction (1987) This psycho thriller is about a happily married man whose one-night stand turns into a series of run-ins with his lover-turned-stalker. Catch great glimpses of the pre-gentrification Meatpacking District.
Kids (1995) Shot in documentary style and starring a bunch of then-unknowns who include Rosario Dawson and Chloe Sevigny, this chilling tale tackles sexual promiscuity, drugs and AIDS.
Law & Order Dick Wolf's long-running series about the city's criminal justice system, set in New York, shot in New York and using real-life stories ripped from the headlines in, where else? New York.
Manhattan (1979) Directed by and starring Woody Allen, as well as Diane Keaton and Mariel Hemingway. A divorced New Yorker dating a high-school student (the adorable, baby-voiced Hemingway) falls for his best friend's mistress in what is essentially a love letter to NYC.
Party Monster (2003) Macaulay Culkin plays the crazed, famed, murderous club kid Michael Alig in this disturbing look into the drug-fueled, club-kid era of the late '80s in downtown NYC.
Project Runway Heidi Klum and adorable Tim Gunn shepherd would-be designers to New York's best fabric stores in the Fashion District as they compete to win $100,000 in this New York–based reality show.
Saturday Night Fever (1977) John Travolta is the hottest thing in bell-bottoms in this tale of a streetwise Brooklyn kid who becomes king of the dance floor.
Sex and the City (2008) The eagerly awaited screen continuation of the cult-TV favorite catches up with the famous foursome, all as witty as ever, as their lives are filled with dramas that include cheating, jilting and kids.
Spider-Man 3 (2007) Tobey Maguire is battling villains with NYC as a backdrop in the darkest, most action-packed film of the three Spideys.
Taxi Driver (1976) Robert DeNiro is a mentally unstable Vietnam-war vet whose urges to lash out are heightened by the high tensions of a much grittier city.
What Not to Wear Shot at Silvercup Studios in Queens, where more than 30 other NY-centric shows are filmed, this reality show teaches women what flatters them most during a Tribeca shopping spree.

DIRECTORY
TRANSPORTATION
ARRIVAL & DEPARTURE
AIR

Multiple direct flights from just about every major city in North and South America and western Europe arrive in New York daily, as do many stopover flights from Asia. Most domestic air travel goes to LaGuardia, international tends to go to John F Kennedy (JFK) and a third, often easier option is Newark Liberty International in New Jersey, only a short drive from Manhattan.

John F Kennedy International Airport

In the far reaches of Queens, **John F Kennedy International Airport** (www .kennedyairport.com) is about 15 miles from Midtown, but it can take 45 to 75 minutes by car, and longer

Travel to/from JFK

	AirTrain/Subway	Taxi	Bus	Car Service
Pick-up point	look for AirTrain signs at terminals that take you to the Rockaway subway station; from there take the A train into Manhattan	outside any terminal; look for the lines, as there are specific pick-up points under 'Taxi' signs	outside any terminal; buses run every 15-20min to midnight	at any JFK terminal
Drop-off point	anywhere on the A train line	anywhere you want	Penn Station, Port Authority Bus Terminal and Grand Central Terminal	anywhere in Manhattan
Cost	AirTrain/Subway $5/2	$45 to Manhattan and most of Brooklyn	$12-15 1-way	$50-75
Duration	1hr	1-2hr	allow 60-75min	1hr
Contact	www.airtrainjfk.com, www.mta.info		for express bus service, ☎ 718-875-8200; www.nyairportservice .com	operators include Big Apple (☎ 718-232-1015), Carmel (☎ 212-666-666), Citywide (☎ 718-405-5822), Dial (☎ 718-743-2877) and Tel Aviv (☎ 212-777-7777)

Travel to/from LaGuardia

	New York Airport Service	Taxi	Train/Subway
Pick-up point	to LaGuardia, buses leave every 20min between 6am and midnight from Penn Station, Port Authority Bus Terminal and Grand Central Terminal	outside any terminal. From the airport, take the M60 to W 106th St and Broadway; the M60 also connects with trains and the subway into Manhattan	a taxi can take you to the N and W trains in Astoria Queens, the 2 4, 5, 6, A, B, C, D subways along 125th St and the 1 subway at 116th, 110th Sts and Broadway
Cost	$15	$15-30	$2
Duration	1hr	20-40min	allow 1hr
Contact	☎ 718-875-8200; www .nyairportservice.com		www.mta.info

in peak traffic. Useful numbers for this airport:

General inquiries (☎ 718-244-4444)
Hotel bookings (☎ 212-267-5500)
Lost and found (☎ 718-244-4225/6)
Medical services (☎ 718-656-5344)
Parking info (☎ 718-244-4444)
Traveler's aid (☎ 718-656-4870; 🕙 10am-6pm) Located in the arrival areas of terminals 1, 3, 4, 6, 7, 8 and 9; helps stranded travelers.

LaGuardia Airport

In northern Queens, **LaGuardia** (www.laguardiaairport.com) is about 8 miles from Manhattan, but traffic can turn that into a two-hour drive. Normally it's not more than 20 minutes. The car services available at JFK Airport are also available at LaGuardia (see the table opposite). Useful numbers for this airport:

General info (☎ 718-533-3400)
Hotel bookings (☎ 212-267-5500)

Lost and found (☎ 718-639-1839)
Parking info (☎ 718-533-3400)

TRAIN

Amtrak trains come right into Midtown, and you can pick them up in Boston, Philadelphia and Washington DC, and at small smaller stops along the way. Long-distance Amtrak and Long Island Rail Road trains arrive at **Pennsylvania (Penn) Station** (☎ 212-582-6875, 800-872-7245; W 33rd St btwn Seventh & Eighth Aves). Commuter trains (MetroNorth) use **Grand Central Terminal** (Map p151, B4; ☎ 212-532-4900; Park Ave at E 42nd St). **New Jersey PATH trains** (☎ 800-234-7284) stop at the World Trade Center site, Christopher St, 14th St, 28th St and 34th St.

PASSPORT

Visitors are now required to have a passport that's valid for at least six months after their intended stay in the USA.

VISA

There are 27 countries whose residents can enter the US without a visa, provided they have a passport and will only stay 90 days. These countries include Australia, France, Germany, Italy, Japan, the Netherlands, Switzerland and the UK (for a complete list, visit www.cbp.gov). Under this program you must have a round-trip ticket that is nonrefundable in the USA, and you will not be allowed to extend your stay beyond 90 days.

Residents of other countries should apply for a visa at the nearest American embassy or consulate to their home before hitting the road. Most applications can be done through the mail. Many of the application forms and further information can be found at the website of the **US State Department** (http://travel.state.gov/visa).

CUSTOMS & DUTY FREE

If you are carrying more than $10,000 in US and/or foreign cash, traveler's checks or money orders when you enter the USA, you must declare it. You can import 1L of liquor (if you are over the age of 21); 200 cigarettes, 50 cigars (provided they are not Cuban) or 2kg of tobacco; and gifts up to a total value of $100 ($800 for US citizens). If you're bringing prescription drugs, make sure they're in clearly marked containers. For updates, check www.cbp.gov.

SECURITY

Security is very visible and tight at all three airports. Allow extra time for check-in and always have your identification on hand. Don't try to carry on metal nail files, Swiss Army knives, pocketknives, razors, corkscrews or any other sharp implements. Of course, any kind of firearm or other weapon, explo-

---

NEWARK LIBERTY INTERNATIONAL AIRPORT

Although it's in another state (New Jersey), many travelers find Newark easier to fly into than either of the very busy New York airports. If traffic is bad, traveling from Newark into Manhattan can take an interminably long time, but public transportation is quick and efficient. Take the **Monorail** (☎ 973-762-5100; 🕑 6am-9pm; tickets $14) from the airport to the NJ Transit train station. From there take a train to Newark's Penn Station (not Manhattan's Penn Station) and get on a **Path Train** (tickets $2; 🕑 24hr) into Manhattan. There's also the **Olympia Express Bus** (☎ 877-863-9275, 212-964-6233, 908-354-3330; tickets $13; 🕑 6am-midnight) from Newark airport to Manhattan, but it could get you stuck in traffic if you take it at peak hour.

CLIMATE CHANGE & TRAVEL

Travel -- especially air travel -- is a significant contributor to global climate change. At Lonely Planet, we believe that all who travel have a responsibility to limit their personal impact. As a result, we have teamed with Rough Guides and other concerned industry partners to support Climate Care, which allows people to offset the greenhouse gases they are responsible for with contributions to energy-saving projects and other climate-friendly initiatives in the developing world. Lonely Planet offsets all staff and author travel.

For more information, turn to the responsible travel pages on www.lonelyplanet .com. For details on offsetting your carbon emissions and a carbon calculator, go to www .climatecare.org.

sives, flammable liquids or solids, or any other hazardous materials are prohibited. Even non-flammable liquids are restricted to 4oz in your carry-on bag; pack the big bottles of perfume in your luggage. Guards are pitiless about making you throw out whatever liquids over 4oz are in your bag at the boarding gate.

....

GETTING AROUND

Subway is generally the fastest, cheapest way to get around Manhattan because busy city streets get clogged by 'gridlock,' when cars sit bumper to bumper waiting for lights to change. City buses can be useful, provided that traffic is moving. Pick up a public transit map from subway ticket booths. Taxis are the most convenient mode of transportation after 1am.

TRAVEL PASSES

MetroCard (☎ 718-330-1234) is the easiest way to pay for travel on New York's public transit system.

Pick one up at any newsstand or subway entrance. The one-day Fun Pass ($7.50) is a major money saver, giving you unlimited access to subways and buses from the first swipe until 3am the next morning. The seven-day ($25) or 30-day ($81) unlimited cards are great deals, but you must let 18 minutes elapse between each swipe, making it harder for two people to share one card. Pay-per-ride options are also available – either a vending machine or subway clerk can put any dollar amount you want on your MetroCard, with bonus rides when you buy several at a time. Be aware that the single-ride cards sold from machines in subway stations expire after two hours. At print time, the single-ride fare was $2, though that's subject to change.

SUBWAY

The subway system (☎ 718-330-1234) runs 24 hours a day. In this

Travel Around New York City

	Theater District	The Met	American Museum of Natural History	Harlem	Dumbo Island	Coney	Williamsburg
Lower Manhattan	subway 10min	subway 15min	subway 15min	subway 25min	subway 10min	subway 45min	subway 30min
Upper East Side	cab 10min	cab/walk 5/10min	cab10min	subway 15min	subway 30min	subway 1hr	subway 30min
Upper West Side	cab/walk 5/10min	cab 10min	walk 5-10min	subway 10min	subway 20-25min	subway 1hr	subway 40min
Theater District	n/a	walk/subway 15/10-15min	walk/subway 15/10min	subway 15min	subway 20-30min	subway 45min-1hr	subway 40min
Southern Brooklyn	subway 40min	subway 30min	subway 40min	subway 45min	subway 20min	subway 30min	subway 35min

book, the nearest subway stop is noted after the 🚇 icon in each listing. If you transfer from the subway to a bus or from a bus to the subway within 18 minutes of paying a fare, there's no double charge – free transfers are permitted. To get the latest bus and subway routes, and up-to-the-minute service changes, visit www.mta.nyc.ny.us and follow the links to NYC Transit. Other useful websites are www.hopstop.com, www.trips123.com and www.public routes.com. These for-profit sites offer free information on traveling around New York and surrounding cities via public transportation.

BUS
City buses (☎ 718-330-1234) operate 24 hours a day and generally run north–south along avenues and crosstown along the major east–west thoroughfares. You need exact coins worth $2 or a MetroCard to board a bus – no bills accepted. The driver will not make change.

BOAT
New York Waterway (☎ 800-533-3779; www.nywaterway.com) ferries make runs up the Hudson River Valley and from Midtown to Yankee Stadium in the Bronx. A popular commuter route goes from the New Jersey Transit train station in Hoboken to the World Financial Center in Lower Manhattan; boats leave every five to 10 minutes at peak times, and the 10-minute ride costs $6 each way.

New York Water Taxi (☎ 212-742-1969; www.nywatertaxi.com; 1 stop $5) is a new service that's really taken off in New York. These yellow taxi boats stop at various piers along Manhattan's West Side and are a wonderful way to travel to Midtown, Lower Manhattan, and parts of Brooklyn and Queens. The Water Taxi Beach (www.watertaxi beach.com) is a favorite pit stop.

TAXI

A taxi is available when the middle of its rooftop number is glowing (as opposed to when the 'off duty' lights on either side of the number are glowing). Fares are metered and start at $2.50; the tip is 10% to 15% (minimum 50¢). There's a 50¢ surcharge from 8pm to 6am.

CAR RENTAL

The main rental agencies in New York City include **Avis** (☎ 800-331-1212), **Budget** (☎ 800-527-0700), **Dollar** (☎ 800-800-4000), **Hertz** (☎ 800-654-3131) and **Thrifty** (☎ 800-367-2277).

PRACTICALITIES
BUSINESS HOURS

Shops are generally open Monday to Saturday from 10am to 6pm and Sunday 11am to 6pm, with some extended hours Thursday nights; many shops close Monday. Some businesses change their operating hours with the seasons, usually resulting in shorter hours in the summer. Banks and institu-

tional businesses keep a 9am to 5pm Monday to Friday schedule, but many also keep 9am to 3pm hours on Saturday.

Museums and art galleries are usually open Tuesday to Sunday from 10am to 5pm. On public holidays, banks, schools and government offices (including post offices) close, and transportation services operate on a Sunday schedule.

....
DISCOUNTS

New York City Pass (www.citypass.com), available online or at major city attractions, buys you admission into the Empire State Building, Metropolitan Museum of Art, Museum of Modern Art, Guggenheim Museum, American Museum of Natural History and a Circle Line cruise for $65 (worth $131 in value). **New York Pass** (www.newyorkpass .com) sells online cards for $69 and gives you daylong access to 40 top attractions (the UN, Statue of Liberty, Guggenheim etc), as well as discounts at 25 stores and restaurants. Two-, three- and seven-day passes are also available, and you can choose to collect them in NYC or have them sent to you before you leave home. The **Entertainment Book** (www.entertainment.com), which you can order for $20 before your arrival, is packed with passes that arm you with dining, shopping and service deals.

ELECTRICITY

Electricity in the USA is 110V and 60Hz. Plugs have two or three pins (two flat pins, often with a round 'grounding' pin). Adapters for European and South American plugs are widely available; Australians should bring adapters.

EMBASSIES & CONSULATES

The UN's presence in New York means that nearly every country in the world maintains diplomatic offices here. Most are listed in the white pages of the phone book under 'Consulates General of (country).' Embassies include the following:

Australia (☎ 212-351-6500; 150 E 42nd St btwn Lexington & Third Aves)
Canada (☎ 212-596-1783; 1251 Sixth Ave btwn 49th & 50th Sts)
Ireland (☎ 212-319-2555; 345 Park Ave btwn 51st & 52nd Sts)
New Zealand (☎ 212-832-4038; 780 Third Ave btwn 48th & 49th Sts)
South Africa (☎ 212-213-4880; 333 E 38th St btwn First & Second Aves)
UK (☎ 212-745-0202; 845 Third Ave btwn 51st & 52nd Sts)

EMERGENCIES

You can always get help by dialing 911 from any phone, including mobiles. There are also emergency-call boxes on many city corners; some look like bright orange bulbs, others are old-fashioned iron boxes

bolted to the crosswalk signals. In either case, push the button and the cavalry comes running.
Police, fire, ambulance (☎ 911)
Police information operator (☎ 212-374-5000)

GAY & LESBIAN TRAVELERS

New York doesn't differentiate much between heterosexual and homosexual – at least, not when it comes to dancing, drinking and eating. For info on the gay and lesbian scene in NYC, see p240.

INFORMATION & ORGANIZATIONS

The free magazines *HX* and *Next* are available at restaurants and bars. Look for *LGNY* and *NY Blade* in street-corner boxes. Pick up the lifestyle magazine *Metrosource* at shops and the LGBT Community Center. *Time Out* features a good events section.

Useful counseling, referral and information centers:
Gay & Lesbian Hotline (☎ 212-989-0999; glnh@glnh.org)
LGBT Community Center (Map pp106–7, C1; ☎ 212-620-7310; www.gaycenter.org; 208 W 13th St at Seventh Ave)

HOLIDAYS

New Year's Day January 1
Martin Luther King Jr Day Third Monday in January
Presidents' Day Third Monday in February

Easter Sunday March/April
Memorial Day Last Monday in May
Independence Day July 4
Labor Day First Monday in September
Columbus Day Second Monday in October
Veterans' Day November 11
Thanksgiving Fourth Thursday in November
Christmas Day December 25

INTERNET
Public libraries offer free web access, and internet cafés are common.

INTERNET CAFÉS
Cyber Café (Map p163, B3; ☎ 212-333-4109; 250 W 49th St btwn Broadway & Eighth Ave; per 30min $6.40, minimum 30min; ☷ 8am-11pm Mon-Fri, 11am-11pm Sat & Sun) High-speed computers with color printers, scanners and web cams, plus there's a coffee and wine bar.

Easy Internet Café (Map p163, B5; ☎ 212-398-0724; 234 W 42nd St; per $2; ☷ 24hr) This is the cheapest, and possibly the biggest, place in town.

LGBT Community Center (Map pp106–7, C1; ☎ 212-620-7310; 208 W 13th St at Seventh Ave; suggested donation $3; ☷ 9am-11pm) The cyber-center here has 15 computers, open to all.

Web2Zone (Map pp92–3, B4; ☎ 212-614-7300; 54 Cooper Sq btwn Astor Pl & Fourth Ave; per hr $5; ☷ 9am-11pm Mon-Fri, 10am-11pm Sat, noon-10pm Sun) Extensive printing and design services, plus computer games.

USEFUL WEBSITES
The **Lonely Planet** website (www.lonelyplanet.com) offers New York City information and links. Other good sites:

New York City Insider (www.theinsider.com)
New York City Search (www.newyork.citysearch.com)
New York Times (www.nytimes.com)
NYC & Co (www.nycvisit.com)

WI-FI
Bryant Park went wireless in 2005, and now all of New York has followed suit. **WiFi Salon** (http://wifisalon.com) has a list of locations, as does www.nyc.wireless.net.

LOST PROPERTY
Public transit (☎ 212-712-4500)
Taxi (☎ 212-692-8294)

MEDICAL SERVICES
New York Hotel Urgent Medical Services (☎ 212-737-1212) offers medical services to visitors, and doctors make 24-hour house (and hotel) calls. Expect to pay top dollar (prices begin at $200). Medical care gets very expensive very fast in the US if you don't have insurance.

DENTAL SERVICES
For tooth situations that can't wait, try **AAA Dental Care** (Map p163, D3; ☎ 212-744-3928; www.emergencydentalnyc.com; Suite 1504, 30 E 60th St).

PHARMACIES
There are a number of 24-hour pharmacies in New York City:
Duane Reade (Map p163, B1; ☎ 212-541-9708; W 57th St at Broadway)

Duane Reade (Map pp106–7, D3; ☎ 212-674-5357; Sixth Ave at Waverly Pl)

HOSPITALS
All hospitals have 24-hour emergency departments that must treat the uninsured.
Bellevue Hospital (off Map p151; ☎ 212-562-4141; NYU Medical Center, First Ave at E 27th St)
Lenox Hill Hospital (Map p183, B3; ☎ 212-434-2000; 100 E 77th St btwn Park & Lexington Aves)
New York Hospital (☎ 212-746-5050; 525 E 68th St btwn York Ave & Franklin D Roosevelt Dr)

MONEY
ATMS
You'll find 24-hour ATMs at banks and most grocery stores, but unless you are using a branch of your bank, expect to pay a $3 fee. Avoid ATMS in nightclubs and try to avoid ATMS set out on streets or in corner shops, especially if they haven't got a security camera pointed at them; many are rigged to steal your number.

CHANGING MONEY
Banks often do better deals than exchange offices, but it's always a good idea to check the rates, commissions and any other charges. Chase, a bank with 80 branches in Manhattan, has no fees.

CREDIT CARDS
Visa, MasterCard (both affiliated with European Access Cards),

American Express and Discover are widely accepted. For lost cards, contact the following:
American Express (☎ 800-528-4800)
Diners Club (☎ 800-234-6377)
Discover (☎ 800-347-2683)
MasterCard (☎ 800-826-2181)
Visa (☎ 800-336-8472)

CURRENCY
The monetary unit used is the US dollar, which is divided into 100 cents (¢). Coins come in 1¢ (penny), 5¢ (nickel), 10¢ (dime), 25¢ (quarter), 50¢ (half-dollar; rare) and $1 denominations. Notes come in $1, $2 (rare), $5, $10, $20, $50 and $100. Some shops won't accept notes higher than $20.

NEWSPAPERS & MAGAZINES
The *New York Times* is the nation's premier newspaper, and covers cultural events extensively in the weekend edition. The weekly *New York Observer* specializes in local media and politics. The *Daily News* and *New York Post* are popular tabloids. The *Wall Street Journal* is the daily business bible.

Time Out New York lists events, restaurants and shops; the *New Yorker* magazine covers high-brow theater, art and music events. Free street papers – such as the *Village Voice*, *AM New York* and *Metro New York* – offer good entertainment listings.

POST

The main **post office** (☎ 212-967-8585; 421 Eighth Ave at 33rd St) is open 24 hours. The post office at the Rockefeller Center (p154) is open Monday to Friday from 9:30am to 5:30pm. The **Franklin D Roosevelt post office** (Map p151, C2; 909 Third Ave) is open Monday to Friday from 9am to 8pm and Saturday from 10am to 2pm.

TELEPHONE

COUNTRY & CITY AREA CODES

The US country code is 1. Manhattan phone numbers are always preceded by a three-digit area code: ☎ 212, ☎ 646 and ☎ 917, although ☎ 646 and ☎ 917 also do double duty as mobile phone and pager area codes. Even when dialing in Manhattan you must use 1 plus the entire 10-digit number. For the outer boroughs, the area codes are ☎ 718 and ☎ 347.

INTERNATIONAL CODES

Dial ☎ 00 followed by the code for the country you're calling.
Australia (☎ 61)
Canada (☎ 1)
Japan (☎ 81)
New Zealand (☎ 64)
South Africa (☎ 27)
UK (☎ 44)

USEFUL NUMBERS

City information (☎ 311)
Clubfone (☎ 212-777-2582)
Collect calls (☎ 0)
Directory assistance (☎ 411)
International access code (☎ 011)
Moviefone (☎ 212-777-3456)
Operator (☎ 0)
Operator-assisted calls (☎ 01 + the number; an operator will come on the line once you have dialed)
Time (☎ 212-976-1616)
Weather (☎ 212-976-1212)

TIME

New York is in the Eastern Standard Time (EST) zone, five hours behind Greenwich Mean Time (GMT). Daylight saving starts on the first Sunday in April (clocks are advanced an hour) and it finishes on the last Saturday in October.

At noon in New York it's 9am in San Francisco, 5pm in London, 6pm in Paris, 7pm in Cape Town and 3am the next day in Sydney.

TIPPING

Waiters work for less than minimum wage, so it is expected that satisfied customers will tip 15% to 20% of the total bill. Tips are not automatically included, but some restaurants add a 15% gratuity to the bills of parties of six or more. Standard tipping amounts:
Baggage carriers $5 for the first bag, $1 for each additional bag.
Bars At least $1 per drink (or more for faster service and stronger drinks).
Cloakroom attendants $2 per item.
Hairdressers 15%

Hotel service personnel $2 for each service performed.
Restaurants 15% to 20% (not expected in fast food, takeout or self-service restaurants).
Room cleaners Minimum $5 per day.
Taxis 10% to 15%
Tour guides $20 per family/group for a full-day tour.

TOURIST INFORMATION

NYC & Co (Map p163, C4; ☎ 212-484-1222; www.nycvisit.com; 810 Seventh Ave at 53rd St; ⏰ 8:30am-6pm Mon-Fri, 9am-5pm Sat & Sun; ⓜ N, R, W, 2, 3 to 42nd St-Times Sq) operates a 24-hour toll-free line with listings of special events and reservation details. Staff are helpful and knowledgeable and the information center is comprehensive.

You'll also find information counters and centers at airports, in Times Sq (Map p163), at Grand Central Terminal (Map p151) and Penn Station.

TRAVELERS WITH DISABILITIES

Federal laws require that all government offices have good elevator and ramp access for wheelchairs and devices to aid the hearing impaired. Almost all major venues offer good bathroom facilities for those with wheelchairs, and all city buses are able to carry wheelchair passengers. Only some subway stations are accessible (see MTA maps or call ☎ 718-596-8585).

WOMEN TRAVELERS

It's a good idea to avoid public transportation after midnight, and watch your drink at all times in a bar – just as a precaution. Carry extra money on you at night in a safe spot so you can grab a cab home, especially if you're traveling alone.

Tampons, pads and condoms are sold everywhere. The contraceptive pill and 'morning after' pill are available in local pharmacies. New York City law stipulates that rape victims be offered the 'morning after' pill while receiving treatment at hospitals, but it's not always automatically offered. If you want to take it, insist upon getting it.

>INDEX

See also separate subindexes for See (p274), Shop (p276), Eat (p277), Drink (p279) and Play (p279).

◎ SEE
Activities
Central Park Bowling Lawns
 176
Chelsea Piers Complex 127-30

000 map pages

000 map pages

000 map pages

INDEX

000 map pages